AQA Compu

AS

Pornpanit (Jiew)

Kevin Bond
Sylvia Langfield

Nelson Thornes

Published in 2008 by:
Nelson Thornes Ltd
Delta Place
27 Bath Road
CHELTENHAM
GL53 7TH
United Kingdom

13 14 15 16 / 10 9 8 7 6 5 4

A catalogue record for this book is available from the British Library

ISBN 978 0 7487 8296 3

Cover photograph: Science Photo Library/Sam Ogden

Illustrations by Fakenham Photosetting
Page make-up by Fakenham Photosetting, Norfolk

Printed and bound in China by 1010 Printing International Ltd

The authors and publisher are grateful to the following for permission to reproduce
photographs and other copyright material in this book:

p6 LS Stockport Ltd; p12 map reproduced by permission of Ordnance Survey on
behalf of HMSO. © Crown copyright 2008. All rights reserved. Ordnance Survey licence
number 100017284; p206 (both) iStockphoto; p219 (top) Rick Friedman/Corbis; p219
used with kind permission of Steve Grand.

Contents

Introduction

Nelson Thornes has worked hard to ensure this book and the accompanying online resources offer you excellent support for your AS or A Level course.

You can feel assured that it matches the specification and provides useful support for these courses.

These print and online resources together **unlock blended learning**; this means that the links between the activities in the book and the activities online blend together to maximise your understanding of a topic and help you achieve your potential.

These online resources are available on **kerboodle** which can be accessed via the internet at **http://www.kerboodle.com/live**, anytime, anywhere. If your school or college subscribes to this service you will be provided with your own personal login details. Once logged in, access your course and locate the required activity.

For more information and help visit **http://www.kerboodle.com**

Icons in this book indicate where there is material online related to that topic. The following icons are used:

💡 Learning activity

These resources include a variety of interactive and non-interactive activities to support your learning:

- Animations
- Simulations
- Maths skills
- Key diagrams
- Glossary

✅ Progress tracking

These resources include a variety of tests that you can use to check your knowledge on particular topics (Test yourself) and a range of resources that enable you to analyse and understand examination questions (On your marks…).

🔢 Research support

These resources include WebQuests, in which you are assigned a task and provided with a range of web links to use as source material for research. These are designed to stretch you and broaden your learning.

🖥 PC activity

This icon identifies where there is a relevant practical activity to be undertaken on a computer. Where indicated, support is provided online.

Web links

Our online resources feature a list of recommended weblinks, split by chapter. This will help you to navigate to the best websites that will aid your learning and understanding of the topics in your course.

How to use this book

The main text of the book covers Units 1 and 2 of the AQA AS Level Computing specification. Unit 1 accounts for 60% and Unit 2 40% of your overall AS Level mark.

Unit 1 is designed to develop your problem solving skills. In this unit you will design then test solutions to problems, ultimately using programming as part of the problem-solving process. Your teacher will help you to choose a programming language for this course, but this book is written with example code from Pascal, VB 2005 and C#. Whichever language you choose, however, remember that problem solving and programming are skills developed and improved through practice. This book and the online resources will provide plenty of opportunity for practising these skills.

Unit 2 covers the fundamental parts of computer hardware, the structure of the Internet and consequences of computing. In this unit you will consider the impact that computing has already had on society and individuals and the direction that new developments may take in the future. The exam for this unit will require both short and long answers, so it is important to practise formulating arguments to support a point of view. The activities in the book and supporting online resources are intended to help you to expand your knowledge and to develop the skills you will need to be successful in your AS examination.

It is recommended that you have plenty of time to develop programming and problem solving skills. The first four sections should be started as early as possible in the course to give you time to develop these skills. Section 5 should be started towards the end of the first half of the course in order to give you an understanding of how data can be coded and Section 7 should follow to give a good understanding of the operation of the internal components of a computer and how they are designed using logic gates. Section 8, Topic 2 should be covered just after halfway through the course. This should be followed by Section 9, which could take up to five weeks of lesson time including practical work. Section 10 can follow next, then Section 8, Topic 1. You should then be able to understand Section 6, which covers how a hardware-software system is created. Following this you should devote time to working with the pre-release material for the COMP1 on-screen examination.

The features in this book include:

Learning objectives

At the beginning of each section you will find a list of learning objectives that contain targets linked to the requirements of the specification. The relevant specification reference is also provided.

Key terms

Terms that you will need to be able to define and understand are highlighted in bold blue type within the text, e.g. **Bluetooth**. You can look up these terms in the glossary.

Key point

Essential points that you should remember for success in this subject.

Did you know?

Interesting facts to bring learning to life.

Activities

Classroom-based tasks to help you apply knowledge and understand key concepts.

Questions

Short questions that test your understanding of the subject and allow you to apply the knowledge and skills you have acquired to different scenarios.

Study tip

Hints to help you with your studies and to prepare you for your exam.

Practice questions

These occur at the end of the book to give practice in questions for particular topics.

Practice questions are reproduced by permission of the Assessment and Qualifications Alliance.

Nelson Thornes is responsible for the solution(s) given and they may not constitute the only possible solution(s).

■ Web links in the book

As Nelson Thornes is not responsible for third party content online, there may be some changes to this material that are beyond our control. In order for us to ensure that the links referred to in the book are as up-to-date and stable as possible, the websites are usually homepages with supporting instructions on how to reach the relevant pages if necessary.

Please let us know at **kerboodle@nelsonthornes.com** if you find a link that doesn't work and we will do our best to redirect the link, or to find an alternative site.

Introduction to this book

The next twenty years will be the most exciting and momentous of times for anyone involved in studying Computing or Computer Science. Computing is a relatively young subject with many great problem solving challenges facing it currently. Today it stands at the crossroads of a revolution in thinking as did Physics at the beginning of the twentieth century. What has heralded this revolution? The answer is the realisation that computation is not just something that computers do but something that nature does and does in a way that is only just being recognised. "In DNA, nature has placed an information process at the foundations of life," claims Nobel Laureate David Baltimore. Coded within DNA in an alphabet of inheritance are the instructions for the creation of life forms as well as the data that represents the forms of life to be produced.

Computer scientists concern themselves with representations of information in patterns of symbols, known as data or data representations, the most appropriate representation for this data and the methods or sets of instructions to transform this data into new representations to provide new information. These methods or sets of instructions must also be represented by patterns of symbols called procedural representations. There are only two essentials of computation therefore:

■ A series of representations
■ A set of instructions for transforming each representation to the next in the series

We draw the conclusion from this that the computer is not essential! The computer is one of many possible media in which computations can happen. What you are embarking on by studying from this book is an understanding of the principles on which computation is based. Computing is a principles-based discipline and it exists in a principles-based framework, unlike ICT, which exists in a technology-based framework. If you want only to acquire skills in using office tools created by computer scientists then studying ICT would be a better option. If you want to be at the forefront of twenty-first century thought and science then study Computing.

Computation is at the heart of the quest to unravel the secrets of life, to understand more about the human brain, the natural sciences and economic systems. This quest began back in 1936 when Alan Turing discussed what is meant by computation in his famous paper on computable numbers. Turing used an imagined machine that has come to be called a Turing machine (this was before the advent of the electronic digital computer) to reason about the act of computation. At the present time, computer scientists use electronic computers as tools to study computation. However, in the future, computer scientists may very well use nature itself, in the form of DNA computers, to study the limits and complexities of computations.

Computer scientists are very much interested in computational procedures for solving problems, such as the mapping of the human genome. These procedures are called algorithms. Algorithms are at the heart of computing. In this book, you will learn to write simple algorithms to describe and control what computers can do. You will also learn about the limitations of algorithms for, despite the awesome power of computers, at present computing machines cannot be controlled to do many things that humans can do easily, such as object recognition. This is one of the great challenges facing computer scientists today. If you are reading this book as you are about to embark on the learning adventure that is Computing, then consider where you might be in ten years time – a fully qualified computer scientist? Will you be one of those computer scientists contributing to the solution of one or more of the great challenges of computer science in the twenty first century? If on the other hand, your future career takes a different route, then rest assured you will have acquired a good grounding in how to think computationally and to solve problems in a logical manner. Thinking computationally is considered an important life skill underpinning many careers. By the way, if you are also considering studying maths, try to take the Decision Maths or Discrete Maths option. You will find these subjects very useful to your future studies in Computing. Good luck in your studies!

Introduction

Study tip

You may wish to choose a language that provides you with a console application that will be the ideal environment to work in for the Unit 1 practical examination. You may wish to choose a language that also allows you to develop windows-based applications, which you may want to use for your A2 coursework.

This section develops your problem-solving skills. Several topics cover programming, but this is not the main aim. Programming is the tool to test out the problem solutions you have developed. It is similar to performing experiments in a laboratory if you are studying physics or chemistry.

Which programming language should you choose? It is not important to choose the latest commercial language. This will change many times in your working life. It is important that you learn the fundamental control constructs required by problem solutions: sequences, decisions, iterations and procedure calls. These are common to most programming languages. Having learnt the principles of computation and the fundamental programming constructs in one language, you will find it easy to learn a new language. Your first programming language should help you with your learning. It should provide you with helpful hints when you make mistakes, have a syntax that is easy to remember, require you to declare variables and decide on the data type before you use them, and not allow you to program in a poor style.

Many modern integrated development environments (IDEs) help you lay out your code in a neat way, indenting where appropriate. They may have auto-complete facilities, so you can write code quickly. They have libraries to provide you with tested routines – built-in functions and procedures.

The programming topics in this book give examples in Pascal, VB 2005 and C#, and you will see that their constructs are similar. All three languages provide console applications and windows-based applications. They all have auto-complete facilities. Whatever language you choose, remember that problem solving and programming are skills developed and improved through practice. If you want to play a musical instrument well, you need to practise. If you want to excel at a sport, you need to train. If you want to be a good problem solver and programmer, you need to practise solving problems and writing programs. You need to solve many more problems than could be set in this book. Look at other programming books. Look around you to find problems to solve. You may find problems to solve by computation in other subjects you study.

To write programs to manipulate data effectively, you need to understand how data is stored in the computer. That is why this unit covers data representation. Developing a computer solution to a problem will follow the system development life cycle, also covered in this unit. Testing your solution with a variety of data and ensuring that only valid data is entered into the computer will minimise errors in your software. The following topics are not designed to be worked through in a linear fashion. You may wish to return to the problem-solving section again and again. The topic on data types is intended for reference when you need to know details about a specific data type.

1 Problem solving

1.1 Principles of computation

Did you know?

Professor Dijkstra, a famous computer scientist, commented: 'Computing is no more about computers than astronomy is about telescopes.'

It is predicted that by 2100 about £500 will buy enough computing power to compute 10,000,000,000,000,000,000,000,000 instructions per second. This power is more than the computing power of the brains of the entire population of the planet.

Key terms

Computation: the act or process of calculating or determining something by mathematical, logical or interactive methods.

Computability: measures what can and cannot be computed.

Computing: the study of natural and artificial information processes.

There has never been a better time to be involved with computing. Exciting new developments such as DNA computing and quantum computing may solve many problems that have proved intractable with conventional computing, problems such as understanding the mind. To comprehend these challenges and perhaps to make a contribution, you will need to know the principles of computing. Two main principles stand out:

- Abstraction
  - What is the right level for thinking about a particular problem?
  - How can we communicate complex ideas simply?
  - How can we decompose problems logically?
- Automation
  - How can we automate an abstraction?

Computation

What is computation?

Before the 1920s, computers were human clerks that performed **computations**, or calculations. Many thousands of computers were employed in commerce, government and research establishments to perform manual calculations such as the calculation of astronomical tables.

After the 1920s, the expression 'computing machine' referred to any machine that performed the work of a human computer. After the late 1940s, 'computing machine' gradually gave way to 'computer' as electronic digital machinery became common. These computers were able to do the calculations originally performed by human clerks.

From the time when computational processes were performed by human clerks, there began the study of computation and **computability** – what can and cannot be computed.

What is computing?

Computing is a natural science. Computation and information processes now underpin many other fields, e.g. biology, chemistry and physics. More importantly, **computing** is not restricted to man-made artefacts such as the personal computer, the Xbox or the iPod. In fact, nature learned a long time ago how to encode information about organisms in DNA and then to generate new organisms from DNA through its own computational methods. Thus computation was present long before computers were invented. The range of phenomena covered by computing is extensive. Here are some fields of current interest:

- **Nanocomputing:** molecular-scale computing, nanites and nanobots.
- **DNA computing:** using strands of DNA to perform computations that would take too long by conventional computers.

■ **Artificial intelligence:** understanding intelligence, robotics, vision, natural language processing, speech.

■ **Nature-inspired computing:** emergent complex behaviour generated from simpler interactions between autonomous agents, cellular automata, fractals.

■ **Quantum computing:** using the quantum states of atoms to perform computations and solve problems that would take too long by a conventional computer.

Computing is also a study of how to compute. **This means a study of the process of computation:**

■ How we do things.

■ How we specify what we do.

■ How we specify what we're processing.

■ Questions

1 What is meant by computation?

2 What did Professor Dijkstra say about computing?

3 What is meant by computability?

4 What is computing?

5 What is artificial intelligence?

💡 Algorithms

A computer can easily total a list of numbers such as 23, 45, 3 and 67. It does it using an **algorithm**, a set of instructions that resemble a cooking recipe. A computer programmer turns the recipe into a computer program in a programming language.

The study of algorithms is one of the foundations of computer science or computing. Computer scientists are interested in what makes a good algorithm. They investigate the fastest and shortest algorithms and algorithms that take up the least amount of space, which problems can and cannot be solved by algorithms, and whether an algorithm is correct or not.

To understand algorithms better, computer scientists have studied real-world problems such as the travelling salesperson problem (TSP). In Fig. 1.1.1 is there a route that takes the salesperson through every

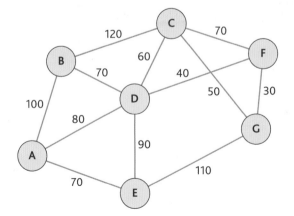

Fig. 1.1.1 *Cities and flight paths with the cost of each in pounds (£)*

city and back to the starting city, A, with a cost no more than a given amount? The salesperson can visit a city only once except for the starting city, which they visit twice, once when they set off and once when they return.

Fig. 1.1.1 represents cities as circles and flight paths between cities as straight lines. The labels represent the cost in pounds (£) of a flight along the chosen path.

Worked example _____

Problem

Look at the flight paths in Fig. 1.1.1. Is there a route that takes the salesperson through every city and back to the starting city A at a cost of no more than £520?

Solution

Yes, ABCGFDEA. Check this for yourself.

_____

▦ Programs and programming

A **program** is a description in a programming language of a process that achieves some result that is useful to someone.

```
Program P(I);
  Write(I*2);
End.
```

An algorithm is a description of a process apart from any programming language. One algorithm may be implemented in many different languages in many different ways in many different programs. An algorithm is run on a computer by translating it into a sequence of computer instructions. These computer instructions are the programs that run on computers.

What does a computer know how to do? Very little. Computers are electronic devices that react to voltages on wires. At this bottom level, the computer only 'knows' about voltages which, for convenience, we interpret as numbers. It is the program running on the computer that interprets the numbers as characters, which can be interpreted in collections such as a web page.

▦ Abstraction and automation

The two main principles of computation are abstraction and automation:

▦ **Abstraction**: what is the right level for thinking about a particular problem, how to communicate complex ideas simply and how to decompose problems logically.
▦ **Automation**: how to automate an algorithm.

Fig. 1.1.2 on p6 shows how a geographically complex layout of railway track and stations can be modelled in a way that is simple and easy to understand, by ignoring detail and concentrating on the essentials. This is an example of abstraction.

Automation involves a programmer turning an algorithm into a computer program for a computer to execute.

▦ Key terms

Program: a description in a programming language of a process that achieves some useful result.

▦ Key point

Programs are not algorithms. An algorithm is a description of a process apart from any programming language. The same algorithm may be programmed in many different languages.

💻 PC activity

Use the Web to research Harry Beck's maps of the London Underground from 1933 onwards.

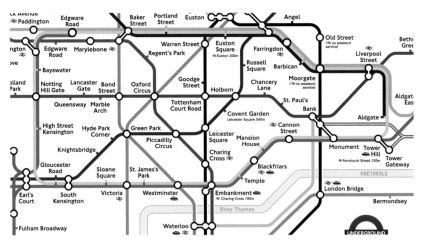

Fig. 1.1.2 *Map of the London Underground*

Questions

6 What is an algorithm?

7 What is the purpose of an algorithm?

8 An algorithm is not the same thing as a computer program. Do you agree? Explain your answer.

9 Is there a route in Fig. 1.1.1 that takes the salesperson through every city and back to the starting city A with a cost of £480 at most?

10 What are the two main principles of computation?

In this topic you have covered:

- principles of computation
- what is meant by computation and computability
- what is meant by computing
- computing as a natural science
- different types of computing
- algorithms and programs.

1.2 Stages of problem solving

> **Key point**
>
> Understanding a problem means turning an ill-defined problem into a well-defined problem stated clearly and unambiguously.

> **Key terms**
>
> **Given:** an initial situation.
>
> **Problem:** a given where it is not immediately obvious how to reach the goal.
>
> **Goal:** a desired outcome.
>
> **Resources:** things that can be used to reach a goal and impose constraints.

During our lives we continually solve a range of problems. Reading a book or holding a conversation is a complex communication problem. When reading, our brains are actively and consciously making sense of what is being read. But when we were learning to read, there was a phase when all our effort went into recognising and verbalising the words. It took thousands of hours to train our brains to recognise and verbalise words with little conscious effort. It takes a similar effort to become a good problem solver in computing.

💡 Understanding the problem

Problem solving involves moving from an initial situation, a **given**, to a desired target situation, a **goal**, using a set of **resources** to help reach the goal and impose constraints along the way. Usually, the term **problem** is used to refer to a situation where it is not immediately obvious how to reach the goal (Fig. 1.2.1).

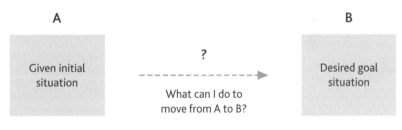

Fig. 1.2.1 *Problem solving: how to achieve a goal*

The first stage of problem solving is to understand the problem. An important aspect of problem solving is realising when you are dealing with an ill-defined problem situation and working to change it into a well-defined problem. You need an initial understanding of the given, the resources and the goal. This requires knowledge of the problem domain – unblocking a blocked waste pipe in your kitchen requires some basic knowledge of the plumbing domain.

> **Case study**
>
> ### Apollo 13 air filter
>
> Apollo 13 was intended to fly to the moon and back. While the main spacecraft, the command and service module (CSM), was orbiting the moon, two astronauts would descend to the surface of the moon in a separate craft called the lunar module (LM). But the LM never went to the moon. At 55 hours and 55 minutes into the mission, all three astronauts heard and felt a 'pretty large bang'.
>
> Two of the three fuel cells in the CSM had gone dead. No one knew quite what had happened, but there was no doubt that the crew was in serious trouble. Fortunately, the LM had an engine to put the crew back on a homeward path, and it carried just enough water, oxygen and power for the four days. The CSM had plenty of lithium hydroxide to remove the carbon dioxide breathed out by the

astronauts in the LM. Unfortunately, these canisters were the wrong size and shape to fit directly into the LM air filter units.

So how could the LM air filter units be adapted to use these oversized canisters? A day and a half after the Apollo 13 accident, the ground teams had designed and built a device that worked. The solution came in the form of an ingenious combination of suit hoses, cardboard, plastic stowage bags and CSM canisters, all held together with gaffer tape (**www.hq.nasa.gov/**). The instructions were uploaded to the Apollo 13 spacecraft and within an hour the solution was working.

We can define four components for this problem:

- ■ Initial situation: lithium hydroxide canisters from the CSM that did not fit air filter units in the LM.
- ■ Resources and constraints:
  a bits and pieces available to the astronauts on board Apollo 13
  b expertise, experience and time of engineers in ground control
  c the lithium hydroxide in the LM canisters would be used up in a given time
  d engineers in ground control could use only bits and pieces on board Apollo 13.
- ■ Goal: adapt the LM air filters to use the lithium hydroxide canisters from the CSM.
- ■ Ownership: team of ground control engineers allocated full time to devise a solution.

■ Defining the problem

A well-defined problem has four components: a clearly defined initial situation given, a clearly defined goal, a clearly defined set of resources and constraints, and ownership. The resources may help you to move from the initial situation to the goal situation; there may be constraints on resources, such as rules, regulations and guidelines about what you are allowed to do in solving a particular problem. You must be committed to using some of your own resources, such as your knowledge, skills and energies to achieve the goal. These four components need to be defined in the problem statement.

If one or more of these components is missing, you have an ill-defined problem situation rather than a well-defined problem. In organisations, a common reason for a problem remaining unsolved is that ownership is not made clear. In teamworking, problem tasks are delegated to individual members of a team. Sometimes it is not made clear who is doing what, so the problem doesn't get solved.

Worked example _____

You are at a river that you want to cross with all your goods. Your goods consist of a chicken, a bag of grain and your dog, Rover. You have to cross the river in your rowing boat but can only take one passenger with you at a time – the chicken, the dog or the bag of grain. You can't leave the chicken alone with the grain as the chicken will eat the grain. You can't leave your dog alone with the chicken as Rover will eat the chicken. However, you know that Rover does not eat grain. How do you get everything across the river intact?

■ Questions

1 Explain what is meant by 'problem'.

2 Explain what is meant by 'problem solving'.

3 Explain what is meant by 'to understand a problem'.

■ Key point

A well-defined problem has four components: givens, resources and constraints, a goal, and ownership.

Problem

- ■ **Initial situation**: you, the chicken, the bag of grain and the dog are on one bank of a river with access to a rowing boat.
- ■ **Resources**: the rowing boat and your knowledge and problem-solving skill.
- ■ **Constraints**: you can take only one passenger, you must not leave Rover with the chicken, you must not leave the chicken with the bag of grain.
- ■ **Goal**: you, the chicken, the bag of grain and the dog on the opposite bank of river.
- ■ **Ownership**: you will be involved in planning the solution and carrying it out.

Solution

1 Take the chicken across the river and leave it on the other side. Return to where you have left Rover and the grain.

2 Take Rover across the river and leave him on the other side. Take back the chicken.

3 Leave the chicken where you started. Take the bag of grain across the river and leave it with Rover.

4 Go back and fetch the chicken and take it across the river with you.

This puzzle requires you to think laterally. Many people are unable to solve the problem because they assume you cannot bring something back on the return trip. In fact, challenging your assumptions is an important part of problem solving. Adding the fact that you are allowed to carry something back across the river would have made the problem definition clearer.

Defining boundaries

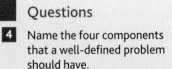

Defining a problem is just as much about clearly **defining boundaries** or the rules of what can and cannot be done. A boundary is a form of constraint. Most problems have other kinds of constraints imposed upon them, including time, available equipment and software (resource constraints). It is vital that you understand clearly what those constraints are, what you can and cannot do. Do not assume constraints that are not true. By using **lateral thinking** you can challenge your assumptions and establish the facts.

The general pattern of lateral thinking is to be consciously aware that we need to add facts to those we start with.

▦ Ask questions. In lateral thinking puzzles, these questions are asked of the person who sets the puzzle but the answers must be yes or no.

▦ Identify the assumptions we are making about the apparent facts in front of us. This means separating what is established from what we haven't established but have unconsciously assumed. One way to do this is to close your eyes and picture the scene that has been described. Next focus on all the details of this picture that were not actually given to you – they are all assumptions.

▦ Make new proposed facts from putting together other facts.

■ Key point

Identify assumptions and challenge them. Establish the real facts.

■ Questions

8 What is meant by defining boundaries in problem solving?

9 What other kinds of constraint occur in problem solving other than boundary constraints?

10 Why is lateral thinking useful in problem solving?

11 How would you use lateral thinking in a problem-solving situation?

💡 Activity

Lateral thinking puzzles

This activity is about false assumptions and you will need a partner. One of you will need to know what happened and answer yes or no to the other's questions. Your teacher can supply the solution to the following lateral thinking problem: Romeo and Juliet are lying dead on the floor, surrounded by water and broken glass. What happened?

Now reverse roles and try this lateral thinking problem. Again, your teacher has the solution. A man lives on the 18th floor of a tower block. Every weekday morning he takes the lift to the ground floor and walks to work. Every weekday evening, he walks from work, takes the lift to the 12th floor and then takes the stairs to the 18th floor. If it was raining in the morning, he takes the lift straight to the 18th floor in the evening. Why does he not use the lift to the 18th floor every weekday evening?

■ Planning a solution

You should determine a plan of action. Ask yourself these questions:

- What strategies will you apply?
- What resources will you use?
- How will you use the resources?
- In what order will you use the resources?
- Are your resources adequate for the task?

Think carefully about possible consequences of carrying out a plan of action. Try to anticipate unwanted outcomes.

A strategy can be thought of as a plan or a possible approach for solving some types of problem. Suppose that every day you have to find a space in the covered bicycle racks at school. Perhaps your strategy is to arrive at school five minutes before anyone else who cycles to school and perhaps it works most of the time.

Breaking big problems into smaller problems, or subproblems, is called a top-down strategy. It may be far easier to deal with a number of smaller problems than one large problem. A big problem can be solved one step at a time. Each of the smaller problems can be worked on independently. This technique is sometimes called divide and conquer or functional decomposition. Writing an essay may be approached by developing an outline then writing small pieces that fill in the details. It is useful to think of the smaller problems as building-block problems – problems that you know how to solve easily and quickly. Increasing your repertoire of building-block problems improves your ability to solve other problems and helps you to get better at using the top-down strategy.

Top-down design

■ Key term

Top-down design: breaks a problem into smaller problems that are easier to work on.

When the top-down strategy is used to plan a solution, it is called **top-down design**. Consider the following problem. Find the values of x which satisfy the equation $x^2 + 3x + 2 = 0$. This is a quadratic equation. A quadratic equation has the form $ax^2 + bx + c$ with $a \neq 0$. Knowledge of the problem domain suggests using the quadratic formula

$$x = \frac{-b \pm \sqrt{b^2 - 4ac}}{2a}$$

to solve the problem. The problem can now be broken down into solving the smaller problems of finding b^2, $4ac$, $\sqrt{b^2 - 4ac}$, $-b \pm \sqrt{b^2 - 4ac}$, $(-b \pm \sqrt{b^2 - 4ac})/2a$ with $a = 1$, $b = 3$ and $c = 2$. In problem solving, note that knowledge of the domain is often required. In this case the domain is mathematics.

We can think of each smaller problem or subproblem as a separate **module** on a chart (Fig. 1.2.2). Each module is a separate procedure or separate stage. The chart is called a hierarchy chart.

> ■ **Key term**
>
> **Module:** a self-contained entity that results when a problem is divided into subproblems; each module corresponds to a subproblem.

■ Activity

Interpret a hierarchy chart

Use the hierarchy chart, working from left to right, to find the values of x which satisfy $x^2 + 3x + 2 = 0$. Check your solution.

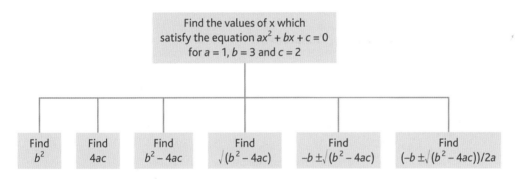

Fig. 1.2.2 *A hierarchy chart breaks a problem into subproblems*

■ Activity

Design a module chart

Use top-down design to draw a hierarchy chart for Topic 1.2 of this book.

Stepwise refinement

Another way of doing top-down design is to start with a big problem and break it into successively smaller problems. This is called **stepwise refinement**. Suppose someone wants to travel from X to Y by car and they ask you for directions. First you would identify the major steps, perhaps two or three. Then you would divide each major step into further simpler steps, and so on. Brain research on short-term memory suggests that we should stop when we have about 7 ± 2 smaller steps.

For example, suppose that you were asked to give directions to someone travelling in Buckinghamshire from Ellesborough to Aston Clinton. Using the map extract in Fig. 1.2.3, you might plan the route as in Table 1, starting at level 0 and stopping at level 2, because you have reached 7 ± 2 chunks of information.

The numbering in Table 1 reflects the stages of refinement and makes it easier for reference. We could show the overall result of stepwise refinement in one go as in Table 2. Indentation indicates a more detailed step. Sometimes the label 0 is omitted and the step numbering becomes 1, 1.1, 1.2, etc. Table 2 is called a **structure table**.

> ■ **Key terms**
>
> **Stepwise refinement:** the process of breaking a problem down through successive steps into smaller problems.
>
> **Structure table:** an indented, numbered list of steps produced by stepwise refinement.

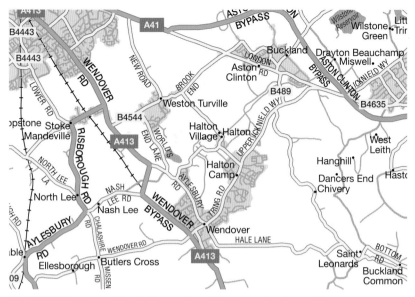

Fig. 1.2.3 *Map extract for the journey from Ellesborough to Aston Clinton*

Table 1 *Stepwise refinement of a problem*

Level 0	Travel from Ellesborough to Aston Clinton
Level 1	1 Travel from Ellesborough to Wendover 2 Travel from Wendover to Weston Turville 3 Travel from Weston Turville to Aston Clinton
Level 2	1.1 Travel from Ellesborough to Butlers Cross 1.2 Travel from Butlers Cross to Wendover 2.1 Travel from Wendover along A413 to junction with B4544 2.2 Travel along B4544 to Weston Turville 3.1 Drive through Weston Turville to junction with A41 3.2 Turn southwards onto A41 to reach Aston Clinton

Table 2 *Structure table for stepwise refinement*

0 Travel from Ellesborough to Aston Clinton
   0.1 Travel from Ellesborough to Wendover
      0.1.1 Travel from Ellesborough to Butlers Cross
      0.1.2 Travel from Butlers Cross to Wendover
   0.2 Travel from Wendover to Weston Turville
      0.2.1 Travel from Wendover along A413 to junction with B4544
      0.2.2 Travel along B4544 to Weston Turville
   0.3 Travel from Weston Turville to Aston Clinton
      0.3.1 Drive through Weston Turville to junction with A41
      0.3.2 Turn southwards onto A41 to reach Aston Clinton

Activity

Use stepwise refinement

Apply stepwise refinement to calculation of the sum and average of any two numbers supplied by another student. Create a structure table in stages so that the final structure table could be used to program a computer to do this task.

■ Carrying out a plan of action

Reflective thinking leads to increased expertise, so carry out a plan of action in a thoughtful manner. Perhaps you will find that you need to go back to an earlier stage. In Table 1 it may turn out that roadworks in Weston Turville delay people's journeys.

Check to see if the desired goal has been achieved by carrying out your plan of action:

1 If the problem has been solved, reflect on what you have learned and how it can be used in other problem-solving situations.

2 If the problem has not been solved, go back to defining the problem or planning a solution.

3 Analyse your steps and your results to see if you have created extra problems to solve.

4 Stop working on the problem. Perhaps you need to acquire more expertise or perhaps there is no solution.

In this topic you have covered:

- the stages of problem solving
- formulation of a well-defined problem
- given, goal, resources, constraints and ownership
- how to define the problem boundaries
- how to challenge assumptions by thinking laterally
- how to plan a solution and draw up an action plan
- top-down design and stepwise refinement
- how to execute and evaluate a plan of action.

1.3 Finite state machines

In this topic you will cover:

- finite state machines

- state transition diagrams with and without outputs

- state transition tables

- decision tables.

Activity

States of a lift

Write down as many states as you can for a lift that serves a three-storey building.

Activity

Lift inputs and outputs

Write down as many lift inputs and outputs as you can.

Did you know?

The Amulet3 mobile phone processor has 500,000 internal states that it can be in. How do you check that all of them are valid?

Key terms

Finite state machine: a machine that consists of a fixed set of possible states with a set of allowable inputs that change the state and a set of possible outputs.

If you have ever used a lift, you have used a finite state machine (FSM). The lift can be in one of a finite number of states at any moment. Finite means countable. For example, one state for a lift serving a three-storey building is 'at the third floor with doors open'. Another is 'travelling between second and third floor with doors closed'.

The lift system has inputs and outputs. One input occurs when a person calls the lift by pressing the lift request button on, say, the second floor. One output occurs to indicate the position of the lift to the person waiting on the second floor.

For the lift to move in the desired direction to the desired floor, it must always know which state it is currently in and what step to take next, so it needs memory to store the current state and a logic device to determine the next step.

When the lift arrives at the second floor, the logic device briefly turns on the door motor to open the doors. The logic device must also update the memory to reflect the new state of the lift – stationary at the second floor with the doors open. Fig. 1.3.1 shows a model of this FSM.

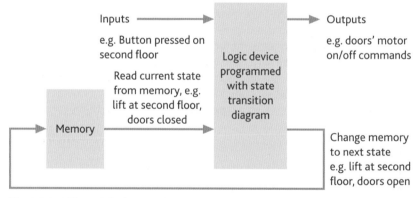

Fig. 1.3.1 *A lift modelled as an FSM*

A **finite state machine** is a machine that consists of a fixed set of possible states, a set of allowable inputs that change the state, a set of possible outputs. The outputs can depend only on the current state, which depends only on the history of the sequence of inputs.

Many types of digital machine, including general-purpose computers, are FSMs. General-purpose computers advance their state at regular intervals and the rate at which they advance is called the clock rate of the machine. Each state is one step towards the solution to a problem. Increasing the clock rate of a computer should enable the computer to solve a problem more quickly.

💡 State transition diagrams

A ballpoint pen is an example of an FSM:

- It has a finite number of states: ballpoint extended and ballpoint retracted.

■ It has a set of allowable inputs: clicking the pen's button.

■ It has a set of possible outputs: retracting or extending the ballpoint.

The behaviour of a ballpoint pen can be described by a **state transition diagram** (Fig. 1.3.2). This diagram consists of two states, 0 and 1, and two transitions indicated by curved arrows. Each curved arrow is labelled with the input that causes each transition, here button clicked.

By repeatedly clicking the button (input), the pen alternates between state 0 (ballpoint retracted) and state 1 (ballpoint extended); the output is determined by which state the pen is in when the button is clicked.

Key terms

State transition diagram: a way of describing an FSM graphically. Each state is represented by a circle and each transition by an arrow labelled with the input that causes the transition plus any output resulting from the transition.

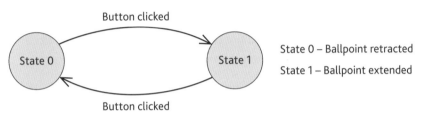

State 0 – Ballpoint retracted

State 1 – Ballpoint extended

Fig. **1.3.2** *State transition diagram for a ballpoint pen*

Worked example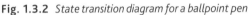

Consider a combination lock that opens only when it is given the sequence 326. Whether mechanical or electrical, this is an FSM with the state transition diagram shown in Fig. 1.3.3. There are no outputs. The initial state of the combination lock is indicated by a small entering arrow pointing to the state 'locked'. When the lock is in state 'locked' and it receives the input 3, the lock moves to the state 'first digit'. When it receives the input 2, the lock moves to the state 'second digit'. When it receives the input 6, the lock moves to the state 'unlocked'. At any stage, if a digit other than the required digit is entered, the lock remains in its current state. The final or halting state is reached when the combination lock is unlocked. The state 'unlocked' is indicated by a double circle because it is the goal state. The goal state is known as the accepting state.

Key point

One reason FSMs are so useful is that they can recognise sequences. The set of recognisable sequences can be legal and valid programs in a given programming language.

Key point

An FSM with no outputs is called a Finite State Automaton (FSA).

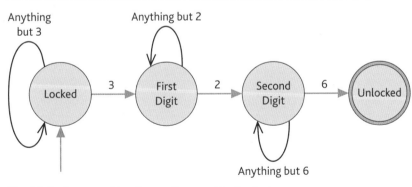

Fig. **1.3.3** *State transition diagram for a combination lock*

Key point

FSAs have an initial state and one or more accepting or goal states. State transition diagrams use a special arrow to indicate the initial state and a double circle to indicate the accepting state, or goal state.

▣ FSM with outputs

An FSM may produce a response when it makes a transition, i.e. an output. This is represented as shown in Fig. 1.3.4 on p14. If the input is A when this machine is in state 1 then the machine moves to state 2 and outputs 'response'. This type of FSM is known as a Mealy machine. It does not have an accepting state.

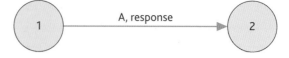

Fig. 1.3.4 *State transition diagram for an FSM that outputs 'response'*

This type of machine is used when we want to do more than just recognise a sequence, such as the sequence for the combination lock. We might want a machine starting in the initial state S_0 to translate a sequence of received 1s, 0s and 2s into plain text consisting of the letters A and B and exclamation mark ! according to the following rules:

- The system begins receiving in the initial state S_0.
- If the received digit is 0 and the system is in state S_0, output the letter A.
- If the received digit is 1 and the system is in state S_0, change state to S_1 and output the letter B.
- If the received digit is 2 and the system is in state S_0, change state to S_2 and output the character !.
- If the received digit is 0 and the system is in state S_1, change state to S_0 and output the letter A.
- If the received digit is 1 and the system is in state S_1, output the letter B.
- If the received digit is 2 and the system is in state S_1, change state to S_2 and output the character !.

Figure 1.3.5 shows the corresponding state transition diagram with outputs for this system.

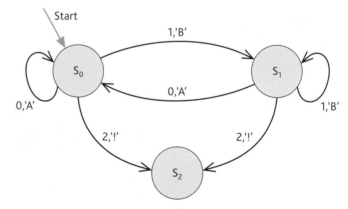

Fig. 1.3.5 *State transition diagram for an FSM that turns 0, 1, 2 into A, B, !*

The sequence 00101102 produces as output AABABBA! Check this for yourself. What does the sequence 101012 produce as output? Answer BABAB!

💡 State transition tables

We can use a table that shows the state that follows for every state and every input. For example, Table 1 summarises the ballpoint pen operation.

Table 1 *State transition table for the ballpoint pen FSM*

Input	Current state	Next state
Button clicked	Ballpoint retracted	Ballpoint extended
Button clicked	Ballpoint extended	Ballpoint retracted

Sometimes the **state transition table** is just called the state table.

If an FSM has outputs, then the state transition table can also show the outputs. Table 2 shows the state transition table for the state transition diagram in Fig. 1.3.5. Check the table entries for yourself.

Table 2 *State transition table for an FSM with outputs*

Input	Current state	Output	Next state
0	S_0	A	S_0
1	S_0	B	S_1
2	S_0	!	S_2
0	S_1	A	S_0
1	S_1	B	S_1
2	S_1	!	S_2

Decision tables

A **decision table** is a precise yet compact way to model complicated logic. Decision tables make it easy to observe that all possible conditions are accounted for.

For example, some logic is written as follows:

```
If X is greater than 6 and Y is less than 7
    Then Output "Pass"
    Else Output "Fail"
```

Table 3 shows the corresponding decision table.

Table 3 *Logical condition expressed as a decision table*

		Rule or condition options: Y means true, N means false			
Conditions	X > 6	Y	Y	N	N
	Y < 7	Y	N	Y	N
Actions	Output 'Pass'	X			
	Output 'Fail'		X	X	X

Note that there are two subconditions in the conditions section of Table 3:

```
X > 6
Y < 7
```

When both conditions are true at the same time, the output is Pass. When either of the conditions is false or both are false, the output is Fail. The Pass or Fail output is indicated by X in the corresponding table cell.

Note that the rules rows are constructed in a systematic way. For example, if there are two condition alternatives, then the first row is constructed with YYNN and the second row with YNYN.

Decision tables

Complete Table 4 for the following logic:

```
If X is greater than 6 and
Y is less than 7 or Z is
equal to 3
   Then Output "Pass"
   Else Output "Fail"
```

Table 4 *Template for a decision table*

		Rule or condition options: Y means true, N means false					
Conditions	X > 6						
	Y < 7						
	Z = 3						
Actions	Output 'Pass'						
	Output 'Fail'						

Questions

1 Fig. 1.3.6 shows an FSM and the state transition diagram with which it is programmed. The machine accepts input sequences consisting of the letters a and b, e.g. aabbbabaaab. The machine has a lamp labelled ACCEPT. The machine starts out in state 1 and the accepting state is also state 1. When the machine is in state 1 after the machine has exhausted the input, the lamp lights. What does this machine detect and indicate with the lamp?

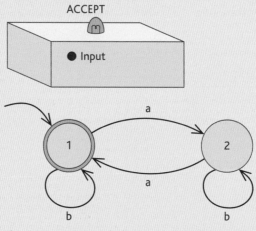

Fig. 1.3.6 *An FSM and its state transition diagram*

2 Draw a state transition diagram for a combination lock with combination 956. Draw the corresponding state transition table.

3 Draw a state transition diagram with outputs for an FSM that gives an output of 1 if and only if the input string read so far ends with 111 otherwise it gives an output of 0.

4 Draw a decision table for the following logic:

```
If X is greater than 6 or Y is less than 7
   Then Output "Pass"
   Else Output "Fail"
```

In this topic you have covered:

- finite state machines, Mealy machines and finite state automata
- state transition diagrams with and without outputs
- state transition tables
- decision tables.

1.4 Algorithm design

Key terms

Algorithm: a description, independent of any programming language, of a process that achieves some task. It is a step-by-step procedure for solving a problem.

Did you know?

Computer science is the study of recipes that can be executed by a computer. In computer science, a recipe defines exactly what has to be done but the recipe is written so it can be implemented in any programming language.

Computer scientists express solutions to problems as algorithms and computer programs. Algorithms are not unique to computing. To understand an algorithm, suppose that a student from the Far East is a guest in your home and you make them a cheese and pickle sandwich. The student asks for the recipe and you write it down for them.

Algorithms

An **algorithm** is a description, independent of any programming language, of a process that achieves some task. It is a sequence of steps, independent of any programming language, that solve some problem.

Activity

Recipe for a cheese and pickle sandwich

a Write down the recipe for a cheese and pickle sandwich. If you need to, look it up on the web.

b Use your recipe to make yourself a cheese and pickle sandwich. Follow the instructions as literally and as exactly as you can.

c After your own experience, do you think that your visitor will be able to follow your recipe?

Writing a recipe for a cheese and pickle sandwich may have seemed trivial at first, but perhaps you found it a little more challenging. If you did not find it challenging, are you sure you did not assume too much?

- Did you specify what cheese to use?
- Did you specify how thick to slice the cheese?
- Did you specify how much cheese to use?
- Did you specify what kind of bread to use?
- Did you specify that the bread should be bought already sliced?
- If not, did you specify that you need a knife for slicing the loaf?
- In which case, did you specify how thick the slices should be?
- Did you specify how much butter to use?
- Did you specify what brand of pickle to use?
- Did you specify whether the same knife could be used for cutting the cheese and spreading the butter?

You probably felt it unnecessary to spell out everything. You probably made assumptions about the knowledge and understanding of the sandwich maker. Algorithms are similar to recipes in that they are loosely drafted and make assumptions about the user's knowledge. They are designed to communicate a computation or a process to humans. Experienced cooks do not need everything spelled out for them, but a computer does. That is why algorithms must be turned into computer programs.

A **program** is a description in a programming language of a process that achieves a useful result. Programs may be large or small. A small program may implement a calculator, whereas a large program may keep track of all the accounts in a bank.

An algorithm is a description of a process apart from any programming language. One algorithm may be implemented in many different languages in many different ways in many different programs.

💡 Planning an algorithm

An algorithm doesn't have to relate to computer programming. For example, suppose that you and your family are travelling in a car and one of its tyres gets a puncture. Let's use stepwise refinement to arrive at a process for changing the flat tyre.

After pulling over to the side of the road, the driver might decide to subdivide the problem of changing a tyre into the following subproblems:

1 Loosen the wheel nuts from the flat tyre.

2 Get the spare tyre from the boot of the car.

3 Jack up the car.

4 Remove the wheel with the flat tyre.

5 Fit the spare tyre and tighten the wheel nuts.

6 Lower the car.

7 Secure the jack and flat tyre in the boot.

Step 3 refinement

3.1 Place the jack under the car near the wheel with the flat tyre.

3.2 Insert the jack handle in the jack.

3.3 Place a brick or wooden block under a wheel to stop the car from rolling off the jack.

3.4 Jack up the car until there is enough room to fit the spare.

Step 3.3 refinement

3.3.1 If the car is facing uphill, place the brick at the back of one of the non-flat tyres; if the car is facing downhill or on the level, place the brick in front of a non-flat tyre.

Step 3.4 refinement

3.4.1 Move the jack handle repeatedly until the car is high enough off the ground for the spare tyre to be put on the wheel.

Three constructs

Note that subproblems 1 and 2 are relatively independent steps and could be done by different passengers from the car. This is a good reason for breaking a problem into subproblems. Step 3.3 requires a bit of decision making. Step 3.4 involves a repetitive action.

We can construct an algorithm for this example from three simple constructs:

▪ **Sequence:** consecutive steps or groups of steps processed one after another in the order that they arise.

▪ **Selection:** a decision-making step, e.g. step 3.3.1.

■ **Repetition or iteration:** a step or sequence of steps that are repeated until some condition is satisfied or while some condition is satisfied, e.g. step 3.4.1.

■ Computer-based problem solving

The problem to be solved should be described in sufficient detail for you to understand it. Read a problem statement carefully, more than once if necessary, so that you get a general idea of what is being asked. Then read it again so that you can answer the following two questions:

■ What data do I have to work with?

■ What information should the solution provide?

The answer to the first question will tell you the desired results, or the problem outputs. The answer to the second question will tell you what data is provided, or the problem inputs.

Worked example _____

- **Problem:** read in two numbers and find and print their sum and average.

- **Discussion:** after identifying the problem inputs and outputs, we must determine the variables for the input data and the output information. We must choose meaningful names for them.

- **Problem inputs:** the first number is assigned to variable Number1 and the second number is assigned to variable Number2

- **Problem outputs:** the sum of the two numbers is assigned to variable Sum. The average of the two numbers is assigned to variable Average.

- **Algorithm:**
    1. Input the first number and store in Number1.
    2. Input the second number and store in Number2.
    3. Calculate the sum of the values stored in Number1 and Number2. Store result in Sum.
    4. Calculate the average of the values stored in Number1 and Number2. Store result in Average.
    5. Output the values stored in Sum and Average.
    Refine step 4: 4.1 Divide value stored in Sum by 2. Store the result in Average.

_____

This algorithm is expressed in structured English. When storing the first number in the variable Number1 we say that we are assigning the first number to variable Number1. The operation of assigning is called **assignment**. We can represent the assignment of a computed value (Number1 + Number2) by a left-pointing arrow as follows:

```
Sum ← Number1 + Number2
```

The computation on the right-hand side of an assignment statement can be any meaningful arithmetic formula.

Questions

8 Name the four major steps to be used in computer-based problem solving.

9 What is meant by assignment?

10 Find and display the largest of three numbers entered through a keyboard. Solve this problem using the four major steps method.

Expressing an algorithm in structured English

Structured English is a very limited, highly restricted subset of the English language. In some ways, structured English resembles a programming language, so programmers find it easy to understand but it is also based on English, so non-programmers should also find it easy to understand.

There is no standard for structured English, but it uses the three basic instruction types: sequence, decision (selection) and repetition.

Sequence of statements

In structured English, sequence consists of command statements of the form 'Do this, do that'. Each command instruction begins with a verb such as SET, DO, MULTIPLY, ADD and SUBTRACT.

```
MULTIPLY hours-worked by pay-rate to get gross-pay
GET next employee-record FROM Employee file
UPDATE employee-record
WRITE updated employee-record to Employee file
INPUT hours-worked
OUTPUT gross-pay
PRINT payslip
```

If we assign the name 'compute gross pay' to the group of statements above, we can use

```
DO compute gross pay
```

In structured English, we assign a value to a variable or a constant using the SET statement, such as

```
SET pi to 3.142
```

Selection statements

In structured English, selection consists of IF THEN, IF--THEN--ELSE and SELECT statements:

```
IF reorder-flag is on
   THEN order more stock
IF stock-level is less than reorder-level
   THEN turn on reorder-flag
   ELSE turn off reorder-flag
SELECT VALUE option
   6 : ADD 1 to counter
   8 : ADD 2 to counter
   10 : ADD 4 to counter
END SELECT
```

In the SELECT statement, the option must match 6, 8 or 10. If it does then the corresponding ADD statement is chosen and the others are ignored.

Repetition statements

In structured English, repetition consists of REPEAT UNTIL, FOR EACH and DO WHILE statements:

```
REPEAT UNTIL last employee-record processed
   ADD next employee-record hours-worked field to total
FOR EACH employee-record
   ADD next employee-record hours-worked field to total
DO WHILE more records to process
   ADD next employee-record hours-worked field to total
```

💡 Expressing an algorithm in pseudocode

Pseudocode is a language for expressing algorithms. An alternative to structured English, it is similar to real programming code but it is not real programming code. Its name comes from the Greek *pseudo* 'false'. The syntax of pseudocode is less strict than the syntax of a real programming language. There is no standard pseudocode and many versions exist. Most incorporate the three structured programming constructs – sequence, selection and repetition – plus input and output instructions. Structured English ignores details such as opening and closing files, initialising counters and setting flags, but they are not ignored in pseudocode.

Sequence of statements

The following sequence consists of two input statements, two assignment statements and one output statement arranged to be executed in the order that they appear. Input and output statements refer to the standard input and output devices, the keyboard and the monitor, respectively.

```
Input Number1
Input Number2
Sum ← Number1 + Number2
Average ← Sum / 2
Output Sum, Average
```

In the following sequence, Read and Write refer to reading and writing operations involving any online storage device. Print refers to any printer.

```
Read x, y From Disk File Temp.Dat
Write x, y To Disk File Result.Dat
Output 'File copied'
Print 'Job finished'
```

Selection statements

Here are some examples of selection pseudocode. Each contains some decision making. The Case statement matches x with 4, 5 or 6 and executes the corresponding statement only if x has that value. If x is 5 then only z ← z − 1 is executed. The other statements are skipped.

Pseudocode

```
If x > 3
  Then y ← 6
EndIf
```

```
If d < 24
  Then
    z ← z + 2
    w ← w - 3
EndIf
If x In [1..10]
  Then y ← 5
  Else y ← 9
EndIf

If w In [1..5, 8, 11]
  Then
    z ← z + 2
    w ← w - 3
  Else
    z ← z + 2
    w ← w - 3
EndIf
Case x Of
  4 : z ← z + 1
  5 : z ← z - 1
  6 : z ← 6
EndCase

Case x Of
  4 : z ← z + 1
      w ← w - 2
  5 : z ← z - 1
  6 : z ← 6
EndCase
```

Repetition statements

Here are some examples of repetition, or iteration, expressed in pseudocode. The block of statements inside the For loop is executed 10 times:

```
For x ← 1 To 10 Do
  y ← y + 2
  z ← z - 5
EndFor
```

In the Repeat Until statement, x ← x + 1 is executed at least once and more times if x is not equal to 6:

```
Repeat
  x ← x + 1
Until x = 6
```

In the While Do statement, x ← x + 1 is only executed while x is less than 5:

```
While x < 5 Do
  x ← x + 1
EndWhile
```

In the For Each loop, x is output for each value, in turn, in the set of values [1,3,5]. Each time x assumes the next value in the set, starting at the first:

```
For Each x In [1,3,5] Do
  Output x
EndFor
```

From pseudocode to program code

This algorithm calculates the sum and average of two numbers. It is written in pseudocode and the high-level language Pascal.

Pseudocode

```
Input Number1
Input Number2
Sum ← Number1 + Number2
Average ← Sum/2
Output Sum, Average
```

Pascal

```
Program FindSumAverage;
Var
   Number1, Number2, Sum, Average : Real;
Begin
   Write('First number? '); Readln(Number1);
   Write('Second number? '); Readln(Number2);
   Sum := Number1 + Number2;
   Average := Sum / 2;
   Writeln('Their sum is ', Sum : 5:2);
   Writeln('Their average is ', Average :5:2);
End.
```

When the program is run and the values shown in Figure 1 are entered, the program outputs the calculated values for the sum and the average.

The sum and average algorithm illustrates several good practices to be followed when constructing algorithms and programs.

▪ Use meaningful names wherever possible, e.g. Number1 instead of N1.

▪ Use indentation to show structure. Statements are indented inside the scope of the main program block (Begin End) and in the Var section. The same guideline applies to loops (For … EndFor) and conditional statements (If … Then).

Program flow charts

A flow chart is a diagram that shows the sequence of operations to solve a problem. Flow charts got a bad name in the 1960s and 1970s because they encouraged unstructured programmed solutions using the GoTo statement but they do have a role to play in describing an algorithm that can be drawn on one side of A4 paper. They are unsuitable for describing anything much larger. Fig. 1.4.2 on p26 shows commonly used program flow chart symbols.

💡 Hand tracing simple algorithms

Verify that an algorithm is correct before you spend time implementing it in a programming language. You can do this as a **hand trace, desk check or dry run**. This consists of a careful, step-by-step simulation on paper of how the algorithm would be executed by a computer. The results of the simulation should show the effect of each step as it is executed on data that is relatively easy to manipulate by hand.

First number? 19.5

Second number? 10.5

Their sum is 30.00

Their average is 15.00

Fig. 1.4.1 *Inputs and outputs for the program FindSumAverage*

Did you know?

Pascal was designed to teach undergraduates good programming style and skills. Developed in the 1970s, it is still the best teaching language. It now retails as Delphi.

Key point

Wherever possible, use meaningful names for variables, etc. Use indentation to show structure.

Worked example _____

The following algorithm calculates the cube of the number in x. Dry run it by completing a trace table as shown in Figure 3.

```
x ← 4
y ← 3
Result ← 1
Repeat
   Result ← Result * x
   y ← y − 1
Until y = 0
```

Key terms

Hand trace, desk check or dry run: a careful step-by-step simulation on paper of how an algorithm would be executed by a computer.

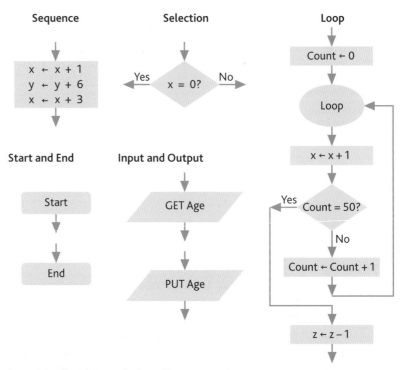

Fig. 1.4.2 *Flow chart symbols used in programming*

a

x	y	Result
4	3	1

b

x	y	Result
4	3	1
4	2	4

c

x	y	Result
4	3	1
4	2	4
4	1	16

d

x	y	Result
4	3	1
4	2	4
4	1	16
4	0	64

Fig. 1.4.3 *Trace table for the cube algorithm: (a) at the start, (b) after the first iteration of Repeat, (c) after the second iteration of Repeat, (d) after the last iteration of Repeat*

Questions

11 Hand trace the following algorithm using as input the numbers 2, 6, 34, 12, 0 in that order.

```
Result ← 0
Repeat
    Input n
    Result ← Result + n
Until n = 0
```

n	Result
	0
2	

12 The following problem has been set. A right-angled triangle has sides a, b and c. Pythagoras' theorem states that $a^2 = b^2 + c^2$. The problem is to create a process that will find and output side a for any given inputs b and c. Express the solution to this problem in (a) structured English and (b) pseudocode.

13 Draw a program flow chart for the algorithm in Question 11.

✔ *In this topic you have covered:*

- the difference between an algorithm and a computer program
- stepwise refinement of an algorithm
- using only sequence, selection and repetition to write algorithms
- the meaning of assignment
- computer-based problem solving
- the difference between structured English and pseudocode
- writing algorithms in structured English and pseudocode
- hand tracing, desk checking and dry running of simple algorithms.

2.1 Input, assignment and output

Key terms

High-level programming language: a language that has English-like keywords and commands to express the basic constructs of sequence, selection (decision) and repetition (iteration).

Pascal: a high-level programming language designed to teach students structured programming.

Visual Basic 2005: a high-level programming language that took the language Basic and redefined it to work with Microsoft's .Net framework.

C#: a high-level programming language based on C++ and Pascal developed specifically for Microsoft's .Net framework.

Variable: a location in memory that contains one or more data values.

Identifier: a unique name given to a variable, a procedure, a function, etc.

In Topic 1.4 you learned about algorithms expressed in structured English and pseudocode. We now consider how to translate an algorithm into a computer program using a **high-level programming language**.

Sections 2, 3 and 4 give a brief introduction to programming. They cover all the key features of high-level programming languages that you need to know and should be able to use. Use online help and local help available in your chosen programming environment.

Programming is a skill like playing a musical instrument or playing a sport. The more you practise, the better you will become. Use the worked examples in this book and try out the constructs by building them into an application. You can use your imagination and expand the examples. You will learn a lot by making small changes and seeing their effects.

This book gives code examples in **Pascal**, **Visual Basic 2005** and **C#**. There are many similarities between programming languages, and learning one language will make it easier to learn another.

Variables

When you solve a problem, you identify the inputs and outputs and determine the variables. You can imagine a **variable** as a box. Each box can usually store one value. Naming a variable is like labelling the box. When you label a box, you write on the outside of the box a description of what you store in the box. When you name a variable you should choose a meaningful name that describes what the variable is going to be used for. This variable name is known as the variable's **identifier**.

Programming languages have rules about what is a valid identifier. They usually allow combinations of alphanumeric characters (letters, numerals and the underscore character) but no spaces or other symbols. Usually, identifiers must start with a letter. Some languages are case sensitive. Some languages require variable identifiers to start with a lower-case letter.

You should follow generally accepted naming conventions for choosing identifiers so that your program code can be easily understood by other programmers. Avoid using keywords as identifiers. Concatenate words – join them together – to describe the purpose of a variable and use casing to indicate the beginning of each word. For example, NumberOfEntries (Pascal case) or numberOfEntries (Camel case). By convention, Pascal and Visual Basic use Pascal case and C# uses Camel case. C# is a case-sensitive language and variable identifiers must start with a lower-case letter.

Don't use single-letter variable identifiers unless this is really appropriate, but there is no need to have a variable identifier of more than 20 characters. Choose sensible identifiers that will read easily in your program code.

Questions

Using the case convention of your chosen programming language, choose meaningful variable identifiers to store these values:

1 The total points scored by player 1 in a game

2 The player number whose turn it is next

3 The number of questions answered correctly

4 The total number of questions in a quiz

5 The number of questions that have been attempted

Study tip

You are allowed to use local help during the AQA COMP1 AS examination, so you should be familiar with how to use the help facility.

Study tip

You may gain marks for choosing sensible variable identifiers.

The assignment statement

To assign a value to a variable we use an assignment statement. Here are some statements to assign the value 7 to a variable with identifier Number1:

Pascal

```
Number1 := 7;
```

VB 2005

```
Number1 = 7
```

C#

```
number1 = 7;
```

Pascal requires a semicolon (;) as a statement separator. Note that the assignment operator in Pascal consists of the combination of a colon and an equals sign (:= with no space between them)

VB expects each statement on a separate line

C# requires a semicolon (;) as a statement separator

The value on the right of the assignment operator is stored in the variable named on the left of the assignment operator. You should read this as 'Number1 becomes equal to 7'.

Although it is possible to write more than one statement on one line, this is not recommended, as it makes your program more difficult to understand and maintain.

An assignment can consist of an expression, a formula, to the right of the assignment operator. This expression is evaluated when the statement is executed and the value is then stored in the variable named on the left of the assignment operator.

If Number1 contains the value 7 and Number2 contains the value 12, when the following statements are executed, Sum will contain the value 19:

Pascal

```
Sum := Number1 + Number2;
```

VB 2005

```
Sum = Number1 + Number2
```

C#

```
sum = number1 + number2;
```

Suppose Count contains the value 5, then after these statements have been executed, Count will contain 6. You can read this statement as 'Increment Count by 1'.

Pascal

```
Count := Count + 1;
```

VB 2005

```
Count = Count + 1
```

C#

```
count = count + 1;
```

An alternative way of writing this is Count += 1

An alternative way of writing this is count += 1;

💡 Arithmetic operators

You can perform arithmetic operations by combining the operators in Table 1.

Table 1 *Arithmetic operators*

Operation	Arithmetic operator	Example
Addition	+	Number1 + Number2
Subtraction	–	Number1 – Number2
Multiplication	*	Number1 * Number2
Division	/	Number1 / Number2

Modular arithmetic

Normal division returns a result that may not be a whole number, but sometimes we are interested in the whole number part only. This is known as **integer division**. Integer division of 17 by 5 gives the result 3.

The modulo operation gives the remainder after a division. For example, the remainder of 17 divided by 5 is 2. Different programming languages use different symbols to represent operators for modular arithmetic.

	Example of integer division	Example of modulo operation
Pascal	`WholeNumberPart := Number1 Div Number2;`	`Remainder := Number1 Mod Number2;`
VB 2005	`WholeNumberPart = Number1 \ Number2`	`Remainder = Number1 Mod Number2`
C#	`int wholeNumberPart = number1 / number2;`	`remainder = number1 % number2;`

Comments

It is good practice to add comments to source code that explain the purpose of a statement or set of statements. These comments are ignored by the **compiler** (Topic 8.2).

	Symbols used to enclose comments which may go over several lines	Symbols to denote that the rest of the line is a comment

Pascal	`{ comments go here}`
	`(* comments go here *)`
		`// comments go here`
		`// and again`
		`// if you need more than one line`

VB 2005		`' comment goes here`
		`' and again`
		`' if you need more than one line`

C#	`/* comments go here */`	`// comments go here`
		`// and again`
		`// if you need more than one line`

Questions

Using the programming language of your choice and sensible variable identifiers, write assignment statements to calculate these values:

6 The number of questions answered wrongly so far in the quiz.

7 The percentage of questions answered correctly from those attempted.

8 The percentage of questions attempted out of the total number of questions in the quiz.

9 How many £5 notes you would get for an amount of money in pounds stored in the variable Amount. (Extension question)

Input and output using a console application

Console application

When you first start a **console application**, the programming environment provides you with a framework where you type your program statements.

Pascal

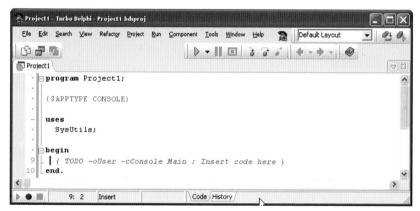

Fig. 2.1.1 *A new Pascal console application*

VB 2005

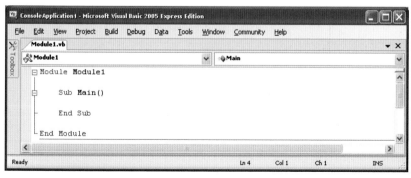

Fig. 2.1.2 *A new VB 2005 console application*

C#

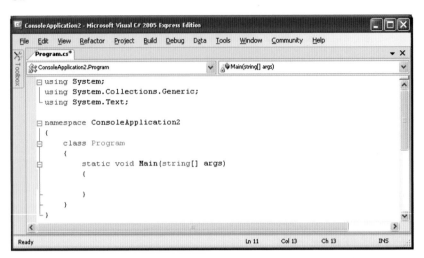

Fig. 2.1.3 *A new C# console application*

Input from the keyboard

Pascal

```
Readln(Number1);
```

VB 2005

```
Number1 = Console.ReadLine()
```

C#

```
number1 = Console.ReadLine();
```

When the above statements are executed, the program will pause and wait for input from the keyboard until the Enter key is pressed. We usually want to prompt the user for a data item that the program is expecting. We need to use write statements to output messages to the console.

Output to the console

	To display a string	To display the contents of a variable
Pascal	Write('Hello World');	Write(Number1);
VB 2005	Console.Write("Hello World")	Console.Write(Number1)
C#	Console.Write("Hello World");	Console.Write(number1);

	To display a string and then move the output stream to a new line	To display the contents of a variable and then move the output stream to a new line	To move the output stream to a new line
Pascal	Writeln('Hello World');	Writeln(Number1);	Writeln;
VB 2005	Console.WriteLine("Hello World")	Console.WriteLine(Number1)	Console.WriteLine()
C#	Console.WriteLine("Hello World");	Console.WriteLine(number1);	Console.WriteLine();

A simple console application

Pascal

```pascal
program Project2;

{$APPTYPE CONSOLE}

uses
  SysUtils;

begin
  Writeln('Hello World');
  Readln
end.
```

Fig. 2.1.4 *Hello World program in Pascal*

VB 2005

```vb
Module Module1

    Sub Main()
        Console.WriteLine("Hello World")
        Console.ReadLine()
    End Sub

End Module
```

Fig. 2.1.5 *Hello World program in VB 2005*

C#

```csharp
using System;

class Program
{
    static void Main(string[] args)
    {
        Console.WriteLine("Hello, World!");
        Console.ReadLine();
    }
}
```

Fig. 2.1.6 *Hello World program in C#*

■ **Key point**

All console applications discussed in this book close the console window when the program finishes execution. Use a readln statement so that you can see the output; this pauses the program and keeps the window open until you press the Enter key. Another method is to change the operating system's default settings for the behaviour of the console window.

Here is how to combine strings and contents of variables into one output stream:

Pascal

```
Writeln(Number1, ' + ', Number2, ' = ', Sum);
```

VB 2005

```
Console.WriteLine(Number1 & " + " & Number2 & " = " & Sum)
```

Alternative method

```
Console.WriteLine("{0} + {1} = {2}", Number1, Number2, Sum)
```

C#

```
Console.WriteLine("{0} + {1} = {2}", number1, number2, sum);
```

Assume Number1 and number1 contain the value 7, Number2 and number2 contain the value 12, Sum and sum contain the value 19. When the above statements above are executed, the console will display 7 + 12 = 19.

Declaring and using variables

Programming languages that require the data types of variables to be declared before they can be assigned values are known as strongly typed languages. This is a desirable feature of a language as the compiler will check that operations are performed on correct variable types. For example, trying to divide one string variable by another is not a legal operation. If you don't need to declare variables, the compiler cannot tell you if you accidentally mistyped the identifier or whether you intend to use a new one. Different languages require variable types to be declared in different ways. See Topic 2.2 for more information about data types.

Pascal

```
Var Number1, Number2, Sum, Average: Real;
Var Max : Integer = 5;
```

The keyword **Var** is followed by a comma-separated list of variable identifiers of the same type followed by : and the data type. You can assign an initial value at declaration time.

VB 2005

```
Dim Number1, Number2, Sum, Average As Single
Dim Max As Integer = 5
```

The keyword **Dim** is followed by a comma-separated list of variable identifiers of the same type followed by the keyword **As** and the data type. You can assign an initial value at declaration time.

C#

```
double number1, number2, sum, average;
int max = 5;
```

The data type is followed by a comma-separated list of variable identifiers. You can assign an initial value at declaration time.

A console application using variables

Pascal

```
Program FindSumAverage;

{$APPTYPE CONSOLE}

Uses
  SysUtils;

Var
  Number1, Number2, Sum, Average : Real;
Begin
  Write('First number? '); Readln(Number1);
  Write('Second number? '); Readln(Number2);
  Sum := Number1 + Number2;
  Average := Sum / 2;
  Writeln('Their sum is ', Sum:8:2);
  Writeln('Their average is ', Average:8:2);
  Readln;
End.
```

Variables are declared before the program block

These numbers format the real number to be displayed to two decimal places. If you don't include this, a real number will be displayed in scientific format

Fig. 2.1.7 *Program FindSumAverage in Pascal*

VB 2005

This statement will force you to declare your variables, a good habit as it will flag up any misspelled identifiers

```
Option Explicit On

Module Module1
    Dim Number1, Number2, Sum, Average As Single
    Sub Main()
        Console.Write("First Number? ") : Number1 = Console.ReadLine
        Console.Write("Second Number? ") : Number2 = Console.ReadLine
        Sum = Number1 + Number2
        Average = Sum / 2
        Console.WriteLine("Their sum is " & Sum)
        Console.WriteLine("Their average is " & Average)
        Console.ReadLine()
    End Sub
End Module
```

Variables are identified here

Fig. 2.1.8 *Program FindSumAverage in VB 2005*

Instead of "Their sum is " & variable, you can write "Their sum is {0}", variable, as in the C# example in Fig. 2.1.9 on p36.

C#

```
using System;
using System.Collections.Generic;
using System.Text;

namespace ConsoleApplication1
{
    class Program
    {
        static void Main(string[] args)
        {
            double number1, number2, sum, average;
            string numberString;
            Console.Write("First Number? ");
            numberString = Console.ReadLine();
            number1 = System.Convert.ToDouble(numberString);
            Console.Write("Second Number? ");
            numberString = Console.ReadLine();
            number2 = System.Convert.ToDouble(numberString);
            sum = number1 + number2;
            average = sum/2;
            Console.WriteLine("Their sum is {0}", sum);
            Console.WriteLine("Their average is {0}",
                                                average);
            Console.ReadLine();
        }
    }
}
```

Variables must be declared before they are used

The Console.ReadLine method only reads strings, so the input string needs to be converted to a real number before we can calculate with it

Fig. 2.1.9 *Program FindSumAverage in C#*

💡 Sequencing instructions

The calculation 4*7+3 gives a different result to the calculation 4*(7+3), because the brackets change the order of evaluation. Similarly, the order in which program statements are executed affects the outcome. When programming with imperative languages, the statements are executed in the sequence the programmer determines. Values need to be assigned to variables before they can be used in calculations, and calculations need to be done before results can be displayed.

In this topic you have covered:

- how to write the code to calculate the result of a formula
- how to write the code to read input from the keyboard and produce output to the screen
- how to declare variable types
- the importance of the sequence of instructions.

🖥 PC activity

In the language of your choice, write programs to do the following:

1. Display the words 'Hello World' on the screen.

2. Display two messages of your choice on the screen, separated by an empty line.

3. Display the sum and average of three numbers entered at the keyboard.

4. Read in two integers and display how many times the first integer divides into the second integer (using integer division). Display the remainder from this division. Hint: use the modulo operation.

5. The user enters an amount of money as a whole number. The program should calculate and display how many £20, £10 and £5 notes and £2 and £1 coins are needed to make up this amount of money. For example, £37 would give 1 × £20, 1 × £10, 1 × £5 and 1 × £2. Hint: use integer division and the modulo operation.

2.2 Data types

All data is stored and processed as a series of bit patterns. We need to declare the type of data values we want to use so that the processor operates on them correctly. For example, we may wish to store whole numbers (integers), text (strings) or numbers with fractional parts (real numbers). The compiler allocates memory space according to the type of data we want to store. For example, integers may be stored using four consecutive bytes and real numbers may be stored using eight consecutive bytes. Programming languages have common data types built in. You may wish to declare your own data types.

Variable declarations

Global variables

Global variables are variables declared at the beginning of the program and accessible from anywhere in the program. It is not always desirable to use a **global variable** as its values may get changed accidentally.

Local variables

Rather than declaring variables globally, it is good programming style to declare variables locally within the block where the variable is going to be used.

When you start writing programs with routines – procedures or functions – you should declare **local variables** within the routines. Any variable value that is required by another routine should be passed as a parameter (Topics 2.5 and 4.2). A routine or subroutine is a subprogram.

Constant definitions

A constant is a value that does not change throughout the program. It is good programming style to declare named constants. Don't use variables because you might change their value by accident. If you choose a meaningful identifier to label a **constant** value then your program will be much easier to understand and maintain.

Imagine you are writing a mathematical program where you require the value of pi. You know that pi is approximately 3.1416. If you use this value wherever required in your program, but later want to calculate it with more accuracy, then you need to change the value throughout. If you declare pi as a named constant and initialise its value at the beginning of your program, you only need to change it in the one place where it is declared.

It is much more meaningful to see an instruction such as
```
Circumference := Radius * 2 * Pi rather than
Circumference := Radius * 2 * 3.1416.
```

	Example	Explanation
Pascal	`Const Pi = 3.141593;`	Constants must be declared before variables. Note that the assignment operator here is =
VB 2005	`Const Pi As Double = 3.141593`	You must declare a type if **Option Strict** is set to **On**
C#	`const double pi = 3.141593;`	You must declare the type as well as give the named constant its value

■ Built-in data types

Integers and bytes

Integers are whole numbers. If the values to be stored are always whole numbers, you should use integer variables rather than real variables. Use integer variables if you are counting the number of items in a list or the number of times some instructions are to be repeated. Integer variables use less memory and store values accurately. Different programming languages support a variety of **integer** types. Table 1 gives the integer types you are expected to know in your language.

Table 1 *Integer data types*

Built-in types	Description	Memory allocated	Range
Pascal			
Integer	Signed 32-bit integer	4 bytes	–2,147,483,648 to 2,147,483,647
Byte	Unsigned 8-bit integer	1 byte	0 to 255
VB 2005			
Integer	Signed 32-bit integer	4 bytes	–2,147,483,648 to 2,147,483,647
Byte	Unsigned 8-bit integer	1 byte	0 to 255
C#			
int	Signed 32-bit integer	4 bytes	–2,147,483,648 to 2,147,483,647
byte	Unsigned 8-bit integer	1 byte	0 to 255

Real numbers

Real numbers are numbers with a decimal point and a fractional part, such as 19.452344668. Different programming languages support a variety of **real number** types. Table 2 gives the real number types you are expected to know in your language.

Table 2 *Real data types*

Built-in types	Description	Memory allocated
Pascal		
Real	Real number	8 bytes
Currency	Used to store monetary values in fixed-point notation (Topic 5.1); it minimises rounding errors	8 bytes
VB 2005		
Single	Single-precision floating-point number	4 bytes
Double	Double-precision floating-point number	8 bytes
Decimal	This data type is used when you want to minimise rounding errors, perhaps for monetary calculations	16 bytes
C#		
double	Double-precision floating-point number. If you want to assign a whole number to a variable of type double, you must use the suffix D, e.g. `double someNumber = 5D;`	8 bytes
decimal	Suitable for monetary calculations. You must assign a money value with the suffix m, otherwise the value is treated as the data type double, e.g. `decimal hourlyRate = 15.20m;`	16 bytes

💡 Characters and strings

A special type of **string** is the empty string (zero characters). This is denoted by opening and closing string delimiters next to each other: `''` in Pascal and `""` in VB and C#.

Table 3 *Character and string data types*

Built-in types	Description	Memory allocated
Pascal		
Char	A variable of this type stores a single ASCII character, e.g. `Symbol := '&';`	1 byte
String	A string is also enclosed in single quotes, e.g. `ExampleString := 'Hello World';`	as required
VB 2005		
Char	A variable of this type stores a single Unicode character, e.g. `Symbol = "&"`	2 bytes
String	A string is also enclosed in double quotes, e.g. `ExampleString = "Hello World"`	as required
C#		
char	A variable of this type stores a single Unicode character, e.g. `char symbol = '&';`	2 bytes
string	Strings are enclosed in double quotes, e.g. `string exampleString = "Hello World";`	as required

You can concatenate strings using the + operator:

Pascal
```
'Hello' + 'World'
```

VB 2005
```
"Hello" + "World"
```

C#
```
"Hello" + "World"
```

You can access individual **characters** of a string by treating the string as a one-dimensional array (Topic 2.6):

Pascal
```
Character2 := ExampleString[2];
```

VB 2005
```
Character2 = ExampleString(1)
```

C#
```
character2 = exampleString[1];
```

Boolean data

The **Boolean data** type supports only two values: **True** and **False** (**true** and **false** in C#).

	Built-in type	**Example**
Pascal	Boolean	Finished := False;
VB 2005	Boolean	Finished = False
C#	bool	**bool** finished = false;

Date and time data

If you want to manipulate a date or a time in your program, here are the built-in data types to use:

- In Pascal use TDateTime.
- In VB 2005 use Date.
- In C# use dateTime.

The date is stored as a real number. The integer part represents the number of days that have passed since 30 December 1899. The fractional part represents the time – the part of 24 hours that has elapsed. See Topic 2.5 for more information on built-in functions.

Pascal
```
Var Today, Tomorrow, DateOfBirth : TDateTime;
DateString : String;
Today := Date();
Tomorrow := Today + 1;
DateString := '1/1/1989';
DateOfBirth := StrToDate(DateString);
Writeln(DateToStr(Tomorrow));
```

There is a built-in function to get the current date

You can manipulate date values

Input and output of dates requires conversion using a built-in function.

VB 2005

```
Dim Today, Tomorrow, DateOfBirth As Date
Today = Now()
Tomorrow = Today.AddDays(1)
DateOfBirth = "1/1/1989"
Console.WriteLine(Tomorrow)
```

C#

```
dateTime today = DateTime.Today;
dateTime tomorrow = today.AddDays(1);
string dateString = "1/1/1989";
dateTime dateOfBirth =
    System.Convert.ToDateTime(dateString);
Console.WriteLine(tomorrow);
```

There is a built-in function to get the current time

You can manipulate date values using class methods

If Option Strict is off, you can input and output dates directly, otherwise you must convert the date string as in C#

There is a property that stores the current date

You can manipulate date values using class methods

Input of dates requires conversion using a built-in function

On output, dates are implicitly converted

User-defined data types

Sometimes we want to work with types that are not built into the programming language we are using. We can declare our own types. A type needs to be defined before we can declare variables of that type.

Record types

A record is a data structure that groups together a number of variables, which need not be of the same type and have no associated ordering. The variables of a **record** are called **fields**.

To use records, we declare the structure as a type then we declare variables of that type. To work with individual fields of a record, we use the dot notation: RecordVariableName.FieldName. You can also declare arrays of records (Topic 2.6) and files of records (Topic 2.7).

Key terms

Record: a data structure that groups a number of variables.

Field: a variable that is part of a record.

Pascal

```
Type TBook = Record // declare a record type TBook
            Title: String[30];
            ISBN: String[13];
            Price: Currency;
            YearOfPublication: Integer;
    End; // of record type declaration
Var Book : TBook;
Book.Title := 'A-Level Computing';
```

VB 2005

```
Structure TBook ' declare a structure type TBook
  Dim Title As String
  Dim ISBN As String
  Dim Price As Decimal
  Dim YearOfPublication As Integer
End Structure
Dim Book As TBook
Book.Title = "A-Level Computing"
```

By convention, the type identifier should start with a T. The identifier for the variable can be similar, without the T.

String fields must be declared as fixed-length fields.

You can declare a variable of the data type TBook

A value can be assigned directly to a field.

A record can be implemented as a Structure. A Structure can also include methods, which makes it almost a class. For more information about classes, see object-oriented programming in A2

You can declare a variable of the data type TBook

A value can be assigned directly to a field

C#

```
struct TBook // declare a structure
    {
        public string Title, ISBN;
        public decimal Price;
        public int YearOfPublication;
    }
TBook book;
book.Title = "A-Level Computing";
```

Array types

In Pascal you may declare an array as a type then declare variables of that type. This is particularly useful when you want to use an array as a parameter (Topic 2.5).

Pascal

```
Type TNameList = Array[1..10] Of String;
Var NameList: TNameList;

Procedure GetData(Var L: TNameList);
Var i:Integer;
Begin
  For i := 1 To 10 Do Readln(L[i]);
End;

Procedure OutputData(L: TNameList);
Var i:Integer;
Begin
  For i := 1 To 10 Do Writeln(L[i]);
End;

Begin
  GetData(NameList);
  OutputData(NameList);
  Readln;
End.
```

Enumerated types

An **enumerated type** defines an ordered set of values. Each value is given an ordinal value, starting at zero. Members of an enumerated type can be used as loop control variables (Topic 2.4), in case statements (Topic 2.3) and as array subscripts (Topic 2.6).

Pascal

```
Program Enumeration;
{$APPTYPE CONSOLE}
Uses SysUtils;
Type TDay = (Sun, Mon, Tue, Wed, Thu, Fri, Sat);
Var x, y : TDay;
Begin
  x := Wed;
  y := Sun;
  Writeln('Wednesday = ', Ord(x));
  Writeln('Sunday = ', Ord(y));
  Readln;
End.
```

VB 2005

```
Module Module1
  Dim x, y As Integer
  Enum Days
    Sun
    Mon
    Tue
    Wed
    Thu
    Fri
    Sat
  End Enum 'Days
  Sub Main()
    x = Days.Wed
    y = Days.Sun
    Console.WriteLine("Wednesday = {0}", x)
    Console.WriteLine("Sunday = {0}", y)
    Console.ReadLine()
  End Sub
End Module
```

C#

```
using System;
using System.Collections.Generic;
using System.Text;

namespace ConsoleApplication1
{
  class Program
  {
    enum Days {Sun, Mon, Tue, Wed, Thu, Fri, Sat};
    static void Main(string[] args)
    {
      int x = (int)Days.Wed;
      int y = (int)Days.Sun;
      Console.WriteLine("Wednesday = {0}", x);
      Console.WriteLine("Sunday = {0}", y);
      Console.ReadLine();
    }
  }
}
```

Sub-range types

In Pascal we can declare a type that is a range of values of an **ordinal type**. Here is an example.

```
Type TCapitalLetter = 'A' .. 'Z';
Var Initial : TCapitalLetter;
:
Initial := 'S';
```

💡 Sets

A set is a collection of values of the same ordinal type. The values of a **set** have no associated order.

Key terms

Ordinal type: defines an ordered set of values such as integer, character, Boolean and enumerated types; real numbers are not of ordinal type.

Set: a collection of values of the same ordinal type with no associated order.

Key point

.Net 3.x will provide hashed sets that will support the set operations in Table 4 as class methods.

Table 4 *Set operators*

Operation	Set operator	Example	Explanation
Union	+	Set3 := Set1 + Set2	Set3 contains each value from Set1 and each value from Set2 but no duplicates
Difference	-	Set3 := Set1 - Set2	Set3 contains only those values from Set1 that do not exist in Set2
Intersection	*	Set3 := Set1 * Set2	Set3 contains only those values that exist in both Set1 and Set2
Membership	In	If 13 In Set1 Then ...	Tests whether the value is in the set. The result is a Boolean value

Pascal

```
Type TLotteryNumbers = Set Of 1..49;
Var Set1, Set2, Set4: TLotteryNumbers;
Set1 := [1, 7, 13, 22, 23, 46];
Set2 := [2, 12, 26, 32, 37, 47];
Set4 := [];
```

[] creates an empty set

VB 2005

```
Dim Set1, Set2, Set3 As New ArrayList
Dim InitialSet() = {3, 4, 5}
Set1.AddRange(InitialSet)
Set1.Add(2)
Set1.Add(7)
If Set1.Contains(7) Then ... ' test whether the value 7 is
                                                    in Set1
```

Sets do not exist; the nearest equivalent is the type ArrayList.

This method adds the contents of the named ArrayList.

This method adds a value to the ArrayList.

ArrayList types do not have the set operators in Table 4. Membership can be tested with the method Contains.

C#

```
ArrayList Set1 = new ArrayList ();
int[] InitialSet = {3, 4, 5};
Set1.Add(7);
Set1.AddRange(InitialSet);
Set1.Add(2);
if(Set1.Contains(7)) ...// test whether the value 7 is in Set1
```

Sets do not exist; the nearest equivalent is the type ArrayList.

This method adds a value to the ArrayList.

This method adds the contents of the named ArrayList

ArrayLists do not have the set operators in Table 4. Membership can be tested with the method Contains.

🔆 Logical bitwise operators

Sometimes we may want to manipulate individual bits in a bit pattern.
In the following examples, *A* contains 13 (00001101 in binary) and
B contains 17 (00010001 in binary).

Table 5 *Logical bitwise operators*

Operator	Result	Explanation
NOT A	11110010	The NOT operator inverts each bit of A, so each 0 becomes a 1 and each 1 becomes a 0
A AND B	00000001	The AND operator sets a bit to 1 if the corresponding bits in A and B are both 1, otherwise it is set to 0
A OR B	00011101	The OR operator sets a bit to 1 if either of the corresponding bits in A and B are 1, otherwise it is set to 0
A XOR B	00011100	The XOR operator sets a bit to 1 if only one of the corresponding bits in A and B is 1, otherwise it is set to 0

Pascal

```
C := Not A;
C := A And B;
C := A Or B;
C := A Xor B;
```

VB 2005

```
C = Not A
C = A And B
C = A Or B
C = A Xor B
```

C#

```
c = ~ a;
c = a & b;
c = a | b;
c = a ^ b;
```

In this topic you have covered:

- global variables: declared at the beginning, accessible from anywhere in the program

- local variables: declared in a program, accessible only within that program block

- constants: values that do not change throughout a program

- built-in data types: integer, byte, real, Boolean, character, string, date and time

- user-defined data types: arrays, records, enumerated types, subrange types and sets

- set operators: union, difference, intersection and membership

- logical bitwise operators: NOT, AND, OR, XOR.

2.3 Selection

Key terms

Boolean expression: returns True or False.

Boolean operators: NOT, AND, OR.

Boolean expressions

Relational operators

Expressions with relational (comparison) operators are known as **Boolean expressions**. When a Boolean expression is evaluated, it returns a Boolean value, True or False.

Table 5 *Relational operators*

	Pascal	VB 2005	C#
Equal to	=	=	==
Less than	<	<	<
Greater than	>	>	>
Not equal to	<>	<>	!=
Less than or equal to	<=	<=	<=
Greater than or equal to	>=	>=	>=

Boolean operators

More complex Boolean expressions can be formed using **Boolean operators**, or logical operators: NOT, AND, OR.

Description	Mathematics	Pascal	VB 2005	C#
Number equal to 1	Number = 1	Number = 1	Number = 1	Number == 1
Number not equal to 1	Number ≠ 1	Number <> 1	Number <> 1	Number != 1
Age 17 or under	Age ≤ 17	Age <= 17	Age <= 17	Age <= 17
Age 17 or more but less than 25	17 ≤ Age < 25	(Age >= 17) AND (Age < 25)	Age >= 17 AND Age < 25	(Age >= 17) && (Age < 25)
Age under 21 or over 65	Age < 21 OR Age > 65	(Age < 21) OR (Age > 65)	Age < 21 OR Age > 65	(Age < 21) || (Age > 65)
Age not under 17	NOT(Age < 17)	NOT (Age < 17)	NOT Age < 17	! (Age < 17)

💡 Simple If statements

Sometimes we want to execute one statement only if a certain condition is met. If the Boolean expression after the If keyword evaluates to True then the rest of the If statement is executed, else control passes to the next statement.

Pseudocode

```
If x > 3
  Then y ← 6
Endif
If d < 24
  Then
     z ← z + 2
     w ← w − 3
Endif
```

Pascal

```
If x > 3
  Then y := 6;
If d < 24
  Then
     Begin
        z := z + 2;
        w := w − 3;
     End;
```

The keywords Begin and End group two or more statements into a block. This is known as making a compound statement

VB 2005

```
If x > 3 Then
  y = 6
End If
If d < 24 Then
  z = z + 2
  w = w − 3
End If
```

Note the position of the keyword Then

C#

```
if (x > 3)
  {
     y = 6;
  }
if (d < 24)
  {
     z = z + 2;
     w = w − 3;
  }
```

The keywords are in lower case

The Boolean expression is enclosed in brackets

Statements are grouped into a block by { and }

If–Then–Else statements

When we want to execute one statement if a certain condition is met, but another statement if the condition is not met, we can use the If–Else construct. If the Boolean expression after the If keyword evaluates to True then the first part of the If statement is executed; if the Boolean expression evaluates to False, control jumps to the statement after the Else keyword.

Pseudocode

```
If x > 3
  Then y ← 6
  Else y ← 9
Endif
If d < 24
  Then
     z ← z + 2
     w ← w - 3
  Else
     z ← z - 2
     w ← w + 3
Endif
```

Pascal

```
If x > 3
  Then y := 6
  Else y := 9;
If d < 24
  Then
  Begin
     z := z + 2;
     w := w - 3;
  End
  Else
  Begin
     z := z - 2;
     w := w + 3;
  End;
```

The keywords **Begin** and **End** group two or more statements into a block. This is known as making a compound statement

VB 2005

```
If x > 3 Then
  y = 6
Else
  y = 9
End If
If d < 24 Then
  z = z + 2
  w = w - 3
Else
  z = z - 2
  w = w + 3
End If
```

Note the position of the keyword **Then**

C#

```
if (x > 3)
  {
    y = 6;
  }
if (d < 24)
  {
    z = z + 2;
    w = w − 3;
  }
else
  {
    z = z − 2
    w = w + 3
  }
```

— The keywords are in lower case.

— Statements are grouped into a block by { and }.

— The Boolean expression is enclosed in brackets.

Nested If statements

A statement in the Then part or the Else part of an If statement may also be an If statement. It is possible to extend the If statement to handle multiple conditions.

Pseudocode

```
If Ch In ['A' .. 'Z']
  Then Output 'uppercase letter'
  Else
    If Ch In ['a' .. 'z']
      Then Output 'lowercase letter'
      Else
        If Ch In ['0' .. '9']
          Then Output 'numeral'
          Else Output'not alphanumeric'
        EndIf
    EndIf
EndIf
```

Pascal

```
If Ch In ['A' .. 'Z']
  Then Writeln('uppercase letter')
  Else
    If Ch In ['a' .. 'z']
      Then Writeln('lowercase letter')
      Else
        If Ch In ['0' .. '9']
          Then Writeln('numeral')
          Else Writeln('not alphanumeric');
```

VB 2005

```
If Char.IsUpper(Ch) Then
  Console.WriteLine("uppercase letter")
ElseIf (Char.IsLower(Ch)) Then
  Console.WriteLine("lowercase letter")
ElseIf (Char.IsDigit(Ch)) Then
  Console.WriteLine("numeral")
Else
  Console.WriteLine("not alphanumeric")
End If
```

 PC activity

In the language of your choice, write programs to do the following:

1. Ask for the user's age to be typed in at the keyboard, then display a message that states whether or not the user is old enough to drive.

2. Ask for two numbers to be typed in at the keyboard, then display the larger of the two numbers.

3. Ask for a number to be typed in at the keyboard, then display a message to say whether or not the number is within the range 0 to 100.

In the language of your choice, write programs to do the following:

1. Ask for a number to be typed in at the keyboard, then display a message to say whether the number is within the range 10 to 20, above this range or below this range.

2. Ask for the user's age to be typed in at the keyboard, then display a message to say whether the user is a child, a teenager or an adult.

3. Ask for three numbers to be typed in at the keyboard, then display the largest one. (Extension activity)

C#

```csharp
if (Char.IsUpper(Ch))
   {
      Console.WriteLine("uppercase letter");
   }
else if (Char.IsLower(Ch))
   {
      Console.WriteLine("lowercase letter");
   }
else if (Char.IsDigit(Ch))
   {
      Console.WriteLine("numeral";
   }
else
   {
      Console.WriteLine("not alphanumeric");
   }
```

💡 Case statements

Nested If statements can get very cumbersome and sometimes a Case statement is preferable. A Case statement presents a list of options that the variable may match. As long as there is no match, control skips to the next option. When a match is found, the associated statements are executed.

Pseudocode

```
Case x Of
   4: z ← z + 1
   5: z ← z − 1
      w ← w − 2
   6: z ← 6
EndCase
```

Pascal

Only one option is executed.

If more than one statement needs to be executed for an option, they must be enclosed between Begin and End.

```
Case x Of
   4: z := z + 1;
   5: Begin
         z := z − 1;
         w := w − 2;
      End;
   6: z := 6;
End;
```

VB 2005

Execution of the statement body begins at the selected statement and proceeds until the next Case or End Select keyword.

```
Select Case x
   Case 4
      z = z + 1
   Case 5
      z = z − 1
      w = w − 2
   Case 6
      z = 6
End Select
```

C#

```
switch (x)
{
  case 4:
    z = z + 1;
    break;
  case 5:
    z = z -1;
    w = w - 2;
    break;
  case 6:
    z = 6;
  break;
}
```

Execution of the statement body begins at the selected statement and proceeds until the **break** statement transfers control out of the **case** body. Execution continues with the statement after the switch block.

🖥 PC activity

In the language of your choice, write programs to do the following:

1. Ask the user for a month number, then display the name of the month; for example, the input 9 should produce a display of September.

2. Ask the user for a year, then display whether that year is a leap year. Hint: use the modulo operation from Topic 2.1.

3. Ask the user for a month number, then display the number of days in that month. For example, the input 9 should display 30.

4. Ask the user for a month number and a year, then display the number of days in that month, taking into account leap years.

5. Input a hexadecimal numeral (Topic 5.1) then display the decimal equivalent.

■ Key point

A year is a leap year when it is exactly divisible by 4. However, a century is not a leap year unless it is divisible by 400.

In this topic you have covered:

- writing Boolean expressions using relational and Boolean operators
- how to code a simple If statement
- how to code an If–Then–Else statement
- how to code a nested If statement
- how to code a Case statement.

2.4 Repetition

> **Key point**
>
> Repetition is often referred to as iteration.

> **Key point**
>
> If you want to repeat several statements, enclose them between Begin and End.

💡 Executing a loop a specific number of times

If we know before entering the loop how many times we want to repeat the group of statements we choose the For loop. The variable, here Count, is known as the loop control variable. The start and end values may be variables but they need to hold a value when the loop is about to be executed.

Pascal

```
Var Count: Integer;
For Count := 1 To 5
   Do Writeln('Line ', Count);
```

VB 2005

```
Dim Count As Integer
For Count = 1 To 5
   Console.WriteLine("Line {0}", Count)
Next
```

C#

```
for (int count = 1; count <= 5; count++ )
   {
      Console.WriteLine("Line {0}", count);
   }
```

🖥️ PC activity

In the language of your choice, write programs to do the following:

1. Display the message 'Hello World' 25 times.

2. Ask the user for a message and the number of times it should be repeated, then display the message with the number of the repetition:
   1 Hello,
   2 Hello,
   etc.

3. Ask the user which times table they wish to see, then display it in the following format:
   1 * 7 = 7
   2 * 7 = 14
   ⋮
   12 * 7 = 84

4. Ask the user to enter 10 numbers. Display the largest number entered.

5. Ask the user how many stars they want to see in one row. Display the row of stars.

6. Expand your solution to Question 5 and ask the user how many rows of stars they want to see. Display the rectangle of stars as specified by the user. Hint: you will need to nest one For loop inside another. (Extension activity)

> **Key point**
>
> The variable count is used here as a stepper (see role of variables, p66).

Executing a loop for each element in an array

This type of loop is especially useful if every item in an array is to be processed. In Pascal, no standard structure is available. You need to establish how many elements are to be processed, i.e. how many elements are in the array, and use a normal For loop.

VB 2005

```
Dim Name As String
  Dim FirstNames() = {"Jack", "Chris", "Tom"}
For Each Name In FirstNames
  Console.WriteLine("Hello {0}", Name)
Next
```

C#

```
string[] firstNames = { "Jack", "Chris", "Tom" };
foreach (string name in firstNames)
{
  Console.WriteLine("Hello {0}", name);
}
```

Executing a loop at least once

If we want to execute a group of statements at least once, then the Boolean expression is evaluated after the first iteration to check whether the loop should be repeated.

Pascal

```
Repeat
  Write('Enter a name, X to finish: ');
  Readln(Name);
Until Name = 'X';
```

VB 2005

```
Do
  Console.Write("Enter a name, X to finish: ")
  Name = Console.ReadLine()
Loop Until (Name = "X")
Do
  Console.Write("Enter a name, X to finish: ")
  Name = Console.ReadLine()
Loop While (Name <> "X")
```

C#

```
do
{
  Console.Write("Enter a name, X to finish: ");
  name = Console.ReadLine();
}
while (name != "X");
```

💡 Executing a loop under certain conditions

If the group of statements is only to be executed under certain conditions, and may not be executed at all, then we need to test the Boolean expression before the iteration starts.

Pascal

```
While Name <>'X'
  Do
    Begin
      Write('Enter a name, X to finish: ');
      Readln(Name);
    End;
```

VB 2005

```
Do While Name <> "X"
  Console.Write("Enter a name, X to finish: ")
  Name = Console.ReadLine()
Loop

Do Until Name = "X"
  Console.Write("Enter a name, X to finish: ")
  Name = Console.ReadLine()
Loop
```

C#

```
while (name!="X")
  {
    Console.Write("Enter a name, X to finish: ");
    name = Console.ReadLine();
  }
```

💻 PC activity

In the language of your choice, write programs to do the following:

1. Ask the user to enter a whole number greater than 99. If the user enters a number less than 100, display an error message and ask them again. Repeat this process until the user enters a valid number.

2. Expand your solution to Question 1 to accept only numbers between 100 and 200.

In this topic you have covered:

- how to decide which type of loop to use
- how to code a loop to be executed a specified number of times
- how to code a loop to be executed at least once
- how to code a loop to be executed zero or more times.

2.5 Procedures and functions

In this topic you will cover:

- the benefits of using procedures and functions

- some useful built-in functions

- the mechanisms for parameter passing

- when to use procedures or functions with interfaces

- the roles played by variables.

Key terms

Function: a routine that is called as part of an expression and returns a value.

Procedure: a routine that may or may not return a value; a procedure call is a statement in its own right, not part of an expression.

These functions return an integer result.

These functions return a real number. To change the result to an integer use the function `CInt(y)`.

These functions return a real number. To change the result to an integer use the function `Convert.ToInt32(y)`.

Key point

In Pascal, a statement block is enclosed between `Begin` and `End`. In VB 2005 a statement block is enclosed by the header and an `End` keyword. In C# a statement block is enclosed in { }.

Routines are also called subroutines or subprograms. They may be **functions**, which return a value, or **procedures**, which may or may not return a value. They are self-contained statement blocks that are given identifiers and can be called from different parts of the program code.

It is good programming practice to group statements into routines, so one routine will do just one task. Routines are declared separately from the main program body. This means the main program body is much easier to understand as it gives an overview of the tasks that make up the solution. The main program body should reflect your problem-solving steps. This will make it much easier to debug programs as each routine can be tested separately.

A routine declaration consists of a routine header followed by a routine body. The routine body is the statement block.

Built-in functions

Routines that are required by many programmers are provided ready for use as built-in functions.

Arithmetic functions

There are many arithmetic functions. One arithmetic function rounds or truncates the real value X to the nearest whole number. Truncation is equivalent to always rounding down.

Pascal
```
y := Round(x)
y := Trunc(x)
```

VB 2005
```
y := Math.Round(x)
y := Math.Truncate(x)
```

C#
```
y := Math.Round(x)
y := Math.Truncate(x);
```

String-handling functions

There are string-handling functions that make it easier to manipulate strings. The following string-handling functions come in useful:

- `Length` or `Len` returns as an integer the number of characters in string s.
- `Pos`, `InStr` and `IndexOf` return the index value (as an integer) of the first character in substring `SubStr` that occurs in string s.
- `MidStr`, `Mid` and `Substring` return the substring of length 1 that appears at position p in string s.
- `Concat` joins strings S1, S2, ..., Sn into a single string s.

Pascal

```
l := Length(s)
p := Pos(SubStr,s)
SubStr := MidStr(s,p,l);
s := Concat(S1,S2, ...,Sn);
```

VB 2005

```
l = Len(s)
p = InStr(s,SubStr)
SubStr = Mid(s,p,l)
```

C#

```
l = s.Length
p = s.IndexOf(substr)
subStr = s.Substring(p,l);
```

> `S := S1 + S2 + ... + Sn;` executes faster than the function Concat.
>
> These methods belong to the string object, so they are invoked using the dot notation.
>
> Indexes count from zero, so the first letter returns an index value of zero

Table 1 *String conversion functions*

Conversion	Pascal	VB 2005	C#
From string to integer	StrToInt(s)	CInt(s)	Convert.ToInt32(s)
From integer to string	IntToStr(n)	CStr(n)	Convert.ToString(n)
From string to real	StrToFloat(s)	CDbl(s)	Convert.ToDouble(s)
From real to string	FloatToStr(r)	CStr(r)	Convert.ToString(r)
From string to datetime	StrToDate(s)	CDate(s)	Convert.ToDateTime(s)
From datetime to string	DateToStr(d)	CStr(d)	Convert.ToString(d)

▍Key point

VB 2005 has no concatenation function. To combine several strings into one, use

```
S = S1 & S2 & ... & Sn
```

C# has no concatenation function. To combine several strings into one, use

```
s = s1 + s2 + ... + sn;
```

The functions in Table 1 convert strings to and from other data formats.

▍Declaring and calling a function

A function header needs to include the data type of the result to be returned. The function body must contain a statement that gives the function a value to return. See p63 for an explanation of `parameterlist`.

Pascal

```
Function Identifier (parameterlist): datatype;
    Var local variable declarations;
    Begin
        statement1;
        statement2;
        .
        .
        statementx;
        Identifier := value;
    End;
```

VB 2005

```
Function Identifier (parameterlist) As datatype
    Dim local variable declarations;
    statement1
    statement2
    .
    .
    statementX
    Identifier := value;
End Function
```

C#

```
static datatype Identifier (parameterlist)
{
    statement1;
    statement2;
    .
    .
    statementX;
    return value;
}
```

Pascal

```
Program Project1;
{$APPTYPE CONSOLE}
Uses
  SysUtils, StrUtils;

Var Number, Answer: Integer;

Function Factorial (n: Integer): Integer;
Var
  Count, Product: Integer;
Begin
  Product := 1;
  For Count :=1 to n
    Do Product := Product * Count;
  Factorial := Product;
End; {of function}

//************Main Program *****************

Begin
  Write ('Type in a number between 1 and 10: ');
  Readln (Number);
  Answer := Factorial(Number);
  Writeln (Answer);
  Readln;
End.
```

Global variable declarations
Parameter list
Data type of return value
Local variable declarations
Function declaration
Statement to provide return value

Main program body
Function call

Fig. 2.5.1 *How to declare and call a function in Pascal*

PC activity

In the language of your choice, write programs to do the following:

1. Read in a name consisting of first name and surname. Extract the initial letter of the first name. Find the position of the beginning of the surname. Hint: look for the space. Extract the first name. Extract the surname.

2. Read a date as a string from the keyboard. Convert it to a date type and add a year. Convert it back to a string and display it on the console.

VB 2005

```
Option Explicit On

Module Module1
    Dim Number, Answer As Integer

    Function Factorial(ByVal n As Integer) As Integer
        Dim Product, Count As Integer
        Product = 1
        For Count = 1 To n
            Product = Product * Count
        Next
        Factorial = Product
    End Function

    Sub Main()
        Console.Write("Input a number between 1 and 10: ")
        Number = Console.ReadLine()
        Answer = Factorial(Number)
        Console.WriteLine(Answer)
        Console.ReadLine()
    End Sub
End Module
```

Labels (VB 2005):
- Global variable declarations → Dim Number, Answer As Integer
- Parameter list → Function Factorial(ByVal n As Integer) As Integer
- Data type of return value → Function Factorial(...) As Integer
- Local variable declarations → Dim Product, Count As Integer
- Function declaration
- Statement to provide return value → Factorial = Product
- Main program body
- Function call → Answer = Factorial(Number)

Fig. 2.5.2 *How to declare and call a function in VB 2005*

C#

```
using System;
using System.Collections.Generic;
using System.Text;

namespace ConsoleApplication1
{
    class Program
    {
        static void Main(string[] args)
        {
            Console.Write("Input a number between 1 and 10: ");
            string numberString = Console.ReadLine();
            int number = Convert.ToInt32(numberString);
            int answer = Factorial(number);
            Console.WriteLine(answer);
            Console.ReadLine();
        }

        static int Factorial(int n)
        {
            int product = 1;
            for (int count = 1; count <= n: count++)
            {
                product = product * count;
            }
            return product;
        }
    }
}
```

Labels (C#):
- Main program body
- Function call → int answer = Factorial(number);
- Parameter list
- Data type of return value
- Function declaration → static int Factorial(int n)
- Local variable declarations → int product = 1;
- Statement to provide return value → return product;

Fig. 2.5.3 *How to declare and call a function in C#*

💡 Declaring and calling a procedure

Pascal

```
Procedure Identifier (parameterlist);
  Var local variable declarations;
  Begin
    statement1;
    statement2;
      .
      .
    statementX;
  End;
```

VB 2005

```
Sub Identifier (parameterlist)
  Dim local variable declarations;
  statement1
  statement2
    .
    .
  statementX
End Sub
```

C#

```
static void Identifier (parameterlist)
  {
  statement1;
  statement2;
    .
    .
  statementX;
  }
```

Look again at the example algorithm in Topic 1.4. The outline solution was:

1 input data,
2 calculate results,
3 output results.

These steps can become procedure calls, as implemented in Figs 2.5.4, 5 and 6; choose the one for the language you are using. The main program body consists of four procedure calls; the final call is to keep the console window visible. The steps to be followed when a procedure is called are outlined in the procedure's declaration. Pascal requires them to be done before the main program body.

Pascal

```pascal
Program FindSumAverage;
{$APPTYPE CONSOLE}
Uses
  SysUtils;
Var
  Number1, Number2, Sum, Average : Real;

Procedure InputData;
  Begin
    Write('First number? '); Readln(Number1);
    Write('Second number? '); Readln(Number2);
  End;

Procedure CalculateResults;
  Begin
    Sum := Number1 + Number2;
    Average := Sum / 2;
  End;

Procedure OutputResults;
  Begin
    Writeln('Their sum is ', Sum:8:2);
    Writeln('Their average is ', Average:8:2);
  End;

Procedure KeepConsoleWindowOpen;
  Begin
    Readln;
  End;

Begin
  InputData;
  CalculateResults;
  OutputResults;
  KeepConsoleWindowOpen;
End.
```

Global variable declarations

Procedure declarations

Main program body consisting of procedure calls

Fig. 2.5.4 *How to declare and call procedures in Pascal*

VB 2005

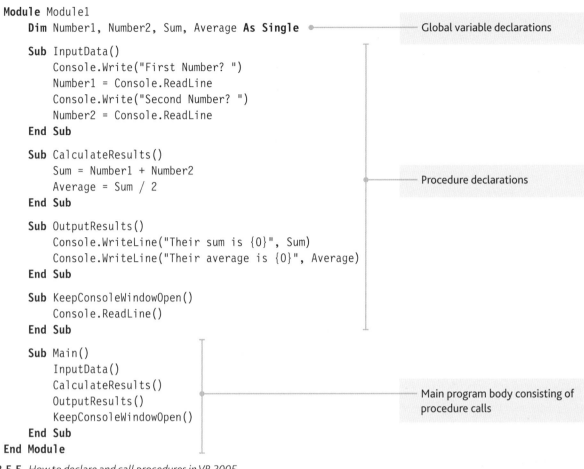

```
Option Explicit On

Module Module1
    Dim Number1, Number2, Sum, Average As Single ●━━━━━━  Global variable declarations

    Sub InputData()
        Console.Write("First Number? ")
        Number1 = Console.ReadLine
        Console.Write("Second Number? ")
        Number2 = Console.ReadLine
    End Sub

    Sub CalculateResults()
        Sum = Number1 + Number2                   ●━━━━━━  Procedure declarations
        Average = Sum / 2
    End Sub

    Sub OutputResults()
        Console.WriteLine("Their sum is {0}", Sum)
        Console.WriteLine("Their average is {0}", Average)
    End Sub

    Sub KeepConsoleWindowOpen()
        Console.ReadLine()
    End Sub

    Sub Main()
        InputData()
        CalculateResults()
        OutputResults()                           ●━━━━━━  Main program body consisting of
        KeepConsoleWindowOpen()                            procedure calls
    End Sub
End Module
```

Fig. 2.5.5 *How to declare and call procedures in VB 2005*

Key point

The variable sum is used here as a transformation.

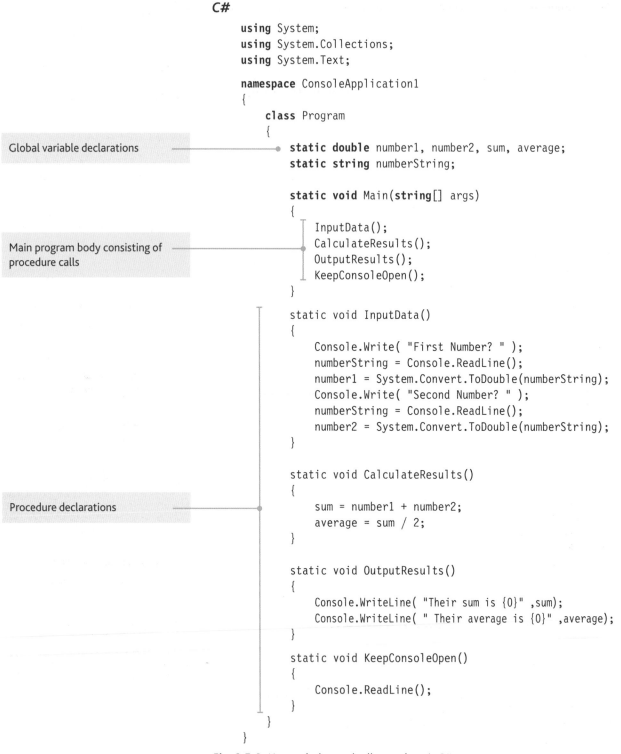

```
                                 C#
                                 using System;
                                 using System.Collections;
                                 using System.Text;

                                 namespace ConsoleApplication1
                                 {
                                     class Program
                                     {
Global variable declarations         static double number1, number2, sum, average;
                                         static string numberString;

                                         static void Main(string[] args)
                                         {
                                             InputData();
Main program body consisting of          CalculateResults();
procedure calls                          OutputResults();
                                             KeepConsoleOpen();
                                         }

                                         static void InputData()
                                         {
                                             Console.Write( "First Number? " );
                                             numberString = Console.ReadLine();
                                             number1 = System.Convert.ToDouble(numberString);
                                             Console.Write( "Second Number? " );
                                             numberString = Console.ReadLine();
                                             number2 = System.Convert.ToDouble(numberString);
                                         }

                                         static void CalculateResults()
                                         {
Procedure declarations                       sum = number1 + number2;
                                             average = sum / 2;
                                         }

                                         static void OutputResults()
                                         {
                                             Console.WriteLine( "Their sum is {0}" ,sum);
                                             Console.WriteLine( " Their average is {0}" ,average);
                                         }

                                         static void KeepConsoleOpen()
                                         {
                                             Console.ReadLine();
                                         }
                                     }
                                 }
```

Fig. 2.5.6 *How to declare and call procedures in C#*

You may feel that the source code is a lot longer when using routines than without them, and that it is too much effort to type more than absolutely necessary. This is fine for a program of just a few lines. As soon as the source code listing extends over more than a page, you will find it easier to keep an overview of what the program is meant to do if the tasks are separated into routines.

Programmers need to write code that is easy to maintain. The code may be maintained by someone other than the original programmer. Very large applications are written by teams of programmers and each programmer's code needs to be easily understandable to the other programmers.

Start your program writing with good habits and use a separate routine for each task. You can reuse code you have written by putting tried and tested routines into a library.

Procedure and function parameters

It is good programming practice to avoid the use of global variables. Variables that are only used within a routine should be declared as **local variables** within that routine. Values that are required by several routines should be passed as parameters. This is known as the **routine interface**. Parameter lists can contain any number of parameters. Routine calls must provide parameters in the same order as declared in the routine header. There are two different mechanisms for passing parameters: **calling by reference** and **calling by value**. The **parameter** list in the routine header shows which is used.

Calling by reference

When a parameter is passed by reference, the variable inside the routine uses a reference to the same memory location as the variable passed as the parameter. Any changes to the contents of the variable in the routine are accessible to the program code from which the routine call was made. It also means that the call must use a variable as a parameter, not an explicit value – you cannot pass 17 by reference.

Pascal

```pascal
Program Project1;
{$APPTYPE CONSOLE}
Uses SysUtils;
Var Number1, Number2: Integer;
Procedure Swap (Var a, b: Integer);
  Var Temp: Integer;
  Begin
    Temp := a;
    a := b;
    b := Temp;
  End; {of procedure}
//************* Main Program *************
Begin
  Number1 := 5;
  Number2 := 7;
  Writeln ('First: ', Number1, ', Second: ', Number2);
  Swap (Number1, Number2);
  Writeln ('First: ', Number1, ', Second: ', Number2);
  Readln;
End.
```

Global variable declarations.

Local variable declaration.

VB 2005

```
Option Explicit On
Module Module1
  Sub Main()
    Dim Number1, Number2 As Integer
    Number1 = 5
    Number2 = 7
    Console.WriteLine("First: {0}, Second: {1}", Number1, Number2)
    Swap(Number1, Number2)
    Console.WriteLine("First: {0}, Second: {1}", Number1, Number2)
    Console.ReadLine()
  End Sub
  Sub Swap(ByRef a As Integer, ByRef b As Integer)
    Dim Temp As Integer
    Temp = a
    a = b
    b = Temp
  End Sub
End Module
```

C#

```
static void Main(string[] args)
  {
    int number1 = 5;
    int number2 = 7;
    Console.WriteLine("First: {0}, Second: {1}", number1, number2);
    swap(ref number1, ref number2);
    Console.WriteLine("First: {0}, Second: {1}", number1, number2);
    Console.ReadLine();
  }
static void swap(ref int a, ref int b)
  {
    int temp = a;
    a = b;
    b = temp;
  }
```

Calling by value

When an argument is passed by value, the routine copies the value of the calling code's variable to the routine's parameter. Changes made to the copy have no effect on the original variable and are lost when the program execution returns to the code from which the routine call was made (Figs 2.5.1, 2 and 3 on pp57–8). Look at this partial program:

```
Procedure Increment (n: Integer);
  Begin
    n := n + 1;
    Writeln(n);
  End; {of procedure}
//************* Main Program *************
Begin
  .
  .
  Number := 7;
  Increment(Number);
  Writeln(Number);
End.
```

The parameter is passed by value. When the procedure is called the value of Number is copied to the parameter n. n changes to 8 within the procedure and this is output. When the control returns to the main program the value of Number is output. This is still 7. So the output from this program is

8
7

Note that if the parameter were passed by reference, the output would be

8
8

PC activity

Modify the partial program so it calls parameters by reference.

PC activity

In the language of your choice, write programs to do the following:

1. Write and test a procedure DisplaySymbols which takes two parameters, an integer x and a character s. The procedure is to display x number of symbol s on the same line. For example, the procedure call DisplaySymbols(3,'*') should display *** in the console window.

2. Expand your solution to Question 1 so that the user is asked how many of the symbols and which symbol should be displayed.

3. Expand your solution to Question 1. Write and test a procedure DisplayRectangle that calls DisplaySymbols so that the output resembles a rectangle of symbols. For example, the procedure call DisplayRectangle(4,3,'%') should display this in the console window:
   ```
   %%%%
   %%%%
   %%%%
   ```

4. Write a program to simulate the game 'Last one loses'. The game is for two players and starts with a set of x counters. The players take turns at removing 1, 2 or 3 counters from the set. The game is over when there are no more counters. The player who took the last counter loses. (Extension activity)

5. Expand your solution to Question 4 to let one user play against the computer. You will need to use random functions to simulate the computer choosing to take 1, 2 or 3 counters. (Extension activity)

The procedure Randomize should be called only once during the execution of the program, to initialise the random number generator.

Random(6) generates an integer in the range 0 to 5. Add 1 to get a number between 1 and 6.

Declare a new object of type Random.

Next(1,6) generates an integer in the range 1 and 6.

Declare a new object of type Random.

Next(1,6) generates an integer in the range 1 and 6.

How to use the built-in random number generator

Pascal

```
Randomize;
Number := Random(6) + 1;
```

VB 2005

```
Dim RandomNumber As New Random
Dim x As Integer
x = RandomNumber.Next(1,6)
```

C#

```
Random randomNumber = new Random();
int x = randomNumber.Next(1,6);
```

The role of variables

A variable is a memory location which we can refer to using its identifier. How do we use variables?

Role	Description	See page
Fixed value	A variable initialised without any calculation and not changed thereafter; for example, we may need to remember the number of array elements in use	91
Stepper	A variable stepping through a systematic, predictable succession of values; for example, during iterations, a variable is used to keep a count of the number of repetitions	52
Most recent holder	A variable holding the latest value encountered when processing a succession of unpredictable values or simply the latest value obtained as input; for example, storing the latest of a series of values input by the user to add to a running total	53
Most wanted holder	A variable holding the most appropriate value encountered so far; for example, when we search through a set of values for the largest value, we store the largest value we have encountered so far	91
Gatherer	A variable accumulating the effect of individual values; for example, when we calculate the total of a series of values, we keep a running total of all the values added so far	223
Transformation	A variable that always gets its new value from a fixed calculation of values of other variables; for example, we might store the result of a conversion of a measurement in inches to a measurement in metres	61
Follower	A variable that gets its new value from the old value of some other data item; for example, before updating a variable its current value is copied to the follower	
Temporary	A variable holding some value for a short time only; for example, it is used as the intermediate storage when swapping values in variables	63

In this topic you have covered:

- functions, which always return a value
- built-in functions for arithmetic and string handling
- call by reference and call by value
- routines with interfaces
- random number generators
- variables taking on different roles.

2.6 Arrays

Did you know?

Edsger W. Dijkstra argued that the first element of a sequence should be numbered 0. Look at this PDF to see why: **www.cs.utexas.edu/users/EWD/ewd08xx/EWD831.PDF**.

Study tip

For AS and A level you need to be able to use one-dimensional arrays, also known as linear lists or vectors, and two-dimensional arrays, also known as tables.

If we store several data values in separate variables and process them individually in a similar way, we have to write very repetitive code. For example, to store the names of four pupils, we need to declare four string variables. This is manageable but what if we wanted to store the names of all the pupils in the school? We need a data structure that allows us to refer to the data values as a group.

An array is an ordered set of data values of the same data type, grouped together and referred to by a single identifier. Arrays may have one or more dimensions. A two-dimensional array can be used to represent a matrix in mathematics.

Arrays occupy contiguous locations in main memory. Individual array elements are referred to using the array identifier and indices, one index per dimension. Some programming languages use ( ) to enclose indices, other programming languages use [ ]. Another name for an index is a subscript.

When you want to use an array as a parameter (Topic 2.5) you may need to declare the array as a type first (Topic 2.2) and then declare a variable of this type.

One-dimensional arrays

Pascal allows you to choose any ordinal type range for array subscripts. Some other languages do not. VB 2005 and C# both number array elements from zero. This means that only the top boundary needs to be specified when declaring an array. If you don't like to work with a zeroth element, you can just leave that element empty and start using the first element. It means that you declare your array one element larger than you need to.

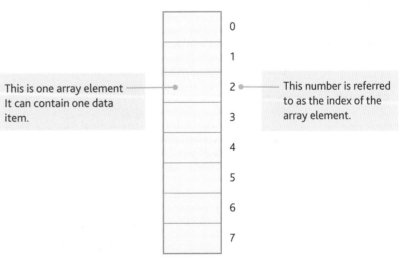

Fig. 2.6.1 *A one-dimensional array*

Student

Fred	0
Jack	1
Chris	2
Ali	3
Harry	4
Bill	5
Zak	6
Phil	7

Fig. 2.6.2 *Array Student*

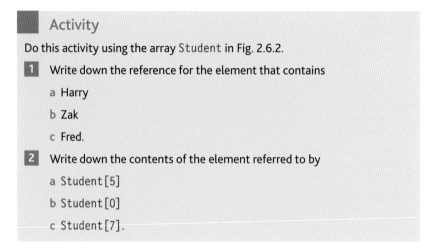

■ Activity

Do this activity using the array Student in Fig. 2.6.2.

1 Write down the reference for the element that contains

a Harry

b Zak

c Fred.

2 Write down the contents of the element referred to by

a Student[5]

b Student[0]

c Student[7].

As with any variable, arrays need to be declared before they can be used in programming code.

The array element index can start at any value. The range is enclosed in [ ].

An array can be declared and initialised in one statement. Array elements can be assigned one at a time.

An array can be declared and initialised in one statement. The index starts at zero.

Individual elements are accessed by the index, enclosed in ( ).

An array can be declared with the final index, enclosed in ( ).

Array elements can be assigned one at a time.

An array can be declared and initialised in one statement. The index starts at zero.

Individual elements are accessed by the index, enclosed in [ ].

An array can be declared with the size of the array, enclosed in [ ].

Array elements can be assigned one at a time.

This loop accesses the array elements in order.

This loop accesses the array elements in reverse order.

This loop accesses the array elements in order.

This loop accesses the array elements in reverse order.

Pascal

```
Var Name : array [0..3] of string=('Fred','Jack','Chris','Ali');
Name[0] := 'Fred';
Name[1] := 'Jack';
Name[2] := 'Chris';
Name[3] := 'Ali';
```

VB 2005

```
Dim Name() As String = {"Fred", "Jack", "Chris", "Ali"}
Console.WriteLine(Name(0))
Dim Name(3) As String
Name(0) = Console.ReadLine()
```

C#

```
string[] name = {"Fred", "Jack", "Chris", "Ali"};
Console.WriteLine(name[0]);
string[] name = new string[4];
name[0] = Console.ReadLine();
```

When we want to access each array element in turn, we can use a loop to do this without repetitive program code.

Pascal

```
For Index := 0 To 3
    Do Writeln(Name[Index]);
For Index := MaxElements DownTo 0
    Do Writeln(Name[Index]);
```

VB 2005

```
Dim Name() As String = {"Fred", "Jack", "Chris", "Ali"}
Dim Index As Integer
For Index = 0 To 3
    Console.WriteLine(Name(Index))
Next
For Index = 3 To 0 Step -1
    Console.WriteLine(Name(Index))
Next
```

C#

```
string[] name = {"Fred", "Jack", "Chris", "Ali"};
for (int index = 0; index <= 3; index++)
   {
     Console.WriteLine(name[index]);
   }
for (int index = 3; index >= 0; index-)
   {
     Console.WriteLine(name[index]);
   }
```

This loop accesses the array elements in order.

This loop accesses the array elements in reverse order.

Worked example

One way of using a one-dimensional array is as a tally chart. If we want to record on a piece of paper how many times we throw each of the numbers on a die, we use a tally chart (Fig. 2.6.3).

How do we implement this as a program? Each of the boxes in Fig. 2.6.3 could be an element of an integer array `Tally`. We could simulate the throws of the die by using the random number generator (Topic 2.5).

- Declare an integer array with indices up to 6.
- Set each element of the array `Tally` to zero; use a loop.
- To simulate throwing the die 200 times, set up a loop to repeat the following steps: generate a random number, increment the corresponding array element by 1.
- Use a loop to display the value stored in each of the array elements.

For example, if the random number is 3, add 1 to the contents of `Tally[3]`. In general, if the random number generated is stored in the variable `Number`, then increment `Tally[Number]`.

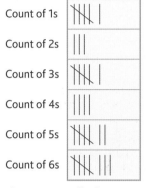

Fig. 2.6.3 *A tally chart*

🖥 PC activity

In the language of your choice, write programs to do the following:

1. Initialise a string array of eight elements with the names shown in the array `Student` (Fig. 2.6.2). Display these names on the console in the order given and then in reverse order.

2. Declare an integer array of 10 elements. Fill the elements with values that the user types in at the keyboard. Display these values on the console.

3. Extend your program from Activity 2 to calculate the sum and average of the numbers stored in the array. Display each number on the console with a message stating whether it is below average, above average or equal to the average.

4. Extend your program from Activity 3 to count how many numbers were above the average and how many below the average. Display your results. (Extension question)

5. Implement the worked example. You can display the value of each element of `Tally` as a number or as symbols that make it look more like a conventional tally chart.

■ Using one-dimensional arrays in parallel

Sometimes we may want to store more than one data item in a row. If these data items are not of the same data type, we cannot use a two-dimensional array. Declaring several one-dimensional arrays with the same number of elements allows us to store and use the required data.

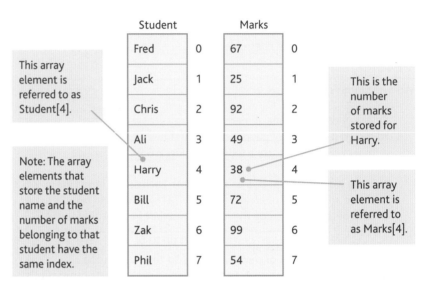

Fig. 2.6.4 *Parallel one-dimensional arrays*

🖥 PC activity

In the language of your choice, write programs to do the following:

1 Initialise a string array of eight elements with the names shown in the array Student (Fig. 2.6.4). Initialise an integer array of eight elements with the marks shown in the array Marks (Fig. 2.6.4). Display the names with the relevant marks next to them on the console.

2 Extend your program from Activity 1 to calculate the average of the number of marks of the students. Display each student's name and their marks on the console with a message stating whether the mark is below average, above average or equal to the average.

3 Extend your program from Activity 2 to count how many students were above average and how many below average. Display your results. (Extension question)

💡 Two-dimensional arrays

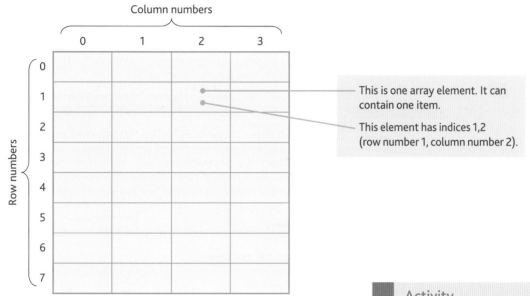

Fig. 2.6.5 *A two-dimensional array*

To store tables of data of the same type, we can declare two-dimensional arrays. For example, the distances between UK cities might be stored in an array Distance.

	London	Manchester	Oxford	Sheffield
London	–	184	56	160
Manchester	184	–	144	38
Oxford	56	144	–	130
Sheffield	160	38	130	–

Fig. 2.6.6 *Array Distance*

Pascal

```
Var Distance : Array [0..3, 0..3] Of Integer;
Distance[1,2] := 144;
```

Declare a two-dimensional array.

This assigns a value to the array element in the second row and third column.

VB 2005

```
Dim Distance(3,3) As Integer
Distance(1,2) = 144
```

Declare a two-dimensional array.

This assigns a value to the array element in the second row and third column.

C#

```
int[,] distance = new int[4,4];
distance[1,2] = 144;
```

Declare a 4 × 4 array.

This assigns a value to the array element in the second row and third column.

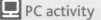

PC activity

In the language of your choice, write programs to do the following:

1 Declare a two-dimensional integer array and store the distance chart values from Fig. 2.6.6. Declare a one-dimensional string array to store the city names. Display on the console the name of each city, except London, and the distance from London.

2 Extend your program from Activity 1 to display the distance chart in Fig. 2.6.6.

3 Find out about the game Battleship (http://en.wikipedia.org/wiki/Battleship_(game)). Declare a 10 × 10 character array and initialise it with some ships. Ask the user to input the coordinates for the target. The program should respond with whether this was a hit or not. When all areas of the ships have been hit, the program should respond with 'Game over' and display the number of shots required. (Extension question)

■ Arrays of records

Instead of using parallel one-dimensional arrays, we can use arrays of records to group data items of different data types together.

Activity

1 Using the array Student in Fig. 2.6.7, write down the data item referred to by Student[5].Name
Student[0].Marks

2 Using the array Student in Fig. 2.6.7, write down the reference for the field that contains

a Harry's marks

b Zak's name.

Student

Name: Fred Marks: 67	0
Name: Jack Marks: 25	1
Name: Chris Marks: 92	2
Name: Ali Marks: 49	3
Name: Harry Marks: 38	4
Name: Bill Marks: 72	5
Name: Zak Marks: 99	6
Name: Phil Marks: 54	7

One array element contains the data of one record. The record consists of two fields, Name and Marks.

This is the index of the array element (one student record).

Fig. 2.6.7 *An array of records*

When you want to use arrays of records, you first need to declare the record type (Topic 2.2) then you can declare an array of this record type.

Declare the record data type.

Declare an array of records.

All the array elements must be initialised before you access them.

Pascal

```pascal
Type
    TStudent = Record
                   Name : String[15];
                   Marks : Integer;
               End;
Var
    Student : Array [0..3] Of TStudent;
    Index: Integer;
Begin
    Student[0].Name := 'Fred';
    Student[0].Marks := 67;
    .
    .
    .

    For Index := 0 To 3
        Do Writeln(Student[Index].Name, Student[Index].Marks);
End.
```

VB 2005

```
Structure TStudent
   Dim Name As String
   Dim Marks As Integer
End Structure
Sub Main()
   Dim Student(3) As TStudent
   Dim Index As Integer
   Student(0).Name = "Fred"
   Student(0).Marks = 67
   .
   .
   .
   For Index = 0 To 3
      Console.Write(Student(Index).Name)
      Console.WriteLine(Student(Index).Marks)
   Next
```

- Declare the structure data type.
- Declare an array of records.
- All the array elements must be initialised before you access them.

C#

```
struct TStudent
   {
      public string Name;
      public int Marks;
   }
static void Main(string[] args)
   {
      TStudent[] student = new TStudent[4];
      student[0].Name = "Fred";
      student[0].Marks = 35;
      .
      .
      .
      for (int index = 0; index <= 3; index++)
         {
            Console.Write(student[index].Name);
            Console.WriteLine(student[index].Marks);
         }
   }
```

- Declare the struct data type.
- Declare an array of records.
- All the array elements must be initialised before you access them.

In this topic you have covered:

- how to use one-dimensional arrays
- how to use two-dimensional arrays
- how to use arrays of records.

🖥 PC activity

In the language of your choice, write programs that do the following:

1. Declare a record type TCar with fields Make and Model (strings), EngineSize (integer) and Price. Declare an array of type TCar to store five cars. Set initial values then display the data on the console.

2. Extend your program from Activity 1 to calculate the average price of the cars. Display the details of each car on the console with a message stating whether the price is below average, above average or equal to the average.

3. Extend your program from Activity 2 to count how many cars have a price above the average price and how many below the average price. Display your results. (Extension question)

2.7 Text files and files of records

Key terms

Text file: a sequence of printable characters, organised line by line; it can be opened and read in a text editor.

CSV file: comma-separated values file; a text file with one record per line and the fields of each record separated by commas.

Binary file: contains mostly unprintable characters.

Key point

In Pascal you can read a character at a time using the command Read rather than Readln. When you come to the end of the line, you need to consume the end of line marker with a Readln command so that the character at the beginning of the next line is the next to be read. If you want individual characters when using VB 2005 or C#, you need to use string-handling functions once you have read a whole line from the keyboard.

Link the file path name to the channel named CurrentFile.

Open or create file for writing.

Read string from the keyboard.

Write string to channel.

Close the file.

So far we have done a lot of programming and data handling, but the data was only stored in variables in main memory as the program was executing. When the program terminates, the contents of the variables are lost. We need some way of storing data in backing store. This can be done using **text files**, **CSV files**, **binary files** or databases; see the A2 book.

Text files

A text file consists of a sequence of printable characters organised into lines, each of which is terminated by an end-of-line marker. A text file can be opened and read in a text editor. When using text files, you read or write a line of text at a time as a string.

You open a text file for reading or writing. You can have more than one file open at any one time, such as one for reading and another for writing.

The next example reads five lines of text from the keyboard and saves them in a text file. The following example reads the text file and displays the lines of text on the console. Use the comments to help you understand the code.

Writing to a text file

Pascal

```pascal
Program WriteToFileProg;
{$APPTYPE CONSOLE}
Uses SysUtils;
Var
  CurrentFile : TextFile;
  FileName, TextString: String;
  Count : Integer;

Begin
  FileName := 'C:\My Files\Programming\Pascal\test1.txt';
  AssignFile(CurrentFile, FileName);
  Rewrite(CurrentFile);
  For Count := 1 To 5
    Do
      Begin
        Write('Input line number ', Count, ': ');
        Readln(TextString);
        Writeln(CurrentFile, TextString);
      End;
  CloseFile(CurrentFile);
  Readln;
End.
```

VB 2005

```
Option Explicit On
Imports System.IO
Module Module1
  Dim CurrentFileWriter As StreamWriter                    Declare a channel for writing.
  Sub Main()
    Dim FileName, TextString As String, Count As Integer
    FileName = "C:\My Files\Programming\VB2005\test1.txt"
    CurrentFileWriter = New StreamWriter(FileName)          Link the file path name to the
    For Count = 1 To 5                                      channel.
      Console.Write("Input line number {0}: ", Count)
      TextString = Console.ReadLine()                       Read line of text from the
                                                            keyboard.
      CurrentFileWriter.WriteLine(TextString)               Write line of text to the channel.
    Next
    CurrentFileWriter.Close()                               Close the channel.
    Console.ReadLine()
  End Sub
End ModuleStreamWriter
```

C#

```
using System;
using System.Collections.Generic;
using System.Text;
using System.IO;
namespace ConsoleApplication1
{
  class Program
  {
    static StreamWriter currentFileWriter;                  Declare a channel for writing.
    static void Main(string[] args)
    {
      string fileName = "C:/My Files/Programming/C Sharp/test1.txt";
      currentFileWriter = new StreamWriter(fileName);       Link the file path name to the
      for (int count = 1; count <= 5; count++)              channel.
      {
        Console.Write(" Input line number {0}: ", count);   Read line of text from the
        string textString = Console.ReadLine();             keyboard.
        currentFileWriter.WriteLine(textString);            Write line of text to the channel.
      }
      currentFileWriter.Close();                            Close the channel.
      Console.ReadLine();
    }
  }
}
```

Reading text from a file

Pascal

```
Program ReadFromFileProg;
{$APPTYPE CONSOLE}
Uses SysUtils;
Var
  CurrentFile : TextFile;
  FileName, TextString: String;
Begin
  FileName := 'C:\My Files\Programming\Pascal\test1.txt';
  AssignFile(CurrentFile, FileName);
  Reset(CurrentFile);
  While Not EoF(CurrentFile)
    Do
      Begin
        Readln(CurrentFile, TextString);
        Writeln(TextString);
      End;
  CloseFile(CurrentFile);
  Readln;
End.
```

Link the file path name to the channel named CurrentFile

Open file for reading

While the end of file has not been encountered

Read a line of text from the channel

Display the line of text on the console

Close the file

VB 2005

```
Option Explicit On
Imports System.IO
Module Module1
  Dim CurrentFileReader As StreamReader
  Sub Main()
    Dim FileName, TextString As String
    FileName = "C:\My Files\Programming\VB2005\test1.txt"
    CurrentFileReader = New StreamReader(FileName)
    Do Until CurrentFileReader.EndOfStream
      TextString = CurrentFileReader.ReadLine()
      Console.WriteLine(TextString)
    Loop
    CurrentFileReader.Close()
    Console.ReadLine()
  End Sub
End Module
```

Declare a channel for reading

Link the file path name to the channel

Until the end of file has not been encountered

Read line of text from the channel

Display line of text on the console

Close the channel

C#

```
using System;
using System.Collections.Generic;
using System.Text;
using System.IO;
namespace ConsoleApplication1
{
  class Program
  {
    static StreamReader currentFileReader;
    static void Main(string[] args)
    {
        string fileName = "C:/My Files/Programming/C Sharp/
        test1.txt";
        currentFileReader = new StreamReader(fileName);
        while (!currentFileReader.EndOfStream)
        {
            string textString = currentFileReader.ReadLine();
            Console.WriteLine(textString);
        }
        currentFileReader.Close();
        Console.ReadLine();
    }
  }
}
```

Declare a channel for reading

Link the file path name to the channel

While the end of file has not been encountered

Read line of text from the channel

Display line of text on the console

Close the channel

▮ CSV files

A comma-separated values (CSV) file is a text file with one record per line and the fields of each record separated by commas (Fig. 2.7.1). CSV files are popular as data files for mail-merge programs.

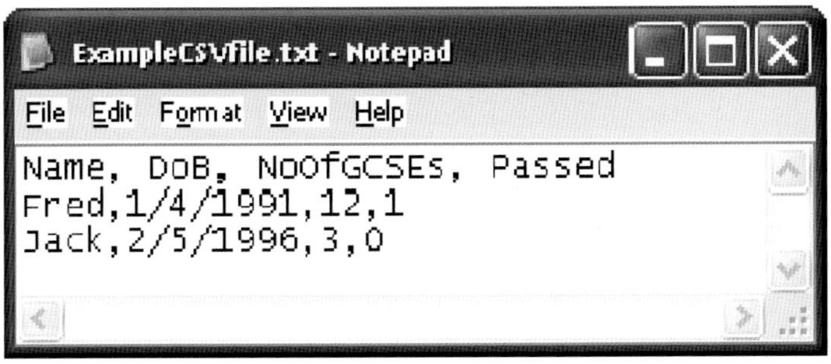

```
ExampleCSVfile.txt - Notepad

File  Edit  Format  View  Help

Name, DoB, NoOfGCSEs, Passed
Fred,1/4/1991,12,1
Jack,2/5/1996,3,0
```

Fig. 2.7.1 Data in a CSV file

Some programming environments, such as the .Net framework, have classes that can handle CSV files directly.

If you wish to create a CSV file more simply, you can create a new text file. Output each record using a separate statement. Put a comma between each field.

Pascal

```
Writeln(CurrentFile, Name, ',', Street, ',', Town);
```

VB 2005

```
TextString = Name + "," + Street + "," + Town
CurrentFileWrite.WriteLine(TextString)
```

Study tip

Programming with classes and objects is beyond the scope of the AS specification.

C#

```
textString = name + "," + street + "," + town
currentFileWriter.WriteLine(textString)
```

Files of records

Files of records are also known as binary files. A file of records usually contains multiple data types. Data types other than strings and characters are stored in internal format and cannot be displayed in a meaningful way in a text editor, which can only interpret character codes (ASCII or Unicode). You need to know the organisation of the record in a binary file to be able to read it.

This example consists of two programs for each programming language. The first reads values for book records from the keyboard and saves them in a file of records. The second reads the file of records and displays the values on the console.

You may wish to read records from a file into an array of records while the program is running and store the contents of the array back into the file before the program terminates.

Writing to a binary file

Pascal

```
Program WriteToFileProg;
{$APPTYPE CONSOLE}
Uses SysUtils;
Type
  TBook = Record
              Title : String[20];
              ISBN : String[13];
              Price : Currency;
              YearOfPublication : Integer;
          End; // of record
Var
  Book : TBook;
  CurrentFile: File Of TBook;
  FileName : String;
  Answer : Char;
Begin
  FileName := 'C:\My Files\Programming\Pascal\test1.bin';
  AssignFile(CurrentFile, FileName);
  Rewrite(CurrentFile);
  Repeat
    Write('ISBN: '); Readln(Book.ISBN);
    Write('Title: '); Readln(Book.Title);
    Write('Price: '); Readln(Book.Price);
    Write('Year Of Publication: '); Readln(Book.
                                    YearOfPublication);
    Write(CurrentFile, Book);
    Write('Do you want to add another record? (y/n) ');
    Readln(Answer);
  Until Answer In ['N', 'n'];
  CloseFile(CurrentFile);
  Readln;
End.
```

Declare a file channel to handle the book record type.

Link the file path name to the channel.

Open or create file for writing.

Write the whole record to the file in one go.

VB 2005

```
Option Explicit On
Imports System.IO
Module Module1
  Structure TBook
    Dim Title As String
    Dim ISBN As String
    Dim Price As Decimal
    Dim YearOfPublication As Integer
  End Structure
  Dim Book As TBook
  Dim CurrentFileWriter As BinaryWriter
  Dim CurrentFile As FileStream
  Sub Main()
    Dim FileName, Answer As String
    FileName = "C:\My Files\Programming\VB2005\test1.bin"
    CurrentFile = New FileStream(FileName, FileMode.Create)
    CurrentFileWriter = New BinaryWriter(CurrentFile)
    Do
      Console.Write("ISBN: ") : Book.ISBN = Console.ReadLine()
      Console.Write("Title: ") : Book.Title = Console.ReadLine()
      Console.Write("Price: ") : Book.Price = Console.ReadLine()
      Console.Write("Year of Publication: ") : Book.YearOfPublication = Console.ReadLine()
      CurrentFileWriter.Write(Book.ISBN)
      CurrentFileWriter.Write(Book.Title)
      CurrentFileWriter.Write(Book.Price)
      CurrentFileWriter.Write(Book.YearOfPublication)
      Console.Write("Do you want to add another record? (y/n) ")
      Answer = Console.ReadLine()
    Loop Until (Answer = "N" Or Answer = "n")
    CurrentFileWriter.Close()
    CurrentFile.Close()
    Console.ReadLine()
  End Sub
End Module
```

C#

```csharp
using System;
using System.Collections.Generic;
using System.Text;
using System.IO;
namespace ConsoleApplication1
{
  class Program
  {
    struct TBook
    {
      public string Title, ISBN;
      public decimal Price;
      public int YearOfPublication;
    }
    static TBook book;
    static BinaryWriter currentFileWriter;
    static FileStream currentFile;
    static void Main(string[] args)
    {
      string fileName = "C:/My Files/Programming/C Sharp/test1.bin";
      string answer;
      currentFile = new FileStream(fileName, FileMode.Create);
      currentFileWriter = new BinaryWriter(currentFile);
      do
      {
        Console.Write("ISBN: "); book.ISBN = Console.ReadLine();
        Console.Write("Title: "); book.Title = Console.ReadLine();
        Console.Write("Price: "); book.Price = Convert.ToDecimal(Console.ReadLine());
        Console.Write("Year of Publication: ");
        book.YearOfPublication = Convert.ToInt32(Console.ReadLine());
        currentFileWriter.Write(book.ISBN);
        currentFileWriter.Write(book.Title);
        currentFileWriter.Write(book.Price);
        currentFileWriter.Write(book.YearOfPublication);
        Console.Write("Do you want to add another record? (y/n) ");
        answer = Console.ReadLine();
      }
      while ((answer == "Y" ) || (answer == "y"));
      currentFileWriter.Close();
      currentFile.Close();
      Console.ReadLine();
    }
  }
}
```

Reading from a binary file

Pascal

```
Program ReadFromFileProg;
{$APPTYPE CONSOLE}
Uses SysUtils;
Type
  TBook = Record
            Title : String[20];
            ISBN : String[13];
            Price : Currency;
            YearOfPublication : Integer;
          End; // of record
Var
  Book : TBook;
  CurrentFile: File Of TBook;
  FileName : String;

Begin
  FileName := 'C:\My Files\Programming\Pascal\test1.bin';
  AssignFile(CurrentFile, FileName);
  Reset(CurrentFile);
  While Not EoF(CurrentFile)
    Do
      Begin
        Read(CurrentFile, Book);
        Writeln('ISBN: ', Book.ISBN);
        Writeln('Title: ', Book.Title);
        Writeln('Price: ', Book.Price:5:2);
        Writeln('Year Of Publication: ', Book.
        YearOfPublication);
      End;
  CloseFile(CurrentFile);
  Readln;
End.
```

Declare a file channel to handle the book record type.

Link the file path name to the channel.

Open file for reading.

While the end of file has not been encountered.

Read whole record into book variable.

VB 2005

```
Option Explicit On
Imports System.IO
Module Module1
  Structure TBook
    Dim Title As String
    Dim ISBN As String
    Dim Price As Decimal
    Dim YearOfPublication As Integer
  End Structure
  Dim Book As TBook
  Dim CurrentFileReader As BinaryReader
  Dim CurrentFile As FileStream
  Sub Main()
    Dim FileName As String
    FileName = "C:\My Files\Programming\VB2005\test1.bin"
    CurrentFile = New FileStream(FileName, FileMode.Open)
    CurrentFileReader = New BinaryReader(CurrentFile)
    Do While CurrentFile.Position < CurrentFile.Length
```

```
                Book.ISBN = CurrentFileReader.ReadString()
                Book.Title = CurrentFileReader.ReadString()
                Book.Price = CurrentFileReader.ReadDecimal()
                Book.YearOfPublication = CurrentFileReader.ReadInt32()
                Console.WriteLine("ISBN: {0}", Book.ISBN)
                Console.WriteLine("Title: {0}", Book.Title)
                Console.WriteLine("Price: {0}", Book.Price)
                Console.WriteLine("Year of Publication: {0}", Book.
                                                   YearOfPublication)
        Loop
        CurrentFileReader.Close()
        CurrentFile.Close()
        Console.ReadLine()
    End Sub
End Module
```

C#

```csharp
using System;
using System.Collections.Generic;
using System.Text;
using System.IO;
namespace ConsoleApplication1
{
  class Program
  {
    struct TBook
    {
      public string Title, ISBN;
      public decimal Price;
      public int YearOfPublication;
    }
    static TBook book;
    static BinaryReader currentFileReader;
    static FileStream currentFile;
    static void Main(string[] args)
    {
      string fileName = "C:/My Files/Programming/C Sharp/test1.bin";
      currentFile = new FileStream(fileName, FileMode.Open);
      currentFileReader = new BinaryReader(currentFile);
      do
      {
        book.ISBN = currentFileReader.ReadString();
        book.Title = currentFileReader.ReadString();
        book.Price = currentFileReader.ReadDecimal();
        book.YearOfPublication = currentFileReader.ReadInt32();
        Console.WriteLine("ISBN: {0}", book.ISBN);
        Console.WriteLine("Title: {0}", book.Title);
        Console.WriteLine("Price: {0}", book.Price);
        Console.WriteLine("Year of Publication: {0}",
                                        book.YearOfPublication);
      }
      while (currentFile.Position < currentFile.Length);
      currentFileReader.Close();
      currentFile.Close();
      Console.ReadLine();
    }
  }
}
```

PC activity

In the language of your choice, write programs for the following tasks:

1 Read from an existing text file and display the contents of the file on the console. You can create a text file in any text editor.

2 Expand your program from Activity 1 to count the number of lines read from the file and display this total.

3 Expand your program from Activity 2 to count the number of words read. Hint: a word terminates with a space, punctuation marks or the end of a line. You need to use string-handling functions to find these characters. (Extension activity)

4 Declare a record type for student details and store in a variable of this type one student's details entered at the keyboard. Before the program terminates, it should save the record to a binary file.

5 Expand your program from Activity 4 to read several students' records into an array of records and store the contents of the array into a file before the program terminates. (Extension activity)

In this topic you have covered:

- the difference between a text file, a CSV file and a binary file of records
- how to read from and write to a text file
- reading records from a binary file
- writing records to a binary file.

3 Programming structure

3.1 Structured programming

Structured approach to program design

During the problem-solving stage (Topic 1.2), we learned to break down the problem into subproblems. The result was a structure table (Table 1 in Topic 1.2). During the program design stage, a system should be divided into modules where each module is self-contained and carries out one task.

The steps identified in a structure table can be developed into modules. The dependence of modules on other modules can be visually represented as a hierarchy chart. A hierarchy chart can be developed further into a structure chart when the module interfaces are also shown – how data is passed in and out of a module. Structure charts also show each major loop as a semicircular arrow and each major decision as a diamond.

To illustrate these design methods, we consider three problems of increasing complexity:

- Problem 1: Fahrenheit to Celsius conversion
- Problem 2: Calculate pay
- Problem 3: Frequency of die scores

Structure tables

A structure table is the result of breaking down the statement of the problem into subproblems and expressing these as a numbered list of steps in structured English (Topic 1.4).

Table 1 *Structure table for Problem 1*

0 Fahrenheit to Celsius conversion
0.1 INPUT degrees Fahrenheit
0.2 CALCULATE degrees Celsius
0.3 DISPLAY result

Problem 1 is a simple problem and the steps at level 1 are sufficient to write procedures for each of these tasks. If the problem is still not broken down into small enough subproblems, the subproblems may be broken down further. Note the numbering system. For each level another digit is added. With Problem 2, we begin at level 0.

    0 Calculate pay

The first step of refinement takes us to level 1:

    0.1 INPUT number of hours worked, pay rate

    0.2 CALCULATE basic pay

    0.3 DISPLAY total pay

Step 0.2 needs further refinement:

    0.2.1 CALCULATE basic pay

    0.2.2 CALCULATE overtime pay

Table 2 *Structure table for Problem 2*

0 Calculate pay
    0.1 INPUT number of hours worked, pay rate
    0.2 CALCULATE total pay
        0.2.1 CALCULATE basic pay
        0.2.2 CALCULATE overtime pay
    0.3 DISPLAY total pay

Table 3 *Structure table for Problem 3*

0 Frequency of die scores
    0.1 INITIALISE a frequency table
        0.1.1 FOR EACH possible die score (1..6)
        0.1.2 SET to zero the entry in the frequency table
    0.2 SIMULATE the throwing of a die 20 times and record score in frequency table
        0.2.1 FOR EACH of 20 goes
        0.2.2 GENERATE a random number between 1 and 6 (the simulated score of a die throw)
        0.2.3 RECORD score in table (INCREMENT by 1 the frequency count of the score)
    0.3 DISPLAY the results
        0.3.1 FOR EACH score in the frequency table
        0.3.2 DISPLAY the score and the frequency of this score

💡 Hierarchy charts

A hierarchy chart shows how the top-level module calls level 1 modules, which in turn may call level 2 modules, etc.

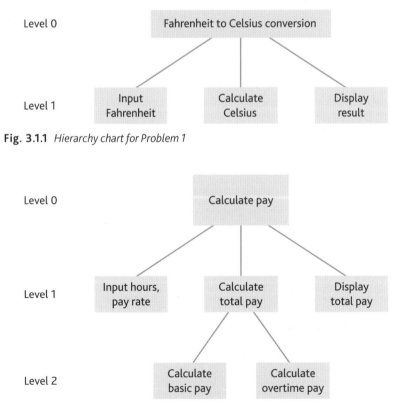

Fig. 3.1.1 *Hierarchy chart for Problem 1*

Fig. 3.1.2 *Hierarchy chart for Problem 2*

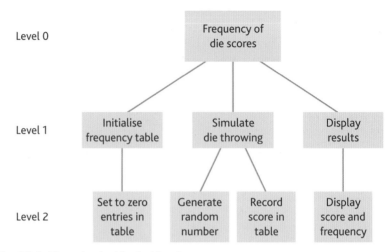

Fig. 3.1.3 *Hierarchy chart for Problem 3*

💡 Structure charts

A structure chart is a hierarchy chart with interfaces and control information. A structure chart does not show the internal specifications of a module; that is, it does not show the local variables and computations.

means import data

means export data

means import and export data

means major decision

means repeat

Fig. 3.1.4 *Structure chart symbols*

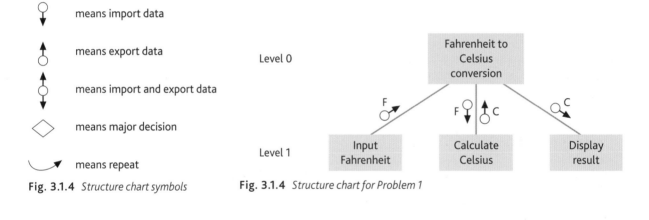

Fig. 3.1.4 *Structure chart for Problem 1*

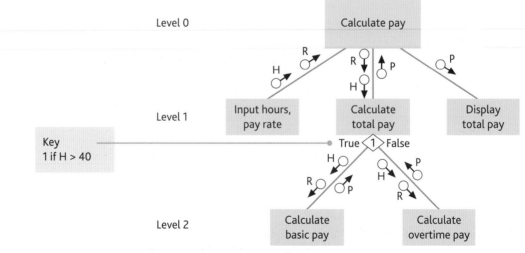

Fig. 3.1.5 *Structure chart for Problem 2*

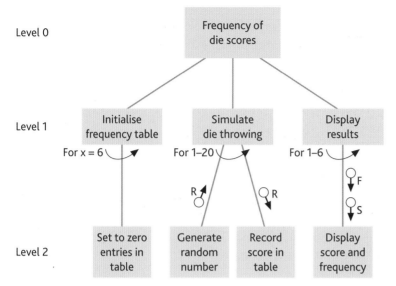

Level 0 Frequency of die scores

Level 1   Initialise frequency table   Simulate die throwing   Display results

For x = 6   For 1–20   For 1–6   F   S   R   R

Level 2   Set to zero entries in table   Generate random number   Record score in table   Display score and frequency

Fig. 3.1.6 *Structure chart for Problem 3*

Developing programs from structure charts

To develop program code from a structure chart, the boxes become procedures or functions and the interface shows the required parameters.

Pascal

Here is some code for Problem 2.

```pascal
Program CalculatePay;
{$APPTYPE CONSOLE}
Uses SysUtils;
Var
  Hours : Integer;
  RateOfPay, TotalPay : Currency;

Procedure InputHours(Var Hours: Integer; Var RateOfPay : Currency);
  Begin
    Write('Enter the number of hours worked: ');
    Readln(Hours);
    Write('Enter the rate of pay: £'); Readln(RateOfPay);
  End;

Procedure CalculateOvertimePay(Hours: Integer;
                               RateOfPay: Currency; Var TotalPay: Currency);
  Begin
    TotalPay := 40*RateOfPay + (Hours-40)*1.5*RateOfPay;
  End;

Procedure CalculateBasicPay(Hours: Integer;
                            RateOfPay: Currency; Var TotalPay: Currency);
  Begin
    TotalPay := Hours*RateOfPay;
  End;

Procedure CalculateTotalPay(Hours: Integer;
                            RateOfPay: Currency; Var TotalPay: Currency);
```

```
Begin
  If Hours > 40
    Then CalculateOvertimePay(Hours,RateOfPay,TotalPay)
    Else CalculateBasicPay(Hours,RateOfPay,TotalPay);
End;

Procedure DisplayTotalPay(TotalPay: Currency);
  Begin
    Write('The pay earned is: £', TotalPay:5:2);
  End;

Begin
  InputHours(Hours,RateOfPay);
  CalculateTotalPay(Hours,RateOfPay,TotalPay);
  DisplayTotalPay(TotalPay);
  Readln;
End.
```

Questions

1 The steps for calculating the average of two numbers are shown as a structure chart in Fig. 3.1.7. What are the missing labels at (a), (b) and (c)?

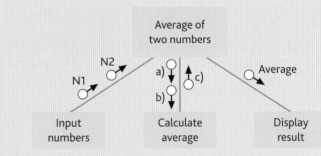

Fig. 3.1.7 *Structure chart for calculating the average of two numbers*

2 The structure chart in Fig. 3.1.8 has been developed for a program to display the times table of a given integer.

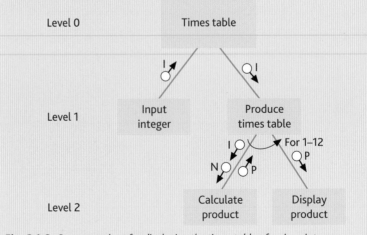

Fig. 3.1.8 *Structure chart for displaying the times table of a given integer*

Complete the missing steps in Table 4 to represent the times table solution.

Table 4 *Structure table for displaying the times table of a given integer*

0 Times table
    0.1 ....
    0.2 Produce times table
        0.2.1 FOR EACH number between 1 and 12
        0.2.2 ....
        0.2.3 ....

Features of structured programming

Good programming style is self-documenting. This means that the code conveys the method of solution without a lot of extra comments added by the programmer. This is achieved by observing the following conventions:

- **Use meaningful identifiers:** the choice of name should reflect the purpose of the variable or subroutine. Adhere to your chosen programming language's conventions for the case of letters. Don't use the underscore character _ to join several words into one identifier. Use uppercase for the first letter of each word only, for example, NumberOfEntries or numberOfEntries.

- **Use indentation:** this should show the structure of the program. For example, all statements within a loop structure should be indented. Some programming environments do this for you automatically. A convention is to use two columns of indentation.

- **Procedures and functions with interfaces:** the program should minimise the use of global variables. Values required by procedures and functions should be passed using parameters.

- **A procedure should execute a single task:** use the steps of stepwise refinement as procedure or function calls.

- **Use structured statements appropriately:** do not use GoTo statements or exit a loop except at the end. If you want to jump out of a For loop before the set number of iterations have been executed, you have chosen the wrong construct. Try a While loop or a Repeat loop instead and use the Boolean expression to exit the loop when required.

Activity

Can you work out what program A and program B are supposed to do? Which program is easier to understand?

Program A	Program B

label1: y=30; **goto** label3;
label2: y=31; **goto** label3;
label4: y=28; **if** z **mod** 4 = 0 **then goto** label5
if (x=1) **or** (x=3) **or** (x=5) **or** (x=7) **or** (x=8) **or** (x=10) **or** (x=12) **then goto** label1;
if (x=4) **or** (x=6) **or** (x=9) **or** (x=11) **then**
goto label2;**if** x=2 **then goto** label4;
label5: y=29; **if** (z **mod** 100 = 0) **and** (z **mod** 400 > 0) **then**
y=28
label3: writeln(x, y);
	Function LeapYear (y: Integer) : Boolean;
	Begin
	  If y **MOD** 400 = 0
	    Then LeapYear := True
	    Else
	      If y **MOD** 100 = 0
	      Then LeapYear := False
	      Else
	        If y **MOD** 4 = 0
	          Then LeapYear := True
	          Else LeapYear := False;
	End;
	Case Month **Of**
	    1,3,5,7,8,10,12: NumberOfDays := 31;
	    4,6,9,11: NumberOfDays := 30;
	    2: **IF** LeapYear(Year)
	                          Then NumberOfDays := 29
	                          Else NumberOfDays := 28;
	End;
	Writeln('Month ', Month, ' has ',NumberOfDays, ' days');

Questions

3 For the following program code, list the features that are poor programming style. Can you identify what this program is calculating?

```
n=Console.ReadLine
x=1 : For y = 1 to n : x=x*y : Next
Console.WriteLine(X)
```

In line 2, please note that : is a statement separator.

4 Rewrite the program in Question 1 and correct the poor features you identified. Use a programming language of your choice.

In this topic you have covered:

- how to construct and use structure tables
- how to construct and use structure charts
- how to construct and use hierarchy charts
- the advantages of the structured approach
- features of structured programming.

3.2 Standard algorithms

In this topic you will cover:

- how to search the contents of a one-dimensional array
- how to sort the contents of a one-dimensional array.

Topic 1.4 explained that an algorithm is a description of a process that achieves some task; it is independent of any programming language. We can express an algorithm using structured English or pseudocode. Searching and sorting are required in many circumstances. If there are a lot of data values, searching or sorting may take quite some time. Different methods have been developed and you will meet more sophisticated techniques in your A2 course.

Student

Name: Fred Marks: 67	1
Name: Jack Marks: 25	2
Name: Chris Marks: 92	3
Name: Ali Marks: 49	4
Name: Harry Marks: 38	5
Name: Bill Marks: 72	6
Name: Zak Marks: 99	7
Name: Phil Marks: 54	8

Fig. 3.2.1 *Array of student records*

Linear search

The most straightforward method for finding a particular element in an unordered list is the linear search technique. The technique involves scanning each element of the list in a sequential manner. The search starts at the beginning of the list. Each element in turn is compared with the required value until a match is found or the end of the list is reached.

For example, if we are looking for Bill's marks in the array Student (Fig. 3.2.1), we start at the first element of the array and check if the name is Bill. The name of the first element is Fred, so we go to the next element, Jack, and the next, and so on, until we get to the sixth element, which stores the name Bill. Then we can retrieve the marks for Bill.

The structure table for the linear search algorithm is shown in Table 1.

Table 1 *Structure table for a linear search*

```
1 GET first element of array
2 REPEAT UNTIL Element Sought is found or end of array
   2.1 IF Current Element is Element Sought
        THEN Element Sought is found
        ELSE get next element
```

We can express the linear search algorithm in pseudocode. Assume the array is called List and the elements are numbered from 1 to Max:

```
ThisElement ← 1
Found ← False
Repeat
   If List[ThisElement] = ElementSought
      Then Found ← True
      Else ThisElement ← ThisElement + 1
Until Found = True Or ThisElement > Max
```

Key point

The variable Max is used here to store a fixed value (see role of variables, p66).

The variable ElementSought is used to store the most wanted holder.

Questions

1 (a) Set up a trace table with the following column headings: ElementSought, ThisElement and Found. Dry run the linear search algorithm to search for Harry in the array Student (Fig. 3.2.1). (b) Set up another trace table with the same column headings and dry run the algorithm searching for Joe in the array Student.

2 In the programming language of your choice, write a function to perform a linear search on a specified list. The function header should be of the form `Search (List, ElementSought)`. Your function should search through the array `List` and return the index value of the item where the element was found. If the sought element does not exist in the list, the function should return `-1`. Test your function by searching for various elements, some of which exist and some of which do not.

💡 Bubble sort

There are several ways to sort elements in a one-dimensional array. The bubble sort is a slow but simple method. The general idea is that, during a pass through the list, neighbouring values are compared and swapped if they are not in order. Several passes are required before all list values are in the correct order. Fig. 3.2.2 shows a set of numbers as they are sorted in a series of passes.

1 **Start** at the beginning of the array.

2 **Compare** the values stored in elements 1 and 2; the values are 67 and 25.

3 **If** they are in the wrong order, swap them; in this case they get swapped.

4 **Compare** the next pair of values, in elements 2 and 3; the values are 67 and 92.

5 **If** they are in the wrong order, swap them; in this case they are in the right order, so do nothing.

6 **Compare** values in adjacent elements until you reach the end of the array.

7 **Repeat** the above steps until no swaps are needed; look at the array after the fourth pass.

Original order		Order after first pass		Order after second pass		Order after third pass		Order after fourth pass	
67	1	25	1	25	1	25	1	25	1
25	2	67	2	49	2	38	2	38	2
92	3	49	3	38	3	49	3	49	3
49	4	38	4	67	4	67	4	54	4
38	5	72	5	72	5	54	5	67	5
72	6	92	6	54	6	72	6	72	6
99	7	54	7	92	7	92	7	92	7
54	8	99	8	99	8	99	8	99	8

Fig. 3.2.2 *Sorting a set of numbers using the bubble sort method*

Have a look at the values in Fig. 3.2.2. What can you tell about the position of the values after the first pass? Which one is already in its final place?

Questions

3 Sort the following numbers into ascending order using the bubble sort method: 78, 56, 45, 34, 23, 12.

(a) Which value is in its final place after the first pass?

(b) Which value is in its final place after the second pass?

Hint: it is easier if you write each number on a separate piece of paper or card and move them around on the table.

4 Sort the following numbers into ascending order using the bubble sort method: 98, 78, 67, 60, 34, 25.

(a) Which value is in its final place after the first pass?

(b) Which value is in its final place after the second pass?

How many times do we need to repeat the steps of the bubble sort algorithm? Each time we make a pass through the list, we get one further element into the correct place. So for n elements we know that after $n-1$ passes all elements must be in their correct places.

Let's write the steps of the bubble sort algorithm for a list of n elements as a structure table (Table 2). This algorithm goes through the array $n-1$ times when we have n elements in the array.

Table 2 *Structure table for a bubble sort*

---

1 FOR elements 1 to (n–1) in the list
  1.1 FOR elements 1 to (n–1) in the list
     1.1.1 COMPARE the contents of element (value1) with the contents of the
         next element in the list (value2)
     1.1.2 IF value1 is greater than value2
         THEN swap the values

What if we have a set of values that are almost in the correct order already, such as 23, 56, 99, 78, 90? After just one pass, this list is in order. What changes can we make to the structure table in Table 2 to stop comparing the elements for several more passes in this circumstance?

If we have no swaps for a whole pass through the list, we know the list is in order, so we can stop (Table 3).

Table 3 *Structure table for a more efficient bubble sort*

---

1 REPEAT UNTIL no swaps done in a pass
  1.1 FOR elements 1 to (n–1) in the list
     1.1.1 COMPARE the contents of element (value1) with the contents of the
         next element in the list (value2)
     1.1.2 IF value1 is greater than value2
         THEN swap the values

Activity

This algorithm can be improved further. Can you work out how?

We can express the bubble sort algorithm in pseudocode:

```
Repeat
    NoMoreSwaps ← True
    For Element ← 1 To NumberOfItems − 1
      Do
        If List[Element] > List[Element + 1]
          Then
            NoMoreSwaps ← False
            Temp ← List[Element]
            List[Element] ← List[Element + 1]
            List[Element + 1] ← Temp
        EndIf
    EndFor
Until NoMoreSwaps = True
```

🖥 **PC activity**

1 Set up a trace table with the column headings NoMoreSwaps, Element, and seven columns for the array elements. Dry run the bubble sort algorithm pseudocode with the numbers 96, 59, 74, 32, 27, 64, 23.

2 In the programming language of your choice, write a program to perform a bubble sort on a set of numbers read in from the keyboard. Your program should display on the console the contents of the list after every pass.

3 Test your program in Activity 2 with different sets of numbers. Include in your tests sets of numbers that are in reverse order and sets that are already in the correct order.

☑ *In this topic you have covered:*

- how to search the contents of a one-dimensional array using a linear search
- how to sort the contents of a one-dimensional array using a bubble sort.

4 Checking for errors

4.1 Validation and error handling

In this topic you will cover:

■ the importance of validating input data

■ how to program simple validation

■ how to handle exceptions.

Key terms

Compilation error: when a program does not compile because of syntax errors or lexical errors.

Run-time error: when the program crashes or gets stuck in a loop.

Logic error: when the programmer has made a mistake and the program output is incorrect.

During the development and use of software there are many opportunities for different types of error to creep in.

You quickly find out about **compilation errors**. Your program does not compile because you have made a syntax error. Depending on the type of programming environment you are using, you will get a more or less helpful message. It is a skill to be able to interpret compiler error messages and correct faulty syntax. When your program compiles, it may not work properly. We distinguish between two different types of operational error: run-time errors and logic errors.

When a program crashes – ends without completing its execution – or locks – gets into an infinite loop – it is known as a **run-time error** (or execution error). This may happen only under certain conditions. No end user thinks highly of software when run-time errors occur. Thorough testing is important (Topic 4.2).

The most difficult type of error to track down is a **logic error**. The program does not crash. It provides the user with answers and all seems well but the programmer's logic is at fault and the output is wrong. For example, in the calculation of an invoice total, we add the cost of the product and postage and packing then apply the VAT rate. If we write the formula as

```
ProductCost + PandP * VATRate
```

this will give a different result from

```
(ProductCost + PandP) * VATRate
```

Both methods give an answer; neither method causes the program to perform a run-time error, but only one method gives the correct result. Users may find it difficult to question the correctness of beautifully formatted and convincingly presented output. Only careful testing will minimise the risk of wrong answers. Before declaring that a program is fully functional, we need to ensure that it gives the correct output, that it does not crash and that it gives the user helpful hints if they try to use it incorrectly.

Every programmer should remember the famous acronym GIGO – garbage in, garbage out. This means that your program cannot possibly produce the correct results if the input data is invalid. There are several reasons for invalid input data:

■ The user mistypes a value.

■ The user types a value in the wrong format.

■ The user uses a value meant for another input.

■ The user misunderstands what data the program expects.

Careful checks are essential so that the data is as accurate as possible. A variety of checks have been devised to minimise the possibility of invalid data.

💡 Validation checks

Validation checks can never guarantee that the data entered is correct. Validation checks can only ensure that the data is reasonable.

If you are programming an interactive user interface, give your user clear messages about what they are expected to enter and in what format. You may decide to put in a loop that does not allow a user to continue until they have entered valid data.

Give examples or a pattern, such as dd/mm/yyyy, for a date to show that leading zeros for day and month are required and the year should be 2008 rather than just 08.

Range checks

The value entered must be within a certain range. For example, when processing marks gained by students in examination papers, the program should check that the students' marks are within the range 0 to 100. Of course this kind of check cannot guarantee that the marks entered are correct.

Worked example _____

> This Boolean expression tests that the number of marks entered is between 0 and 100 inclusive:
>
> (NumberOfMarks > = 0) AND (NumberOfMarks <= 100)

Format checks

Codes, such as product codes, are often difficult to type correctly. A format check can ensure the code conforms to certain rules. For example, National Insurance numbers have two letters, six digits and one optional letter. You can use string-handling functions (Topic 2.5) to check the characters of a string. If you program a Windows-type application, most visual programming environments provide text boxes where formats can be set without any explicit programming of code from you; they are called input masks.

Length checks

When processing strings you can check whether the string length is as expected.

Type checks

Entering text when a number is expected is a common error. To avoid the program crashing, you should read input as a string then convert it when the type has been checked (p98).

Lookup checks

If a user is expected to input one of a list of values, the program could look up this value in a list or database. This is a popular method for checking the correctness of postcodes. The postcode entered by the user is looked up in a database and the addresses covered by this postcode are displayed. The user will quickly see whether the code was entered correctly. This is especially important if the user is transcribing a handwritten or spoken code. The full address is used to verify the postcode. You can keep acceptable values in an array or file and search it to check that the user has entered valid data.

Check digits

There is the risk of typing errors when entering long numbers or codes. A check digit is calculated from the other digits and appended to the code. An example is the International Standard Book Number (ISBN). The last digit is the result of a calculation that uses all the other digits and their positions. This allows transposition errors to be detected. From 1 January 2007 the old 10-digit ISBNs were replaced by new 13-digit ISBNs, called ISBN-13.

The check digit of ISBN-13 is calculated as follows. Starting from the left, each digit (excluding the check digit) is multiplied alternately by 1 or 3. These products are added together and the modulus of 10 is calculated. This will give a value from 0 to 9. This value is subtracted from 10, which leaves a value between 1 and 10. A 10 is replaced by a 0, so in all cases a single check digit is the result.

Worked example _____

Here is the calculation to check the ISBN 9781904467298, which has check digit 8.

$(1 \times 9) + (3 \times 7) + (1 \times 8) + (3 \times 1) + (1 \times 9) + (3 \times 0) + (1 \times 4) +$
$(3 \times 4) + (1 \times 6) + (3 \times 7) + (1 \times 2) + (3 \times 9)$

$$= 9 + 21 + 8 + 3 + 9 + 0 + 4 + 12 + 6 + 21 + 2 + 27$$

$$= 122$$

$$122 \bmod 10 = 2$$

$$10 - 2 = 8$$

The check digit is correct, so this is a valid ISBN.

> ### Activity
> Find out how the ISBN-10 check digit was calculated. Look up the ISBN-10 from a book you have and calculate its check digit. See if it matches the check digit printed in the book.

Presence checks

Some data values may be optional. Other data values are essential to the correct functioning of the program. The presence check ensures that all required values are entered. You may decide not to allow a user to continue until they have entered a required data value; you can do this by using a loop construct.

> ### Questions
> **1** What validation checks would you use to ensure the date of birth entered for a job application is valid?
>
> **2** What validation checks would you use to ensure the account number for a bank account is valid?

Exception handling

When you write code where you think something might cause a run-time error, such as invalid user input or division by zero, use exception handling to recover from the error without crashing the program. If an error occurs when the program tries to execute the statements in block Try, program execution moves to block Except or block Catch. This gives the programmer a chance to avoid the program crashing by trapping the error and handling it.

Consider this simple example. If the user enters characters other than digits, the input cannot be converted into an integer as intended by the statement in block Try. Calling the string conversion function with incorrect data would normally result in an execution or run-time error and the program would terminate. As this is a situation that can be anticipated, the programmer can write code to handle this error and put it in block Except or Catch. In this case the user is alerted that the input was not a valid data type and the program continues with the statement after the block Except.

Integrated debugging must be turned off for this to work

Pascal

```pascal
Var NumberString: String; n: Integer;
Write('input an integer: ');
Readln(NumberString);
Try
  n := StrToInt(NumberString);
Except
  Writeln('This was not an integer');
End; // of exception
```

VB 2005

```vb
Dim NumberString As String
Dim n As Integer
Console.Write("input an integer: ")
NumberString = Console.ReadLine()
Try
  n = Convert.ToInt32(NumberString)
Catch
  Console.WriteLine("This was not an integer")
End Try
```

C#

```csharp
Console.Write("input an integer: ");
string numberString = Console.ReadLine();
try
{
  int n = Convert.ToInt32(numberString);
}
catch
{
  Console.WriteLine("This was not an integer");
}
```

 PC activity

1   In the language of your choice, write a program that asks the user to enter the measurements of a swimming pool. The program should display the number of litres of water required to fill the pool. It should not crash if a run-time error occurs.

2   Extend your program from Question 1 to allow for a swimming pool with a shallow end and a deep end. Ensure that your program cannot crash. (Extension activity)

In this topic you have covered:

- the importance of validating input data to check that it is reasonable
- range checks, format checks, length checks, type checks, lookup checks, presence checks
- how to calculate check digits
- how to use exception handling to trap run-time errors.

4.2 Testing

Did you know?

Software systems are by far the most complex systems built by humans.

Key terms

Robust system: a system that is unlikely to malfunction.

Did you know?

The further we go in system development, the more costly it becomes to correct any faults.

Study tip

For the AS course you will not be expected to write a large program that is difficult to test thoroughly. But you will be expected to specify how you are going to test a program, select appropriate test data and test a program using selected test data.

```
Count := 0;
Total := 0;
Readln(Number);
While Number >= 0
  Do
    Begin
      Count := Count + 1;
      Total := Total + Number;
      Readln(Number);
    End;
Average := Total / Count;
```

However carefully you design and code your program, it is very unlikely it will work perfectly first time round. The longer the source code of a program, the more errors there are likely to be. Good program layout, a modular approach and good use of routines with interfaces and local variables will improve your chances of debugging your program. When do we know that a program works correctly? We cannot be certain that a large program will never malfunction. No testing devised so far can prove that a program works under all circumstances. The bigger a piece of software, the more likely it is that it may fail sometime. Testing can only reveal the presence of errors. Thorough testing can provide us with some assurance that we have a **robust system**.

Some testing strategies

Dry-run testing

Dry-run testing is used to test an algorithm or program code without the use of a computer. The programmer follows through the code manually using test data to check that the algorithm or program code is correct. This is normally done with a small part of the program, such as one routine. During dry-run testing, a trace table is usually completed to make it easier to check the contents of variables.

Black-box testing

Black-box testing is sometimes known as functional testing. It is carried out without looking at the program code. Carefully selected test data is used and expected results are compared to actual results. This will show whether the program, or program part, functions correctly.

White-box testing

White-box testing is also known as structural testing. Tests are devised to check each possible path through the program code.

Questions

1. You are asked to test some software. You are not given a copy of the program code, only the system objectives that outline the proposed functionality of the software. What type of testing can you perform?

2. You have written a program and used your test plan to check that your program functions correctly. One test does not give the expected result. What should you do to locate the error in your program code?

3. Dry run the program code opposite by completing the trace table. Use the values 5, 7, 23 and –1 as input.

Count	Total	Number	Average

4 Does the dry run in Question 3 show any errors in the program code?

5 Devise test data to do white-box testing for the program code in Question 3. Does your white-box testing find any errors?

💡 Selection of test data

The purpose of testing is to reveal the presence of errors. When designing tests, it is important to use the inputs that users are likely to generate. This includes valid data but also invalid data. Choose test data very carefully. You need to test as thoroughly as possible, but you do not want to type in large amounts of test data. Think about how you are going to test your solution before you start coding. This may make you more aware of any special cases, boundary values and the sorts of values that should not be acceptable as valid data.

Worked example

You are asked to write a program that calculates the current age in years of a person from their date of birth. How will you test whether your solution does this correctly for all possible dates of birth?

One way of testing might be that you type in your own date of birth and check the answer. You know how old you are, so that is the expected result. Does the actual result from your program match this? If it does, does this mean your program works?

You should ask yourself the following questions:

1 Will it give the correct age if the birthday is later in this year? Example: test in May for a birthday in August.

2 Will it give the correct age if the birthday was earlier this year? Example: test in May for a birthday in February.

3 Will it give the correct age if the birthday is tomorrow, today or yesterday?

4 What should the program do if the user types in a date in the future?

5 What should the program do if the user types in a date that is not a valid date, e.g. 31/2/1999?

6 What should happen if the program is asked to calculate the age of a person born on 29 February in a leap year?

■ Activity

1 Check today's date. Now think of some test data and expected results to test Questions 1 and 2 in the worked example.

2 Check today's date. Now think of some test data and expected results to test Questions 3 and 6 in the worked example.

3 Check today's date. Now think of some test data and expected results to test Questions 4 and 5 in the worked example.

Normal data

Probably a large number of values can be classed as normal data. If you choose values that are just inside a boundary, you are also doing part of the boundary testing. This means you will save yourself time and effort. Choose values that are realistic but that do not make it unduly difficult to do calculations by hand. You need to be able to work out the expected result accurately so you can compare it with the actual result.

Boundary data

A boundary value is a value where the processing is different for values below and above this value. It is very common that a programmed solution does not handle boundary values quite as expected. For example, if an online ordering site offers free delivery on orders over £100, do you have to pay the charge if you order goods for exactly £100? Do you have to order goods worth £100.01 or £101.00 for free delivery?

Erroneous data

When you set up validation checks, you will need to test that they work as intended. An erroneous input might be pressing a key at the wrong time. A typical error is to press the Enter key before typing in any data, effectively inputting an empty string.

■ Evidence of testing

Present any test data so it is clear what you are trying to test and what are your expected results. It is a good idea to use a table for your **test plan** with space to fill in the actual results when you do the testing (Table 1). Give a reference to a screenshot that shows the result of the test, your **evidence of testing**. Your screenshot should always show the data entered as well as the result from this data entry. An error message without the accompanying data is unlikely to be sufficient.

Table 1 *Test plan for a program that calculates age from a date*

Test number	Test data	Reason for choice	Expected result	Actual result
1	Today's date: 1/9/2008 Date of birth: 7/8/1978	Normal data Birthday month before current month	30	
2	31/2/1999	Invalid date	Should give error message	See Figure 1
3				

PC activity

Design a test plan for the program to calculate the volume of a swimming pool (Question 1, p98). Choose sufficient test data to fully test your program. Include evidence of testing for each type of test data.

Fig. 4.2.1 *Evidence of testing that shows the data entered and the error message*

Activity

Look at the values you have chosen in the three activities on p100. Do you think you are testing the solution thoroughly enough?

Questions

6 A routine is to calculate weekly gross pay for employees paid by the hour. The input consists of the hourly rate of pay and the number of hours worked in the week. The rules are that the first 35 working hours are paid at the normal rate. Working hours 36 to 48 are paid at 1.5 times the normal rate. No one is allowed to work more than 48 hours. a Give the minimum number of normal and boundary data values to test that the routine works correctly for all valid data input. b Give two types of erroneous data values that the program should reject.

7 Choose the minimum number of normal and boundary data values to test the coins and notes program (Question 5, p36).

✓ *In this topic you have covered:*

- the importance of testing to reveal the presence of errors
- how to select appropriate test data
- boundary data
- how to produce evidence of testing.

5 Data representation

5.1 Binary and hexadecimal numbers

Key terms

Binary: a number system that uses two digits, 0 and 1.

Bit: a binary digit; it can be 0 or 1.

Byte: a group of 8 bits.

Word: a group of bytes.

Denary number system: a number system that uses the digits 0 to 9.

Bits, bytes and words

The storage locations in digital computers are built using electrical circuits that can exist in one of two states – low voltage and high voltage. Therefore we need two symbols to represent these states, 0 (low voltage) and 1 (high voltage). This is known as a **binary** system. The smallest possible storage location contains either a 0 or a 1; it cannot be empty. Digital computers use the binary system for storing program instructions and data of all types – numbers, characters, sound, pictures, and so on. A binary digit, or **bit**, is a 0 or a 1. A group of 8 bits is known as a **byte**. A group of bytes is known as a **word**. How many bytes make up a word depends on the type of computer. For example, a 64-bit machine has a word size of 64 bits = 8 bytes.

💡 Representing numbers: binary and denary

Denary and binary number systems

First, let's remind ourselves how our ordinary decimal or **denary number system** works. It uses the 10 digits 0 to 9.

Worked example

> Consider the number 146. These three digits represent one hundred, four tens and six ones:
>
> | 100 | 10 | 1 |
> |-----|-----|-----|
> | 1 | 4 | 6 |

As we move from right to left each digit is worth ten times as much as the previous one. This is the base 10 number system, or denary number system. The number base specifies how many digits are used and how much each digit is multiplied by as we move from right to left – the place values.

The binary system is a base 2 system, using only the two digits 0 and 1. As we move from right to left, each digit is worth twice as much as the previous one. Note that the place values are powers of 2.

Worked example

> The binary number 10010010 can be set out under place values as follows:
>
> | 128 | 64 | 32 | 16 | 8 | 4 | 2 | 1 |
> |-----|-----|-----|-----|-----|-----|-----|-----|
> | 1 | 0 | 0 | 1 | 0 | 0 | 1 | 0 |

This represents 128 + 16 + 2 = 146. Using only one byte to hold a number would limit the computer to storing only small numbers. Usually four or more consecutive bytes are used to store numbers.

Converting from binary to denary

Put each binary digit under the correct heading in the table.

Worked example

To translate 01001001 into decimal, arrange the digits in the table as follows:

128	64	32	16	8	4	2	1
0	1	0	0	1	0	0	1

This gives 64 + 8 + 1 = 73.

Converting from denary to binary

To convert 21 from denary to binary, write down the place values. Then find the largest place value that is less than or equal to 21; it is 16. Write a 1 in the column headed 16. Subtract 16 from 21 and you get 5. Now find the largest place value that is less than or equal to 5; it is 4. Write a 1 in the column headed 4. Subtract 4 from 5 and you get 1. Write a 1 in the column headed 1. Fill in empty columns with 0. You end up with this:

128	64	32	16	8	4	2	1
0	0	0	1	0	1	0	1

So 21 in binary is 00010101.

Binary addition

Let's first remind ourselves how we add two numbers in denary. When we add two digits which produce a result greater than 9, we use place values and carry a 1 to the next column on the left. Binary addition works in the same way.

Here are the rules of binary addition:

0 + 0 = 0
0 + 1 = 1 + 0 = 1
1 + 1 = 10 (0 and carry 1)
1 + 1 + 1 = 11 (1 and carry 1)

Worked example

```
  00011001      25
+ 00011010    + 26
  00110011      51
```

Binary multiplication

Let's first remind ourselves how we multiply two numbers in denary. If we want to multiply 7 by 4, we could interpret this as adding 7 four times. This is fine for small numbers, but how do we do multiplication with large numbers? We use the place values of digits.

Activity

Convert the following binary numbers to decimal: (a) 0100, (b) 0101, (c) 1010, (d) 01000010, (e) 01011001.

Key point

Denary and decimal refer to the same thing, i.e. a number based on the digits 0–9.

Activity

 Convert the number 227 to binary.

2 Convert the following numbers to binary: (a) 3, (b) 9, (c) 19, (d) 28, (e) 76, (f) 129.

Activity

 (a) Add 0101 and 0010, (b) add 01101010 and 01000011, (c) add 01010101 and 01111110. Check your results by converting to denary.

2 Add 01010111 and 10101001 and comment on your result.

Multiplying 7 by 10 gives 70; we have just moved the 7 into the next column to the left. Multiplying 7 by 100 gives 700; we move the 7 two columns to the left. Binary multiplication works in the same way.

Here are the rules of binary multiplication:

$0 \times 0 = 0$
$0 \times 1 = 1 \times 0 = 0$
$1 \times 1 = 1$
$1 \times 10 = 10$

If we want to multiply a binary number by 2 (10_2), we move the binary pattern one place to the left and put a zero in the vacated binary place.

If we want to multiply a binary number by 4 (100_2), we move the binary pattern two places to the left and put a zero in each of the vacated binary places.

Remind yourself how to do long multiplication in denary by looking at the next worked example. Binary long multiplication works in the same way, but is much easier as we only need to multiply by 1 and shift the binary pattern to the left by the number of 0s of the binary value we want to multiply by.

Worked example

```
        11000          24
   ×    10001      ×   17
   110000000          168
       11000          240
   110011000          408
```

Activity

Check that this rule is true by multiplying the following bit patterns by 2 and converting the numbers before and after multiplication to denary: 101, 110, 1001, 10101, 1100, 1000.

Activity

a Multiply 0101 and 0010,

b multiply 01001010 and 00000011,

c multiply 01000001 and 00000110.

Check your results by converting into denary.

Questions

1 What is the largest binary number that can be held in (a) 8 bits, (b) 16 bits, (c) 32 bits and (d) 64 bits?

2 How many bits make one byte?

3 What are the possible values that one bit can take?

4 Convert the decimal numbers 20 and 10 into binary. Add the binary numbers for 20 and 10; show your working. Then convert the result back to denary to check your answer.

5 Convert the decimal numbers 5 and 6 into binary. Multiply the binary numbers for 5 and 6; show your working. Then convert the result back to denary to check your answer.

Representing numbers: negative numbers

Two's complement

Negative numbers can be represented using a system called **two's complement**. To understand how this works, imagine the milometer of a car set at 00000 miles. If the car goes forward one mile, the reading becomes 00001. If the milometer is turned back one mile, the reading becomes 99999 miles. This can be interpreted as –1 mile.

Figure 1 shows how two's complement works in the same way.

Key terms

Two's complement: a system for representing negative numbers.

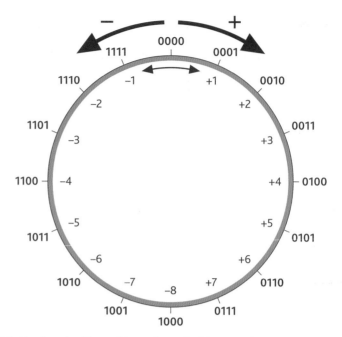

Fig. 5.1.1 *Number wheel for positive and negative binary numbers*

Worked example

When we add the binary equivalents of 5 and –5, we obtain

```
    1011
+   0101
(1) 0000
```

We ignore the carry of 1.

Here is the procedure for converting a negative denary number to two's complement binary:

1 **Find** the binary value of the equivalent positive denary number.
2 **Change** all the 0s to 1s and all the 1s to 0s.
3 **Add** 1 to the result.

And here is a method for changing the sign of a binary number:

1 **Starting** from the right, leave all the digits alone up to and including the first 1.
2 **Change** all the other digits from 0 to 1 or from 1 to 0; for example –00101100 becomes 11010100.

Converting a negative two's complement number to denary

- **Method 1**: flip the bits, add 1 then work out the denary equivalent.
- **Method 2**: use the place values. Write the binary digits down under the place values 1, 2, 4, 8, etc. Note that the leftmost bit has a negative place value. Add up all the place values which have a 1 under them.

Worked example

Convert the two's complement number 10011010 to denary.

-128	64	32	16	8	4	2	1
1	0	0	1	1	0	1	0

This gives -128 + 16 + 8 + 2 = -102.

> ### Activity
> Convert the following two's complement numbers to denary:
> (a) 10101010, (b) 10000001,
> (c) 11111111, (d) 00010111.

Binary subtraction

The easiest way of performing binary subtraction is to convert the number to be subtracted to a negative number and then add it.

Worked example

Subtract 13 from 17 using 1 byte for each number.

00001101	13

11110011	-13
+ 00010001	+ 17
00000100	4

> ### Activity
> **1** Subtract 25 from 28 in binary and show your working.
>
> **2** Subtract 23 from 123 in binary and show your working.

The most or least significant bit

A positive number always has 0 as the most significant bit (MSB). A negative number always has 1 as the MSB. An even number always has 0 as the least significant bit (LSB). An odd number always has 1 as the LSB. -1 is represented by a 1 in every bit, whatever the word size.

> ### Questions
> **6** What is the largest negative number that can be held in 8 bits using two's complement?
>
> **7** Convert the decimal numbers 11 and 9 to binary. Using 8 bits for each number, show your working in binary of subtracting 9 from 11.
>
> **8** Convert the decimal numbers 17 and 15 to binary. Using 8 bits for each number, show your working in binary of subtracting 17 from 15.
>
> **9** Convert the decimal numbers 96 and 40 to binary. Using 8 bits for each number, show the binary pattern for -96 and -40. Comment on your result of adding these two patterns together. (Extension question)

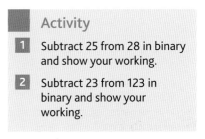 Representing numbers: hexadecimal

Digital computers represent everything using the binary system, but binary patterns are very inconvenient for humans to read, as even a relatively small number such as 254 requires eight digits to represent it in pure binary.

To make it easier for a human to read the contents of main memory or a computer file, binary numbers are commonly put into groups of four bits and displayed using the **hexadecimal number system**.

> ### Key terms
> **Hexadecimal number system:** a number system that uses the digits 0 to 9 and the letters A to F.

> ### Key point
> Hexadecimal is used as a shorthand notation for binary number patterns.

Table 1 *Numbers 1 to 16 in denary, binary and hexadecimal*

Denary	Binary	Hexadecimal
1	1	1
2	10	2
3	11	3
4	100	4
5	101	5
6	110	6
7	111	7
8	1000	8
9	1001	9
10	1010	A
11	1011	B
12	1100	C
13	1101	D
14	1110	E
15	1111	F
16	10000	10

Key point

It is useful to remember that 1010 in binary is 10 in denary and A in hexadecimal. Also remember that 1111 is 15 in binary and F in hexadecimal. You can work out the other numbers as required.

Activity

Convert the denary number 126 into (a) binary and (b) hexadecimal.

Activity

1 Convert the binary number 0110 1101 into (a) denary and (b) hexadecimal.

2 Convert the following binary patterns into hexadecimal numbers: 1111 1110 1110 1101 1101 1010 1101. What is the message?

Hexadecimal numbers are numbers to base 16, and use the digits 0 to 9 and the letters A to F. Table 1 shows the numbers 1 to 16 in denary, binary and hexadecimal.

Converting from denary to hexadecimal

Worked example

Convert the denary number 213 to hexadecimal. First convert the denary number to binary. Divide the bits into groups of four, starting from the right. Then convert each group of four digits into hexadecimal.

128	64	32	16	8	4	2	1
1	1	0	1	0	1	0	1

Thus, denary 213 = D5 in hexadecimal. Notice that this is the same as $13 \times 16 + 5$. Each digit in a hexadecimal number is worth 16 times as much as the one on its right.

Converting a hexadecimal number to denary

Method 1

Convert each hexadecimal digit into its binary equivalent:

	A				3		
8	4	2	1	8	4	2	1
1	0	1	0	0	0	1	1
128	64	32	16	8	4	2	1
1	0	1	0	0	0	1	1

So the hexadecimal number A3 equals $128 + 32 + 2 + 1 = 163$ in denary.

Method 2

Use the hexadecimal place values. To translate the hexadecimal number A3 to denary, do $10 \times 16 + 3 = 160 + 3 = 163$ in denary.

Questions

10 The following hexadecimal numbers represent 16-bit two's complement numbers: B13C, 7010, 1FFF, 8A1E, 9000, F73F. Can you tell which ones represent negative numbers? Convert the hexadecimal numbers into binary and check your answers.

11 Where have you seen hexadecimal numbers used? What were they used for?

Representing numbers: real numbers

Fixed-point binary numbers

So far we have only been able to represent whole numbers. Calculations often have fractional results, so we need to be able to store real numbers. There are an infinite number of fractions, but only a limited number of bits available to represent them. Trying to map an infinite number of values onto a limited number of bit patterns results in loss of precision.

We can easily extend the system we used for integers to include fractions. Look at the place values of denary numbers:

100	10	1	.	1/10	1/100
0	6	8	.	2	5

The number 68.25 represents 6 tens, 8 units, 2 tenths and 5 hundredths. In binary, the equivalent place values are

128 64 32 16 8 4 2 1 . 1/2 1/4 1/8 1/16

Worked example _____

The number 68.25 can be expressed as 68 + 1/4, and using the place values above converts to

128	64	32	16	8	4	2	1	.	1/2	1/4	1/8	1/16
0	1	0	0	0	1	0	0	.	0	1	0	0

Notice that the first digit after the point, called the binary point, is worth one-half, whereas in the decimal system the equivalent digit is only worth one-tenth. This means that with the same number of digits after the point, the binary system is less precise. For example, if we write down an amount in pounds sterling to 2 decimal places, the amount is accurate to the nearest penny. If we convert the amount to binary and allow only two digits after the binary point, we can only hold .00 (0 pence), .01 (25 pence), .10 (50 pence) or .11 (75 pence) as the fractional part, so the amount is only accurate to the nearest 25 pence.

Fixed-point notation assumes a binary point in a set position as there is no third symbol available to store it explicitly. Here are some decimal fractions and their binary equivalents.

Binary fraction	Fraction	Decimal fraction
0.1	1/2	0.5
0.01	1/4	0.25
0.001	1/8	0.125
0.0001	1/16	0.0625
0.0000 1	1/32	0.031 25
0.0000 01	1/64	0.015 625
0.0000 001	1/128	0.007 8125
0.0000 0001	1/256	0.003 906 25
0.0000 0000 1	1/512	0.001 953 125
0.0000 0000 01	1/1024	0.000 976 5625

An advantage of fixed-point notation is that it makes the arithmetic simple – the same as integer arithmetic – so processing is faster. A disadvantage of fixed-point notation is that it is of limited range:

increasing the number of bits after the binary point for precision decreases the range, and vice versa, in a fixed number of bits.

Another method of representing real numbers is as floating-point numbers; this is covered in the A2 part of the course.

Questions

12 Using one byte to hold each number, with an imaginary binary point fixed after the fourth digit, convert the following decimal numbers to binary: (a) 3.75, (b) 5.1875, (c) 7.562, (d) 7.5627.

13 Convert the following numbers to decimal, assuming 4 bits after the point: (i) 0000000001011000 and (ii) 0000000000110010.

14 What is (i) the largest positive number and (ii) the smallest positive number that can be held in two bytes, assuming four bits after the point?

15 Using one byte to hold each number, with an imaginary binary point fixed after the fourth digit, what is the largest number that can be stored? What is the difference between two consecutive values? How could the precision of storing a fractional number be improved? What effect would this have on the range of numbers that could be stored? (Extension question)

In this topic you have covered:

- a bit can take the values 0 or 1
- a byte is a group of 8 bits
- a word is a group of bytes
- place values of binary integers double moving to the left
- place values halve moving to the right
- two's complement has the same place values as unsigned numbers except the leftmost bit, which has a negative place value
- negative binary numbers have a 1 as the most significant bit; positive binary numbers have a 0 as the most significant bit
- binary subtraction works by adding the two's complement of the number to be subtracted
- hexadecimal digits are used to represent a group of 4 bits.

5.2 Character coding schemes

In this topic you will cover:

■ ASCII and Unicode, which are the standard coding systems for coding character data

■ the difference between the character code representation of a denary digit and its pure binary representation

■ error detection and correction using parity bits and Hamming code

■ why and where Gray code is used.

In Topic 5.1 we learned how numbers are represented inside the computer. When we want to store text in computer memory, we need to represent each character with a different binary pattern.

There are various coding schemes in use. The most important ones are American Standard Code for Information Interchange (ASCII) and Unicode.

Activity

1 How many different patterns do we need to represent all the characters on a computer keyboard? Hint: upper-case and lower-case letters, 10 digits and other symbols.

2 How many bits do we need to give us that number of patterns?

ASCII

ASCII uses 7 bits and can therefore represent 128 different characters. A different binary number is assigned to each character. Here are some examples:

> Character A is coded as 65: 1000001
> Character B is coded as 66: 1000010
> ⋮
> Character a is coded as 97: 1100001
> Character b is coded as 98: 1100010
> ⋮
> Character 0 is coded as 48: 0110000
> Character 1 is coded as 49: 0110001
> Character 2 is coded as 50: 0110010

Some of the characters are control codes, such as Line Feed and Tab. The eighth bit in a byte of this coding scheme is used for error checking (p112). Extended ASCII uses the eighth bit in a byte to code more characters, such as © Œ ® è Ç.

Digits have different binary representations when they are stored as text than when they are stored as numbers. For example, the characters '48' are represented by 00110100 00111000 whereas the number 48, if stored in a 16-bit word, is represented by 00000000 00110000.

Questions

1 The ASCII code for the character '2' is 50. What is the ASCII code for the character '5'?

2 If 8 bits are used to store one character, what is the bit pattern when the string '35' is stored in a 16-bit word?

3 If binary integers are to be stored using 16 bits, what would be the bit pattern to represent the number 35?

4 What is the numeric difference between the bit pattern of the digits '0' to '9' and their pure binary equivalents? (Extension question)

Unicode

Unicode uses 16 bits to represent characters. Unicode provides a unique number for every character, whatever the platform, whatever the program, whatever the language.

The character A is coded as 0000000001000001_2 (0041_{16}); it is 65_{10}. In fact, the extended ASCII codes are incorporated into Unicode representations. Go to **www.unicode.org/charts** for a complete list of Unicode character codes.

Questions

5 How many different characters can be coded with 16 bits?

6 Find out what the Unicode is for the characters ® ∞ €.

7 Can you find a similarity between the ASCII codes and the Unicode codes for our alphabet? (Extension question)

Error checking and correction

Single parity bit

An extra bit, or parity bit, is added to the bit pattern for error checking. A computer system uses either odd parity or even parity. In an odd-parity system the extra bit (parity bit) is set so that the total number of 1 bits in a bit pattern is an odd number.

Worked example

> The ASCII code for the character f is 1100110. Adding a parity bit would make the pattern 11100110 (odd parity).

In an even-parity system the parity bit is set so that the total number of 1 bits in a bit pattern is an even number.

Worked example

> The ASCII code for the character f is 1100110. Adding a parity bit would make the pattern 01100110 (even parity).

If an ASCII character is transmitted using even parity, the receiver will check the parity after transmission and if the parity is now odd there was an error in transmission.

Key point

If the parity bit is correct, we cannot guarantee that there are no errors. If two bits are transposed, i.e. swapped, the parity bit will remain the same, so a transposition error is not noticed. Similarly, if there is an even number of errors in a bit pattern, this parity check will not flag an error.

Activity

1 A computer system uses even parity. Complete the following bit patterns: (a) _0100001, (b) _1010011, (c) _1000011, (d) _1001001.

2 A computer system uses odd parity. Which of the following bit patterns contain an error? (a) 11010011, (b) 11100011, (c) 01101001, (d) 11100101, (e) 11101110, (f) 11100011, (g) 01100101.

Majority vote

Error detection is good, error correction is better. How can we increase the chances that the data reaches its destination correctly? One method is to send each bit three times and use the idea of a majority vote to determine the correct bit. This is a very expensive method as three times the volume of data is transmitted.

Worked example

To send the bit pattern 010 111 01 the following would be transmitted: 000 111 000 111 111 111 000 111. If there is a lot of interference, the pattern might be received as 010 110 100 110 011 101 000 011. If every triplet is now checked and if the majority of the bits are 1, the bit is taken to be a 1; if the majority of the bits are 0, the bit is taken to be a 0.

💡 Hamming code

Richard Hamming invented a system which can self-correct single errors using a few parity bits in a bit pattern.
All bit positions that are powers of 2 are used as parity bits: positions 1, 2, 4, 8, 16, ….
All other bit positions are for the data to be encoded: positions 3, 5, 6, 7, 9, 10, 11, 12, 13, 14, 15, ….

Each parity bit calculates the parity for some of the bits in the code word. The position of the parity bit determines the sequence of bits that it alternately checks and skips. Even parity is used.

- Position 1 ($n = 1$): skip 0 bits ($0 = n - 1$), check 1 bit (n), skip 1 bit (n), check 1 bit (n), skip 1 bit (n), …
- Position 2 ($n = 2$): skip 1 bit ($1 = n - 1$), check 2 bits (n), skip 2 bits (n), check 2 bits (n), skip 2 bits (n), …
- Position 4 ($n = 4$): skip 3 bits ($3 = n - 1$), check 4 bits (n), skip 4 bits (n), check 4 bits (n), skip 4 bits (n), …
- Position 8 ($n = 8$): skip 7 bits ($7 = n - 1$), check 8 bits (n), skip 8 bits (n), check 8 bits (n), skip 8 bits (n), …

General rule for position n: skip $n - 1$ bits, check n bits, skip n bits, check n bits, ….

Table 1 *Transmitting ASCII character M with Hamming code parity bits*

Bit position	11	10	9	8	7	6	5	4	3	2	1
Data bit or parity bit	D	D	D	P4	D	D	D	P3	D	P2	P1
Data	1	0	0		1	1	0		1		
P1	1		0		1		0		1		?
P2	1	0			1	1			1	?	
P3					1	1	0	?			
P4	1	0	0	?							
Code with parity bits	1	0	0	1	1	1	0	0	1	0	1

Worked example

The ASCII code to transmit 'M' is 1001101. Note that each data bit in Table 1 is checked by at least two parity bits. The parity bits are not checked. If a single error has occurred with one of the data bits, at least two parity bits will flag an error.

In Table 2, P2 and P3 are flagging an error. Adding the position numbers of these failing parity bits (P2 is in bit position 2 and P3 is in bit position 4) gives a bit position of 6. This is where the error occurred. Flipping the bit in position 6 will correct the error. Stripping the parity bits out reveals the original data: 1001101.

Table 2 *Transmitting ASCII character M with an error*

Bit position	11	10	9	8	7	6	5	4	3	2	1
Data bit or parity bit	D	D	D	P4	D	D	D	P3	D	P2	P1
Code received	1	0	0	1	1	0	0	0	1	0	1
P1	1		0		1		0		1		1✓
P2 (recalculated)	1	0			1	0			1	1	
P3 (recalculated)					1	0	0	1			
P4 (recalculated)	1	0	0	1✓							
Code received	1	0	0	1	1	0	0	0	1	0	1
Flip bit 6 as 2 + 4 = 6						1					
Code with parity bits	1	0	0	1	1	1	0	1	1	1	1
Recover correct data	1	0	0		1	1	0		1		

P1, P2, P3, P4 are grouped as "recalculated".

Activity

What happens if the single error occurred in a parity bit?

Hamming code is still used today because it provides a good balance between error correction and error detection. Wireless communication is one application that uses Hamming code.

💡 Gray code

There are some applications where it is advantageous to use a binary representation in which two consecutive values differ in only one bit. Frank Gray invented a binary code where this is true even when the maximum value resets to zero. The full name of this code is binary reflected Gray code (BRGC).

If you compare the Gray codes for 0 to 7 and 8 to 15, you will see that they are symmetrical apart from the most significant bit (MSB), hence the name binary reflected Gray code. Notice too that bit 0 follows a repetitive pattern of two (11, 00, 11 etc.) and bit 1 follows a pattern of four, bit 2 follows a pattern of eight. Gray codes can be generated for any number of bits.

The Gray code is popular because it prevents some data errors that can occur with pure binary during state changes. For example, in a circuit with sluggish system response, a pure binary state change from 0011 to 0100 could cause the counter to see 0111 or 0110 or 0101. This sort of error is not possible with Gray code, so the data is more reliable.

The Gray code is used in angular movement systems where angular positions have to be known. A radial line of sensors reads the code off the surface of the disc and if the disc is halfway between two positions, each sensor might read its bit from both positions at once but since only one bit differs between the two, the value read is guaranteed to be one of the two valid values.

A Gray code counter toggles only one output bit at a time, whereas a pure binary counter may toggle multiple bits. Gray code counters consume only half the electrical power of an equivalent binary counter. Digital logic designers use Gray codes extensively for passing multibit count information between synchronous logic that operates at different clock frequencies. It is fundamental to the design of large chips that operate with many different clocking frequencies.

Questions

8 What type of error could be detected with a single parity bit in a computer word?

9 Explain how a single parity bit is used to detect whether an error has occurred during transmission.

10 What type of error could be detected using Hamming code?

11 Why is Hamming code still used today?

12 What is the difference between pure binary representation and Gray code?

13 Why is Gray code used?

In this topic you have covered:

- ASCII uses 8 bits (1 byte) and Unicode uses 16 bits (2 bytes)
- parity bits are extra bits added to a bit pattern for error checking
- odd parity: the number of 1s in the bit pattern is odd
- even parity: the number of 1s in the bit pattern is even
- if the parity of the bit pattern has changed after transmission, there was an error in transmission
- Hamming code uses several parity bits in a bit pattern and can correct single bit errors
- BRGC is designed so that only one output bit changes when a counter is built
- BRGC is fundamental to the design of large chips that operate with different clocking frequencies.

Table 3 *Four-bit Gray codes*

Decimal	Pure binary	(BRGC)
0	0000	0000
1	0001	0001
2	0010	0011
3	0011	0010
4	0100	0110
5	0101	0111
6	0110	0101
7	0111	0100
8	1000	1100
9	1001	1101
10	1010	1111
11	1011	1110
12	1100	1010
13	1101	1011
14	1110	1001
15	1111	1000

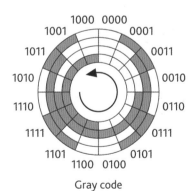

Gray code

Fig. 5.2.1 *Four-bit Gray code encoder*

5.3 Bitmapped and vector graphics

Key terms

Pixel: the smallest addressable area or smallest solid block of colour in an image.

Bitmap: created when the pixels of an image are mapped to positions in memory that store binary codes representing the colour of each pixel.

■ Bitmapped graphics

In bitmapped graphics, an image is divided into a grid of picture elements called **pixels**. Fig. 5.3.1(a) shows an image with an 7 × 7 grid superimposed on it. The process that produces Fig. 5.3.1(b) samples the colour in each grid cell of Fig. 5.3.1(a) then assigns and stores a binary code to represent the average colour in each grid cell. The stored binary codes are used to reproduce a copy of the scanned original. The size of each grid cell in Fig. 5.3.1 is too big to allow an accurate copy of the original to be reproduced. Reducing the size of each cell improves the resulting image (Fig. 5.3.2) but the cell size is still too large to produce an accurate copy.

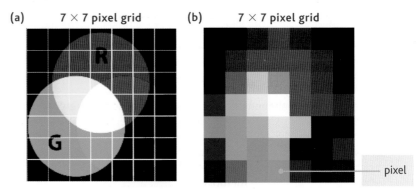

(a) 7 × 7 pixel grid   **(b)** 7 × 7 pixel grid

pixel

Fig. 5.3.1 *An image (a) before scanning and (b) after scanning*

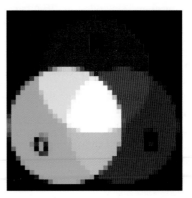

Fig. 5.3.2 *Effect of using a smaller grid cell when the image is scanned*

Memory bitmaps

The binary codes for each pixel are stored in memory (before being written to a file) when an image is scanned. The file contains the bitmapped representation of the image. An image is displayed on a visual display unit by first transferring the binary codes from a file back into memory. Fig. 5.3.3 shows a fragment of memory that holds the binary codes for the image in Fig. 5.3.1(b). The term **bitmap** arises because the pixels of the image are mapped to specific positions in memory where binary codes – one per pixel – are stored. These codes represent the colour or greyscale value of each pixel for images made up of black, white and shades of grey.

These binary codes set
the colour of the pixels

7 x 7 pixel screen

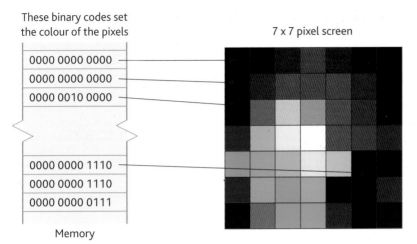

Memory
0000 0000 0000
0000 0000 0000
0000 0010 0000
0000 0000 1110
0000 0000 1110
0000 0000 0111

Memory

Fig. 5.3.3 *Binary codes mapped to a bitmapped image*

The screen of a visual display unit (VDU) is divided into pixels. The higher the resolution, the greater the number of pixels for a given size of screen. An image is created on the screen by selectively lighting the pixels in the required colours. The colour selected for each pixel is coded in a fixed number of bits. For example, 8 bits per pixel gives 256 possible colours. The bits controlling a particular pixel are stored in a specific memory cell in the main memory or screen (video) memory of the computer connected to the VDU. Consecutive memory cells are used to store all the binary codes that control the display on the screen. The computer scans this block of memory and generates the required picture from the stored codes. To change part of a displayed picture, the computer must locate the corresponding memory cells and alter the codes.

Resolution

The **resolution of a VDU screen** is expressed as the number of pixels per row by the number of pixels per column. Some typical resolutions are 1024 × 798, 800 × 600, 640 × 480. A VDU screen resolution setting of 1024 pixels × 798 pixels (817,152 pixels) contains more pixels than a screen resolution of 640 pixels × 480 pixels (371,200 pixels). It is not the number of pixels that determines the sharpness of an image but the size of each pixel. The smaller the better. So we must take into account the number of pixels and the physical size of the image. A small image size containing a large number of pixels should produce the sharpest image. Therefore, a better definition of resolution is the number of dots/pixels per inch or centimetre. Fig. 5.3.4 shows the effect on an image with a fixed number of pixels of reducing the display's resolution.

Fig. 5.3.4 *Effect on an image with a fixed number of pixels of reducing the display's resolution*

Colour depth

The number of bits used to represent the colour or greyscale value of a single pixel in a bitmapped image is called the **colour depth**. The colour of a single pixel can be coded using the RGB colour model, which mixes red, green and blue additively to produce a specific colour. In this model, the relative brightnesses of red (R), blue (B) and green (G) are encoded separately. To produce white, the values for R, G and B are all set to 100%; black is produced when the values are all set to 0%; red when the R value is 100% and the G and B values are set to 0%.

1-bit colour

A black and white image is known as a monochrome image. One bit is allocated to each pixel, restricting the colour of each pixel to black or white. A bit value of 0 sets a pixel to black; a bit value of 1 sets a pixel to white.

12-bit direct colour

In 12-bit direct colour, 4 bits (2^4 or 16 possible levels) are allocated for each of the R, G, and B components, enabling 4,096 ($16 \times 16 \times 16$) different colours. This colour depth is sometimes used in devices with a limited colour display, such as mobile telephones.

True colour

True colour can mimic many colours found in the real world, producing 16.7 million distinct colours. This approaches the level at which the human eye can distinguish colours for most photographic images. 24-bit true colour uses 8 bits to represent red, 8 bits to represent blue and 8 bits to represent green, giving 2^8 (256) levels of each of the three colour components. They can therefore be combined to give a total of 16,777,216 ($256 \times 256 \times 256$) colours.

32-bit colour

32-bit colour is really true colour with an extra 8 bits chosen because the word size of modern PCs is 32 bits or 64 bits. The extra 8 bits are either ignored or used to represent an alpha channel, which is a way of providing partial transparency.

Memory requirements

Suppose a bitmapped image, size 8 pixels $\times$ 8 pixels, uses 8 bits to encode the colour of each pixel – 3 bits for red, 3 bits for green and 2 bits for blue because the eye is less sensitive to blue.

If the image has a size of 8×8 pixels (64 pixels in total), a minimum of 64 bytes is required to store the image's bitmap. If 16 bits are used per pixel – 4 bits for red, 4 bits for green, 4 bits for blue and 4 bits unused – then a minimum of 128 bytes are needed for the bitmap. Using 32 bits per pixel requires 256 bytes.

If we use a higher resolution for the image, keeping its dimensions the same, we need to create a bitmap of more pixels. For example, if we double the size in pixels in each dimension from 8×8 to 16×16, we increase the number of pixels by a factor of 4, so our minimum memory requirement must also increase by a factor of 4. Using 32 bits per pixel will require a minimum of 1,024 bytes.

Bitmap file calculations

Increasing the resolution of a bitmapped VDU screen increases the amount of memory required to display graphics, as does increasing the colour depth. For example, a screen set to a resolution of 1024 × 768 and a colour depth of 32 bits needs a memory of 1024 × 768 × 4 bytes = 3,145,728 bytes = 3 MB. Therefore, at least 3 MB of file space is required to save the displayed graphic in a file. Actually, the file space requirement will be slightly greater because the resolution and the colour depth information must be saved at the beginning of the file in an area called the header.

Activity

Face pasting

Create an image against a uniformly coloured background, e.g. use a digital camera to capture an image of a person's face against a blue background. Find a suitable royalty-free image on the Internet to use as the new background. Now, using a simple program written for the task or some image manipulation software, merge the two images so that the face is imposed onto the second image. The pixels of the blue background surrounding the face should not be copied onto the second image. In image manipulation software these would be set to transparent. If you write your own program, you need to check for blue pixels and intentionally not copy them across to the new image.

Questions

1. What is a pixel?
2. What is a bitmap?
3. What is meant by the resolution of an image?
4. What is meant by colour depth?
5. Calculate the minimum file size of a 1024 × 768 pixels bitmapped image that uses a colour depth of 24 bits.

Vector graphics

Instead of dividing a graphic image into pixels, a **vector graphic** identifies the objects that make up the image – the lines, arcs, curves, circles, ellipses, rectangles, polygons, etc. Even text is broken down into straight lines and curves. Vector graphics record information about these objects to define the image. Pixels do not enter into this process. For example, a line 100 pixels long needs just a few bytes to describe it in vector graphics whereas 100 × 3 bytes are required in a bitmap using 24-bit colour. Vector drawing software uses the commands that create **objects** as the source of information needed to describe the graphic. If you are converting a bitmapped graphic to a vector graphic, the software uses techniques that identify the graphic components of the bitmap.

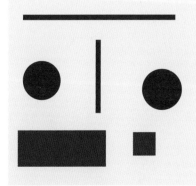

Fig. 5.3.5 *Vector graphic*

Drawing list

Object information (in vector graphic format) is recorded in a file. This format lists all the objects making up the graphic with necessary information about each object as a list of drawing commands – the **drawing list**. These drawing commands can be used to recreate the graphic. For example, the graphic in Fig. 5.3.5 corresponds to the drawing list in Table 1.

Table 1 *Drawing list for a vector graphic*

Drawing list	Explanation
line (20,10,180,20, red, 4)	Draw line from 20,10 to 180,20 in red, 4 pixels wide
line (90,50,90,140, red, 4)	Draw line from 90,50 to 90,140 in red, 4 pixels wide
circle (30,80,10, red, filled, white)	Draw circle centre 30,80 radius 10 filled in red, white border
circle (170,90,10, red, filled, white)	Draw circle centre 170,90 radius 10 filled in red, white border
rect (10,110,100,180, blue, filled, none)	Draw rectangle top left 10,110 bottom right 100,180 filled in blue, no border
rect (130,112,140,122, blue, filled, none)	Draw rectangle top left 130,112 bottom right 140,122 filled in blue, no border

■ **Key terms**

Vector graphic: records geometric and other information about the objects that make up an image.

Object: a component of a vector graphic, such as a line, a rectangle or a circle.

Drawing list: the list of drawing commands that recreate a vector graphic.

Property: of a vector graphic object, describes things such as the size, direction, thickness, shading, font size or typeface.

🖥 PC activity

Investigate the effect of magnification on bitmap and vector graphics.

Properties of objects

To recreate a vector graphic, the **properties** of every object in the drawing list must be specified. Properties or attributes are position, size, direction (possibly using endpoint coordinates), line thickness, font size and typeface, shading, the mathematical description of the curves, whether a closed shape is filled or not, the fill colour, whether the closed shape has a border, the colour and thickness of any border.

💡 Comparing bitmapped and vector graphics

When a bitmap is scaled, the pixels enlarge. As the magnification increases, the pixels can become visible, leading to a staircase effect (Figure 6). Vector graphics avoid such distortion when magnified because scaling is applied to a line's endpoints, taking into account the change in line thickness in a way that avoids creating a staircase effect. The scaling is geometric because vector graphics deal with objects not pixels. Vector graphics are defined by the relative positions of objects in a three-dimensional or two-dimensional coordinate system. If you increase the

Scaled bitmapped graphic

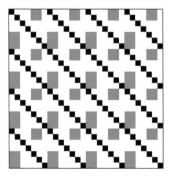

Scaled vector graphic

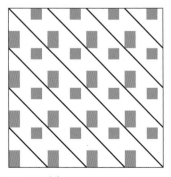

Fig. 5.3.6 *Scaling images: (a) a distorted bitmap graphic and (b) a vector graphic*

size of the coordinate system, the drawing increases in size. You do not lose resolution when you enlarge a true vector drawing, because it has no intrinsic resolution.

Here are the advantages and disadvantages of bitmapped and vector graphic images:

- Geometric images require fewer bytes in vector graphic format than in bitmapped format.
- Images that have continuous areas of colour, such as photographic images, take up fewer bytes in bitmapped format than in vector format.
- Geometric images load faster from secondary storage (magnetic disk) and download faster over the Internet in vector graphic format.
- Vector graphic images scale without distortion whereas bitmapped images do not.
- Some vector graphic formats can be searched for particular graphic objects which may then be manipulated; it is much harder to do this in bitmapped graphics.

Basic compression techniques

The purpose of **data compression** is to squeeze data into a smaller number of bytes than the data would occupy if uncompressed. Bitmapped graphic files can be very large, e.g. 3 MB for a resolution of 1024×768 and a colour depth of 32 bits, but it is possible to reduce the size of bitmapped files by various compression techniques.

Run-length encoding

Run-length encoding (RLE) is a simple compression technique that takes account of the fact that some images have long runs of pixels of the same colour. Consecutive memory cells of the bitmap are compared. If three or more consecutive cells contain the same bit pattern, then a run of cells has been found that can be encoded in two bytes. The first byte stores the number of identical consecutive (contiguous) memory cell bytes and the second byte stores the colour code. For example, Fig. 5.3.7 encodes a block of six memory cells with the colour 1000 0000.

Run-length encoding is a lossless compression technique. Decompressing an RLE-compressed image produces the original uncompressed image exactly, i.e. without loss. RLE is used in the PCX image file format developed for PC Paintbrush, one of the first widely accepted imaging standards. PCX has since been succeeded by more sophisticated image formats such as GIF, JPEG, and PNG. GIF and JPEG use RLE compression stages.

Lossy compression

Lossy compression methods discard information which is not considered important, e.g. background scenery is saved with reduced resolution. Decompressing an image compressed with a lossy compression method results in an uncompressed image that is different from the original but is close enough to be useful. The human eye is good at seeing small differences in brightness over a relatively large area – gradual changes in pixel brightness values that occur over many pixels – but not so good at distinguishing the exact strength of a high-frequency brightness variation – drastic changes in pixel brightness values that occur over a narrow range of pixels. This makes it possible to get away with greatly reducing

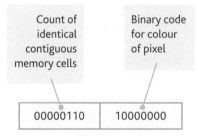

Fig. 5.3.7 *Run-length encoding*

the amount of information in the high-frequency components. It is also possible to exploit the sensitivity of the eye by reducing the number of bits per pixel for colours that the eye is least sensitive to, such as blue.

Case study

Image formats and compression

JPEG, pronounced jay-peg, is a commonly used method of compression for photographic images. The name JPEG stands for Joint Photographic Experts Group, which is the committee that created the standard. The JPEG standard specifies the compression-decompression algorithm, or codec, and the format of the file used to store the image. The codec defines how an image is compressed into a stream of bytes and decompressed back into an image. The compression method is usually lossy compression, meaning that some visual quality is lost in the process.

Graphics Interchange Format (GIF) is an 8 bit per pixel bitmap image format used widely on the web. The format uses a palette of up to 256 distinct colours from the 24-bit RGB colour space. The bitmap uses one byte per pixel but the value of each byte is used as the address of an entry in a 256-cell table. Each cell contains a 24-bit value coding the red, green and blue components of a pixel in true colour. The limitation of only 256 different colours, albeit 24-bit colours, makes the GIF format unsuitable for reproducing colour photographs and other images with continuous colour, but it is well-suited for simpler images such as graphics or logos with solid areas of colour. It also supports animations and allows a separate palette of 256 colours for each frame. GIF images are compressed using the Lempel–Ziv–Welch (LZW) lossless data compression technique to reduce the file size without degrading the visual quality.

Portable Network Graphics (PNG) is a bitmapped image format that employs lossless data compression. PNG was created to improve on and replace the GIF format, as an image file format not requiring a patent licence. PNG is pronounced ping. It supports palettes of 24-bit RGB colours and greyscale images. It was designed for transferring images across the Internet.

Scalable Vector Graphics (SVG) is a language for describing two-dimensional graphics and graphical applications in Extensible Markup Language (XML). It is relatively new and was designed especially to provide vector graphics on web pages. It is text based, which makes it easy to search and perform graphics transformations.

Shockwave Format (SWF) and Flash format are two similar formats from Macromedia, now part of Adobe. They are primarily vector formats but they can incorporate small bitmapped images. Both are used to create animations for web browsers that have the required plug-ins. SWF and Flash use a binary format rather than a text format, which provides few hooks for text searching or image extraction.

Questions

11 What is meant by data compression?

12 Describe the image compression technique of run-length encoding.

13 What is the difference between lossless compression and lossy compression?

14 Name two ways that lossy compression achieves data reduction.

In this topic you have covered:

- a pixel is the smallest addressable area or solid block of colour in an image
- a bitmap is created when the pixels of an image are mapped to binary codes for their colours
- image resolution is the number of dots/pixels per inch or per centimetre
- screen resolution is the number of pixels in the horizontal dimension by the number of pixels in the vertical dimension
- colour depth is the number of bits to represent the colour of a single pixel in a bitmapped image
- the size of a bitmap in bytes is its size in pixels multiplied by its colour depth in bytes
- a vector graphic records information about the objects that make up an image
- a vector graphic object is a graphic component such as a line, a rectangle or a circle
- a drawing list is the list of drawing commands that create the vector graphic
- properties of a graphic object describe its size, direction, thickness, shading, font size, typeface, etc.
- data compression squeezes uncompressed data into fewer bytes
- run-length encoding is a lossless method of image compression
- lossy image compression reduces the resolution of the background; it uses fewer bits for colours to which the human eye is less sensitive and fewer bits for low-intensity colours
- scaled bitmapped graphics become distorted whereas scaled vector graphics do not distort
- geometric images take up less memory and load faster as vector graphics
- photographs with lots of continuous colour take up less memory as bitmapped graphics.

5.4 Representing sound in a computer

In this topic you will cover:

- how sound is represented and recorded in a computer

- the difference between analogue and digital data and analogue and digital signals

- sampling, sampling resolution and sampling rate

- the principles of operation of an analogue-to-digital converter

- sound synthesis

- streaming audio.

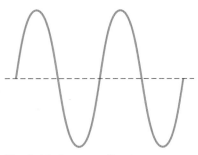

Fig. 5.4.1 *Pure tone vibration*

Fig. 5.4.2 *A superposition of pure tones*

Sound and data

Sound

Sound is an air pressure wave that is sensed by our ears. In an analogue sound system, the pressure wave is captured by a transducer, often a microphone, that produces an electrical voltage or current that varies in proportion to the sound pressure. The electrical signal can then be transmitted by telephone, broadcast by radio, preserved on magnetic tape (audio cassettes) or used in other ways. At the other end, the electrical signal is used to recreate sound by vibrating some mechanical surface in a loudspeaker or an earphone, reproducing the original pressure wave with varying degrees of fidelity so that we can hear the sound. The higher the pitch of the sound, the more rapid the vibration. A pure tone is a regular sine wave (Fig. 5.4.1). A more complicated sound is a superposition of these waves and might look like Fig. 5.4.2.

A vinyl LP record exploits the shape of the sound wave by fixing a similar shape in the long spiral groove running across the surface of the record. The groove stores data about the sound in analogue form. When the record is played, a fine needle follows the changes in the groove and creates an electrical signal proportional to the changes. The signal is amplified then fed to a loudspeaker. In the days of wind-up gramophones, the needle vibrated a mechanical surface directly to produce the sound.

Today almost all sound systems are digital. The electrical signal from a transducer such as a microphone is converted into a sequence of numerical values proportional to the strength of the signal and those numerical values are stored, transmitted, processed, etc., before they are converted back to an analogue electrical signal and then to sound. For example, an audio CD contains about an hour's worth of sampled voltage values: 44,100 samples per second in each of two stereo channels. Each sample is 16 bits, representing one of 65,536 possible voltage values; multiplying this out gives about 650 MB for an hour, or roughly 10 MB per minute.

What is analogue data?

Physical quantities such as temperature and pressure vary continuously in the real world. They are known as analogue quantities. Fig. 5.4.3 shows how the temperature in a classroom varies with time over a period of 12 hours.

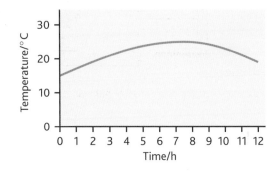

Fig. 5.4.3 *Analogue temperature data*

Data is anything that is collected and submitted for processing. **Analogue data** is data that varies in a continuous manner, such as speech conveyed from speaker to listener by sound waves.

What is digital data?

Digital quantities vary in discrete steps – they are discontinuous. Here are three sets of digital quantities: 1, 2, 3, 4 (set 1); 0, 1, 1, 0, 1, 0 (set 2); A, B, C, D (set 3). When analogue physical quantities are sampled and their values recorded, in the appropriate units, they become **digital data**. Digital data takes the form of discrete values. The denary number 57 is an example of digital data. Another example of digital data is the binary number 10101100. Fig. 5.4.4 shows digital data in the form of temperature readings taken at hourly intervals.

Hour	Temperature	Hour	Temperature
1	17	7	25
2	18	8	25
3	19	9	24
4	20	10	21
5	21	11	19
6	24	12	18

Fig. 5.4.4 *Digital temperature data*

Key terms

Analogue data: data that varies in a continuous manner.

Digital data: data that takes the form of discrete values.

Analogue signal: an electrical signal that varies in a continuous manner.

The difference between data and signals

To process analogue data, it must be sensed then converted into an equivalent electrical form. The electrical equivalent is called an analogue electrical signal or just an analogue signal. An **analogue signal** is an electrical signal that varies in a continuous manner. The device that does this is known as a transducer. A transducer is designed to convert energy from one form to another. A microphone is an example of a transducer. It converts continuously varying sound pressure waves into a continuously varying electrical signal. Another example of a transducer is a loudspeaker. A loudspeaker converts electrical energy into sound energy.

Fig. 5.4.5 shows a typical electrical circuit for converting sound energy into electrical energy. Fig. 5.4.6 shows the variation in pressure produced by the speaker whistling a pure tone. Fig. 5.4.7 shows the equivalent analogue signal.

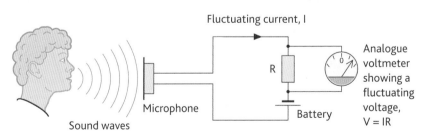

Fluctuating current, I

Microphone

Sound waves

R

Battery

Analogue voltmeter showing a fluctuating voltage, $V = IR$

Fig. 5.4.5 *A typical electrical circuit for converting sound energy into electrical energy*

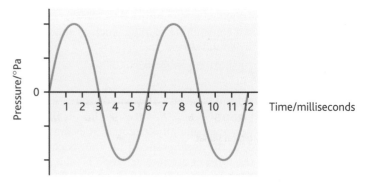

Fig. 5.4.6 *Variation in pressure produced by the speaker whistling a pure tone*

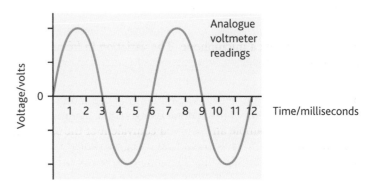

Fig. 5.4.7 *Equivalent analogue electrical signal*

Key terms

Digital signal: an electrical signal with voltage changes that are abrupt or in discrete steps.

Table 1 *Coding binary in voltages*

Voltage level	Binary
7.5	011
5	010
2.5	001
0	000
0	100
−2.5	101
−5	110
−7.5	111

Table 2 *Coding binary data by binary signals*

Voltage level	Binary
5	1
0	0

Fig. 5.4.8 shows a **digital signal**. In this example the voltage levels available to the signal were −7.5, −5, −2.5, 0, 2.5, 5, 7.5.

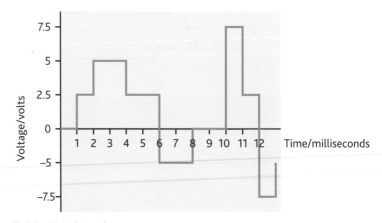

Fig. 5.4.8 *Digital signal*

Each voltage level encodes a single item of binary data (Table 1). The most significant binary digit is a sign bit: 0 represents + and 1 represents −. Unfortunately, this leads to two binary patterns for zero.

It is possible to use just two voltage levels, 0 volts and 5 volts (Fig. 5.4.9). The digital signal is then a binary digital signal.

Each voltage represents a single item of binary data: 5 volts is binary 1 and 0 volts is binary 0 (Table 2).

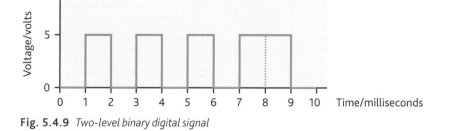

Fig. 5.4.9 *Two-level binary digital signal*

The stream of voltage pulses shown in Fig. 5.4.9 encodes the binary data 0110101010; the least significant digit is the first pulse to be produced.

💡 Analogue to digital conversion

Sound waves may be converted into an equivalent analogue electrical current or voltage using a microphone. The variation in frequency (pitch) and the variation in amplitude (loudness) of the sound are reproduced in electrical form.

A computer may be used to record sound, but first the sound must be converted into digital form. This is done using an analogue-to-digital converter, or **ADC**, to sample an electrical equivalent of the sound and to convert the samples into a digital signal using two voltage levels. To play back the recorded sound, a digital-to-analogue converter, or **DAC** is used to convert the digital signal representing the recorded sound into an analogue electrical signal that is then played through a loudspeaker to produce sound. Fig. 5.4.10 shows how sound could be recorded and played back through the sound card of a computer system. The system relies heavily on a technique called pulse code modulation (**PCM**).

■ Key terms

ADC: analogue-to-digital converter; converts an analogue signal into an equivalent digital signal.

DAC: digital-to-analogue converter; converts a digital signal into an equivalent analogue signal.

PCM: pulse code modulation; a process for coding sampled analogue signals by recording the height of each sample in a binary electrical equivalent.

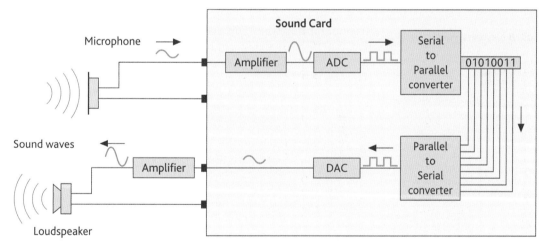

Fig. 5.4.10 *How sound could be recorded and played back through the sound card of a computer*

The PCM form of an analogue signal is produced by an ADC as follows:

1 Samples are taken of the analogue signal at fixed and regular intervals of time (Fig. 5.4.11). The sampling frequency, or sampling rate, must be at least twice the highest frequency in the analogue signal. These samples are represented as narrow pulses of height proportional to the value of the original signal. This process is known as pulse amplitude modulation (**PAM**).

■ Key terms

PAM: pulse amplitude modulation; a process that samples analogue signals at regular time intervals and produces electrical pulses of height proportional to the original signal's amplitude at the instant of sampling.

Fig. **5.4.11** *Sampling*

2 To produce PCM data, the PAM samples are quantised. That is, the height of each PAM pulse is approximated by an n-bit integer. For example, if $n = 3$, then $8 = 2^3$ levels are available for approximating PAM pulses (Fig. 5.4.12).

Fig. **5.4.12** *Quantisation*

3 Finally, the height of each PCM pulse is encoded in n bits to produce the digital output in binary signal form. For Fig. 5.4.12, using $n = 3$, the PCM pulses are coded in binary as follows: $4 \rightarrow 100_2$, $7 \rightarrow 111_2$, $3 \rightarrow 011_2$.

The output from the PCM encoder is a sequence of fixed-height pulses (Fig. 5.4.13) least significant bit first. The train of pulses may then be stored in memory in groups, where each group consists of 3 bits (Fig. 5.4.14).

Sample no

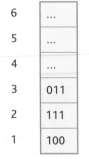

Fig. **5.4.14** *Encoding*

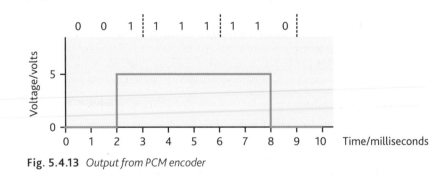

Fig. **5.4.13** *Output from PCM encoder*

The process is reversed using a DAC. The DAC produces an analogue signal that is an approximation of the original analogue signal (Fig. 15). The staircase effect is a result of approximation during PCM quantisation. The deviation from the original is known as **quantisation noise**. Fig. 5.4.15 shows a higher sampling rate than was shown in the previous diagrams.

This electrical signal, sometimes after amplification, is used to recreate the sound by vibrating a mechanical surface in a loudspeaker or an earphone.

Key terms

Quantisation noise: the difference between the original amplitude and its sampled value.

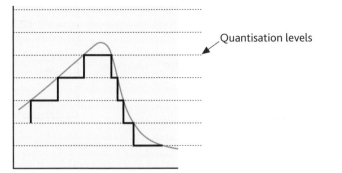

Fig. 5.4.15 *DAC output: an analogue signal that approximates the original analogue signal*

Worked example

Problem

An analogue signal of frequency 1,000 Hz is converted to a PCM digital signal by sampling at a frequency of 2,000 Hz = 2,000 samples per second. Each sample is encoded in 8 bits using PCM coding. How many bytes of storage are required for the PCM-coded result if recording 10 seconds of analogue signal?

Solution

A sampling frequency of 2,000 Hz means that 2,000 samples are taken per second. In 10 seconds this means that 20,000 samples are taken. One byte (8 bits) is required for each sample. Therefore 20,000 bytes of storage are required.

Questions

1 A sound wave is digitised using a circuit containing an ADC that uses PCM coding. The sampling frequency is 40 kHz. (a) What device is required in addition to the ADC? (b) Each sample is coded in 16 bits. How much storage is required in bytes for one minute of recorded sound?

2 Explain by example the difference between analogue and digital data.

3 Explain the difference between an analogue signal and analogue data.

4 What converter will convert a digital signal into an analogue signal?

▥ Managing and manipulating sound

Sampled sound and Nyquist's theorem

The sampling rate, or sampling frequency, defines the number of samples that are taken per second when digitising a continuous signal. For time-varying signals, the sampling rate is measured in hertz (Hz). The sampling resolution is the number of bits assigned to each sample. More bits per sample means a more accurate representation of the signal being sampled.

Here are some questions to consider when sampling an analogue signal.

▥ How often do we sample? Sampling more often means that we can track the changes in a rapidly varying signal more accurately. If we don't sample often enough, we miss meaningful changes in the signal. **Nyquist's theorem** states that we must sample at a frequency at least twice the rate of the highest frequency in the sampled signal.

▥ How accurately do we sample? More bits per sample means a more accurate representation of the signal wave.

▥ How much space do we need to store the sound? More frequent sampling and more accurate samples mean more data, which can add up very quickly.

▥ How much bandwidth do we need to transmit sound in electrical form? Bandwidth is information-carrying capacity. It takes more capacity to preserve all the low and high frequencies that might be

■ Key terms

Nyquist's theorem: sample at a frequency at least twice the rate of the highest frequency in the sampled signal.

■ Key point

More bits per sample means a more accurate representation of the signal wave. More frequent samples means a more accurate representation of the signal wave. More bits per sample means more data. More frequent samples means more data. More bits per sample means more bandwidth required for transmission. Higher sampling frequencies mean more bandwidth required for transmission.

■ Key point

For a given duration of audio in seconds, MIDI files require less storage space than MP3 files and MP3 files require less storage space than WAV files. MP3 is used for most music available on the Internet. WAV is used for audio CDs.

■ Key terms

MIDI: Musical Information Digital Interface; a way of representing the sounds made by an instrument.

Synthesise sound: use digital means to generate audio signals resembling instrument sounds or the human voice.

needed, perhaps for hi-fi sound, whereas it takes much less bandwidth if only some frequencies need to be transmitted, perhaps for telephone speech.

■ How do we convert back from numbers to an analogue waveform? If the original waveform is to be reproduced with reasonable fidelity, we have to do this carefully too.

Storing sound in files

There are several file formats for storing digitised sound. The most notable is the WAV format supported in Windows 3.1, 95, 98, NT, 2000, ME, XP and Vista. One minute of sound saved to a WAV file requires 2.5 MB of disk space. The WAV format is used when audio is stored on CDs.

Another file format is MPEG audio, which uses extensions .mp2, .mpa, .mp3, .mp4. MPEG is primarily a compression algorithm that can be applied to a number of audio formats, e.g. WAV. However, it also exists as an audio file format. MPEG is based on psychoacoustic modelling that removes frequencies the brain and ear will not miss. This substantially reduces the file size before other compression techniques are applied. Files of one-tenth their WAV size with no apparent loss in quality are achievable with MPEG CD quality. For MP3, one minute of CD-quality audio can be cut down from 2.5 MB to about 0.25 MB (**www.MP3-tech. org**). MP3 is the compressed format that is used for most music available on the Internet.

We can also use the properties of human speech to compress telephone speech significantly (**www.data-compression.com/speech.html**). This is used in mobile phones. Compression techniques for speech do not work as well for music.

When sound is converted into digital form it is possible to mix sounds from multiple sources and to store the combination in a single file. There is a lot on the Web about sound. Visit **www.music.arts.uci.edu/dobrian/ digitalaudio.htm**.

Synthesising sound

According to **www.webopedia.com/TERM/MIDI.html**, Musical Information Digital Interface, or **MIDI**, is a widely used representation for instrumental music that does not store sound waves at all. Instead it stores a digital representation of the notes to be played, including what note, what instrument and what duration. The resulting form is very compact and very flexible for many purposes. It is easy to transpose into a different key, play on different instruments and synthesise musical notation from it.

The device that is going to produce the sounds has to create or **synthesise sounds** from an internal definition of what they sound like. For example, a typical low-end synthesiser can approximate 64 instrumental sounds. Depending on the synthesiser, the approximation to the real instrument may go from very good to very bad. Piano sounds can be approximated fairly well but the human voice is not well approximated.

Streaming audio

Many Internet audio sources stream the sound to a streaming client, such as RealPlayer, on your machine. As the streaming client receives the audio data, it puts it in a buffer to be stored until it is used. A few seconds after the client starts receiving audio data, the client player starts reading the data from the buffer and playing it. As long as the player is not trying to access data that hasn't been received yet, streaming will be successful. If the buffer runs out of audio data, the player will pause until it receives more. Streaming avoids the need to download and store large sound files. The sounds come in as they are needed but without occupying file space on your hard drive. The other reason that many sources stream audio is that, in theory, it prevents copying.

💡 Editing sound

Once a sound wave is stored in digital form, it may be edited to remove notes, add new notes, change the frequency of notes, and reduce or eliminate background noise. A sound-editing package such as Goldwave or Audacity can take separate digital recordings of sound waves then merge or mix them into one file in different ways.

☑️ *In this topic you have covered:*

- the difference between analogue and digital data

- the difference between analogue and digital signals

- sampling and digitising using PAM and PCM

- sampling rate and sampling resolution

- analogue-to-digital converter and quantisation noise

- sampled sound and Nyquist's theorem

- factors that affect the quality of recorded sound

- file formats for storing sound data in files

- sound synthesis, streaming audio, editing sampled sound.

Questions

5 State Nyquist's theorem.

6 State two factors likely to affect the quality of the recorded sound and the file size of a digital audio recording.

7 Take each factor in your answer to Question 2 and explain how it affects the quality and the file size.

8 What is meant by synthesising sound?

9 Explain the process of streaming audio.

The system life cycle

6.1 Stages in hardware and software development

Key terms

System: a whole composed of parts in orderly arrangement.

Systems analysis: the study of a complex process in order to improve its efficiency.

Manual system: a system that does not involve computers.

♀ What is a system?

The Oxford English Dictionary defines a **system** as a whole composed of parts in orderly arrangement according to some scheme or plan. It defines **systems analysis** as the analysis of a complex process or operation in order to improve its efficiency, especially by applying a computer system.

Many people are required to develop a large system. It often takes many man-years to go from initial concept to completed solution. Formal procedures are essential to ensure that everyone involved can contribute effectively to deliver the required solution. There are various methods but they all have these basic stages: analysis, design, implementation, testing and evaluation. Any system, however well produced, will eventually cease to be adequate, and the whole process will start all over again. This gives us the concept of the systems development life cycle (Fig. 6.1.1).

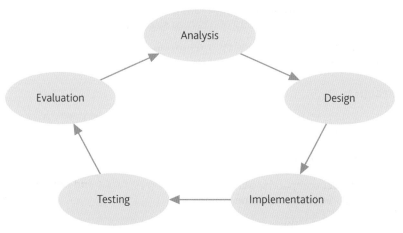

Fig. 6.1.1 *The systems development life cycle*

Analysis phase

A system may be perceived to be in need of change for a variety of reasons; here are three:

■ **Changes in the organisation:** a business starting to trade on the Internet will require an online ordering system.

■ **Technical developments:** unlike bar codes, RFID tags can be read from a distance, which allows a change in stock control or tracking systems.

■ **Outdated practices:** perhaps a system cannot respond quickly to support customers.

The current system may be a **manual system**, where no computer is involved. The system consists of a set of procedures and work practices followed by people working in the organisation. Information is stored on paper in folders or filing cabinets. On the other hand, the current system may be a computerised system which no longer provides the required information quickly enough.

A new computer system is a major investment for an organisation. It is vitally important that money and time are spent wisely to improve the system. The first step during the analysis stage is to define the problem: what exactly is wrong with the current system?

A feasibility study then identifies whether it is technically and financially feasible to implement a solution. When it has been decided that it is worth proceeding, a full analysis is done. This means gathering detailed facts about the current system and the issues. Here are some fact-gathering methods:

▦ **Interviews:** people involved in the current system as operators, supervisors or managers may be asked about their part in the system, what the problems are and what they require from a new system.

▦ **Observation:** a systems analyst may observe the working practices of staff, noting where bottlenecks occur and where efficiency could be improved.

▦ **Questionnaires:** sometimes it is not possible to interview all those affected by the system. To get a wider view, carefully designed questionnaires may be used to gather information from staff and customers.

▦ **Examination of documentation:** an analyst may examine job descriptions, written procedures, guidelines, the forms and reports used by the organisation, and other documents.

The result of the analysis stage is a **requirements specification** with system objectives.

Design phase

A new system must be designed carefully before it can be developed. A good design will be detailed enough to allow teams of specialists to produce the system as the designer intended. These system components need to be specified:

▦ **Hardware:** computers, network requirements, input and output devices, online and off-line storage.

▦ **Software:** programs, development environment.

▦ **Data files:** structure and expected size.

▦ **User interface:** method of operation.

▦ **Required inputs:** data requirements and method of capture.

▦ **Required outputs:** layouts of screens and printed reports.

▦ **Manual procedures:** operational procedures.

▦ **Test plan:** method of testing and test data.

Implementation phase

▦ Development of software by coding and testing.

▦ Installation of the hardware.

▦ Installation of the software.

▦ Preparation of the data files.

▦ Training of the users.

▦ Writing the system documentation.

▦ **Key terms**

Requirements specification: a set of system objectives.

Testing phase

Testing is vital. During program design and program writing, spend a substantial part of the time on testing (Topic 4.2). When the parts are put together and the software has been installed, the whole system needs to be tested before it goes live.

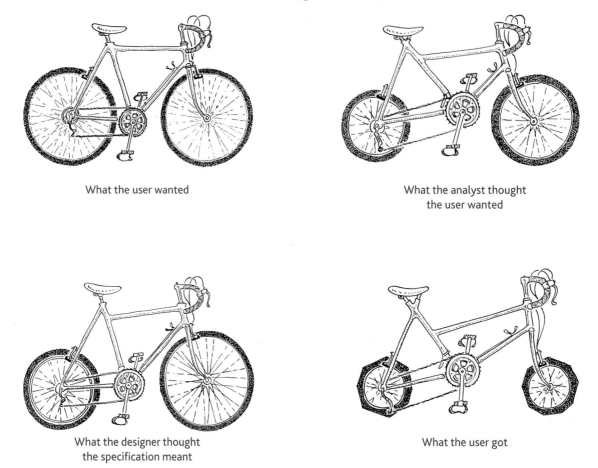

What the user wanted

What the analyst thought
the user wanted

What the designer thought
the specification meant

What the user got

Fig. 6.1.2 *Translating requirements into applications*

Case study

Find out about one major failure of software systems, such as the grounding of all aircraft at Heathrow when a system upgrade went wrong; the explosion of the Ariane 5 rocket in 1996; Patriot missile failure during the 1991 Gulf War; the failure of the system used by the London Ambulance Service; the 2003 blackout in North America; the Y2K problem; the Therac-25 accidents (1985–87). What caused the failure? What were the consequences? What was done to remedy the situation and how long did it take?

Evaluation phase

When the new system is fully operational, reflect on how successful it is:

■ Does the new system meet its original system objectives and requirements?

■ How effective is the new system in solving the original problem?

■ Can users operate the new system without making mistakes or working under stressful conditions?

During the systems development life cycle you will often need to refer back to an earlier stage. For example, during the design stage it may become apparent that not enough information was gathered about a particular aspect of the system and further analysis needs to be done. During the implementation stage some of the design work may prove to be incomplete, so further design work will be needed. During system testing, errors in the software or hardware configuration may require further development work.

Most software is regularly updated. This is known as **software maintenance**. Errors, or bugs, in software need to be fixed as soon as they are discovered. Users change their requirements; for example, a manager may request another type of report. External requirements, such as a change in taxation, may also impose changes.

Questions

1 During which stage of the system development life cycle would a user be asked what part they play in the functioning of the system and what they think the problems are?

2 How could a systems analyst find out what the customers who regularly shop at a builders' merchant thought of the current billing system?

3 A wholesale bakery employs sales staff to collect orders by phone. The bakers start baking when they get the quantities of goods to be produced for the next morning. They complain that they get this information so late that the product is often not ready when the deliveries need to be packed. The sales staff insist they work as hard as they can. How can a systems analyst find out where the problem lies?

4 Information is stored in filing cabinets. During which stage of the systems development life cycle is this information typed into computer files for use by a new computerised system?

5 Why is system testing necessary when the programmers have tested their code as they developed it?

6 Why is it necessary to check that the completed system meets the original requirements?

✔ *In this topic you have covered:*

■ a system is a whole composed of parts in orderly arrangement

■ a manual system is a process that does not involve computers

■ stages of systems development: analysis, design, implementation, testing, evaluation, maintenance

■ analysis: study of a complex process to produce a requirements specification or system objectives

■ design: specification of all software, hardware, data files, test plans

■ implementation: software development, installation, data preparation, training, documentation

■ testing: during program development and before the whole system goes live

■ evaluation: see whether the system solves the problem effectively

■ maintenance: update a program to correct faults or improve features.

Introduction

This unit consists of three main areas:

- the fundamental parts of the computer hardware
- the structure of the Internet including web page design
- consequences of Computing.

To understand what new developments we might make in the future, we need to understand the fundamental concepts of current computer design. How do processors work? How is hardware made to do the things we want it to do? What types of software are there? Why are there so many different programming languages? At the most basic level of processor design is Boolean algebra. Processors are built from logic gates. To understand the limitations and possibilities of this design we need to know how the components interact. The first computer was a mechanical device invented by Charles Babbage in 1822. The first electronic computers were programmed by plugging connections and setting dials. While the computer was being set up to run a new program it could not be used for anything else. The first computer that could store a program in memory started the development of the computers that are in common use today. The stored program concept was a huge step forward in the usefulness of the computer. A program could be loaded into memory very quickly and each of its instructions was fetched into the processor and executed, one after the other, in the sequence the programmer determined.

This unit introduces the structure of the Internet, and the protocols used to provide the various services. You should also have some practical experience of setting up web pages using HTML and style sheets. You need to understand that HTML should be used for content and structure only and that style sheets are used for style and layout of web pages.

Computers are very good at calculating but not so good at recognising hand writing, faces and patterns that the human brain is very good at processing. One of the many challenges facing computer scientists is to make the computer perform 'intelligent' processing. There are many exciting projects currently under way, for example, see www.cs4fn.org or www.aaai.org/AITopics/.

Computers are everywhere. As a budding computing scientist you will need to think about the moral consequences of this, such as the invasion of privacy because of constant surveillance and recognition systems. As you produce new systems you need to understand your responsibilities. As computers are used in new situations, what impact does this have on society as we know it?

As well as short, single sentence answers, the exam for this unit may include questions that require you to organise a longer response clearly and coherently, using specialist vocabulary. You should practise formulating arguments to support a point of view, such as whether digital rights management is a good or a bad thing; or open source software versus proprietary software.

7.1 Logic gates and Boolean algebra

Key terms

Boolean variable: may have two discrete possible values, e.g. true or false.

In 1847 George Boole, an English mathematician, introduced a shorthand notation for a system of logic originally set forth by Aristotle. Aristotle's system dealt with statements considered either true or false. Here are two examples:

It is raining today.

Today is my birthday.

In Boole's shorthand, the first statement could be represented by the variable X and the second by a variable Y. Variables in Boole's shorthand system, or **Boolean variables**, may have two discrete possible states or values, often called true or false. Table 1 shows the use of X to indicate whether or not it is raining today. Boole's shorthand logic system is a form of algebra known as Boolean algebra.

Table 1 *Using Boolean variable X to indicate if it is raining today*

X	Meaning
True	It is raining today
False	It is not raining today

Boolean algebra had very little practical use until digital electronics and computers were invented. Digital computers use the binary number system, which has only two states, 0 and 1. Boolean algebra is ideal for this. Table 1 may be recast using 1 for true and 0 for false (Table 2).

Table 2 *Using Boolean variable X with the binary number system to indicate if it is raining today*

X	Meaning
1	It is raining today
0	It is not raining today

Truth tables

The binary states of Boolean variables may be conveniently represented by a simple switch with two states: switch open (0) and switch closed (1). The switch in Fig. 7.1.1 connects an electrical supply to a lamp. When the switch is closed the lamp is lit, otherwise it is not lit.

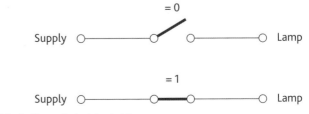

Fig. 7.1.1 *Coding switch states in binary*

Key terms

Truth table: a table that shows the result of applying the logical function to all possible combinations of inputs.

OR function: the output is true if either or both inputs are true.

Fig. 7.1.2 shows three ways of representing the state of the lamp for given states of the switch. The tables in Fig. 7.1.2 are known as **truth tables**: Lamp On = True (1) when Switch Closed = True (1) and Lamp On = False (0) when Switch Closed = False (0).

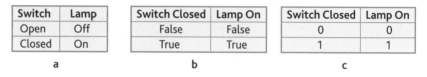

Switch	Lamp
Open	Off
Closed	On

Switch Closed	Lamp On
False	False
True	True

Switch Closed	Lamp On
0	0
1	1

a   b   c

Fig. 7.1.2 *Three ways of representing the state of the lamp for a given state of the switch*

OR function

If switches are wired as in Fig. 7.1.3, then for a connection to be made between the supply and the lamp, switch X OR switch Y must be closed. Fig. 7.1.3 also shows a truth table for this **OR function**.

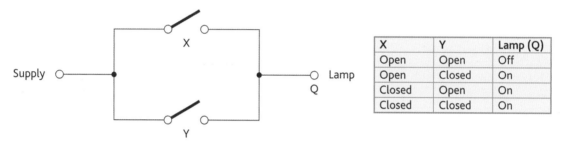

X	Y	Lamp (Q)
Open	Open	Off
Open	Closed	On
Closed	Open	On
Closed	Closed	On

Fig. 7.1.3 *OR function: switch arrangement and truth table*

Key terms

Boolean equation: an equation that expresses a Boolean output Q in terms of Boolean inputs, X, Y, Z, etc., to which one or more Boolean functions, such as OR, AND and NOT, are applied.

AND function: the output is true if all inputs are true.

Table 3 *Truth table for $X + Y = Q$*

X	Y	Q
0	0	0
0	1	1
1	0	1
1	1	1

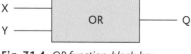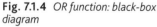

Fig. 7.1.4 *OR function: black-box diagram*

The lamp is on if switch X is closed OR if switch Y is closed OR if both are closed, otherwise the lamp is off. The switches X and Y are Boolean variables because they each have two states, **open** or **closed**. The state of the lamp, Q, is a Boolean variable because the state has two possible values, **off** or **on**. Therefore we can write a **Boolean equation**:

(Switch X closed) + (Switch Y closed) = (Lamp On)

or just

$X + Y = Q$

The + sign is used here quite differently from the way it is used in ordinary arithmetic; it means OR. Table 3 shows the truth table for the OR function based on an analogy with the switch–lamp scenario. For X and Y, **0** means **open** and **1** means **closed**; for Q, **0** means **off** and **1** means **on**.

Table 3 describes the two-input OR function, which can be represented by a black-box diagram (Fig. 7.1.4). The inputs X and Y are transformed by the OR function into output Q.

AND function

If a situation described by Boolean variables gives a desired result only when all of several external situations are satisfied, then it obeys the Boolean **AND function**. For example, the light inside a refrigerator is either on or off, so this is a Boolean variable. The light is on if the electrical supply to the refrigerator is on AND the refrigerator's door is open:

Lamp on if supply on AND door open

Each of the three variables in the above situation has two possible states:

- The lamp is either on or not on.
- The electrical supply is either on or off.
- The door is either open or shut.

Therefore, Boolean algebra may be used to express this situation using the full stop symbol (.) for AND. The word AND is the logical connective for the AND function. The following Boolean equation represents the relationship between the door, the supply and the lamp:

(Supply On).(Door Open) = (Lamp On)

Using the Boolean variable X for the supply switch, Y for the door switch and Q for the lamp, the Boolean equation becomes

$X.Y = Q$

If we use a switch analogy, we see that the AND function may be represented as in Fig. 7.1.5.

X	Y	Lamp (Q)
Open	Open	Off
Open	Closed	Off
Closed	Open	Off
Closed	Closed	On

Fig. 7.1.5 *AND function: switch arrangement and truth table*

Table 4 shows the truth table for the AND function based on an analogy with the switch–lamp scenario. For X and Y, **0** means **open** and **1** means **closed**; for Q, **0** means **off** and **1** means **on**.

NOT function

The **NOT function** can be represented by the truth tables in Fig. 7.1.6 using the Boolean variable X for the state of the switch and Q for the state of the lamp. When the switch is open the lamp is on, and vice versa. The second truth table uses **0** for switch state **open** and **1** for switch state **closed**, **1** for lamp **on** and **0** for lamp **off**.

X	Q
Open	On
Closed	Off

X	Q
0	1
1	0

Fig. 7.1.6 *NOT function: truth tables*

Notice that the NOT function inverts the input. The Boolean equation for this is

$Q = \text{NOT } X$

or

$Q = \overline{X}$

where $\overline{X}$ means NOT X. Fig. 7.1.7 shows a black-box diagram for the NOT function.

Combinations of AND and OR

It is possible to have more complex Boolean algebra expressions than just a single AND or OR function. Consider the switch arrangement in Fig. 7.1.8.

Table 4 *Truth table for X.Y = Q*

X	Y	Q
0	0	0
0	1	0
1	0	0
1	1	1

Key terms

NOT function: the output is the inverse of the input.

Fig. 7.1.7 *NOT function: black-box diagram*

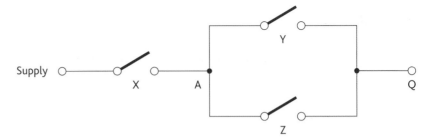

Fig. 7.1.8 *A switch arrangement for a combination of AND and OR gates*

We define a condition Q, where $Q = 1$ when there is a connection between the supply and Q, and $Q = 0$ when there is no connection. There are two ways of tackling the problem to obtain a Boolean equation for Q.

The first way is just to inspect the diagram to see that there is a connection to Q if both X and Y are closed or if both X and Z are closed:

$$Q = (X \text{ AND } Y) \text{ OR } (X \text{ AND } Z)$$

$$Q = X.Y + X.Z$$

With more complex arrangements it is not easy to obtain an answer just by inspection. A useful approach is to split the arrangement into parts. If we divide the arrangement at point A in Fig. 7.1.8, we can state that we need a connection from the supply to A and a connection from A to Q. In Boolean terms, this means

$$Q = X \text{ AND } (Y \text{ OR } Z)$$

$$Q = X.(Y + Z)$$

This is the same result as by the first method when we realise that, as with normal algebra, we can multiply out the bracketed terms as follows:

$$X.(Y + Z) = X.Y + X.Z$$

Questions

1 Draw the truth tables for the AND, OR and NOT functions.

2 What logic function is performed by the switch arrangement in Fig. 7.1.9?

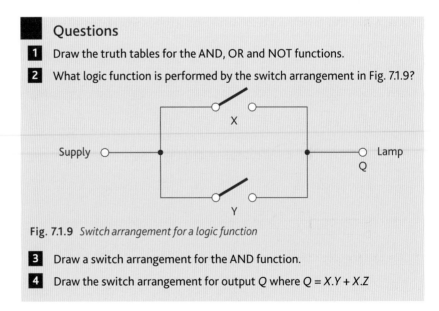

Fig. 7.1.9 *Switch arrangement for a logic function*

3 Draw a switch arrangement for the AND function.

4 Draw the switch arrangement for output Q where $Q = X.Y + X.Z$

💡 Logic gates

Electronic circuits that perform the Boolean functions are called **logic gates**. Several symbols are used for logic gates. The symbols used in this book (Fig. 7.1.10) are widely used and follow the standard ANSI/IEEE Std 91a-1991. Logic gates form the basis of all logic circuits. Inputs to and outputs from electronic logic gates are in the form of voltages; a high voltage represents one state, logic 1, and a low voltage represents the other state, logic 0.

(a)

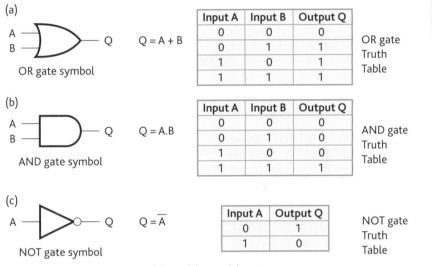

Input A	Input B	Output Q
0	0	0
0	1	1
1	0	1
1	1	1

OR gate symbol $Q = A + B$ OR gate Truth Table

(b)

Input A	Input B	Output Q
0	0	0
0	1	0
1	0	0
1	1	1

AND gate symbol $Q = A.B$ AND gate Truth Table

(c)

Input A	Output Q
0	1
1	0

NOT gate symbol $Q = \overline{A}$ NOT gate Truth Table

Fig. 7.1.10 *Logic gate symbols: (a) OR, (b) AND, (c) NOT*

Combinations of logic gates

AND, OR and NOT gates may be connected to perform a variety of Boolean functions. The output of one gate is used as the input to other gates. In Fig. 7.1.11 we see that

$E = A.B$

$F = C.D$

$Q = E + F$

therefore

$Q = A.B + C.D$

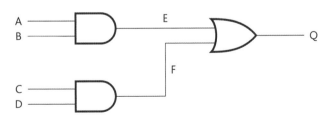

Fig. 7.1.11 *Three gates connected to perform a Boolean function*

Suppose we require an output Q from three inputs A, B, C such that $Q = 0$ when A is present (1) and B is present (1) or when B is not present (0) but C is present (1):

$\overline{Q} = A.B + \overline{B}.C$

This is the same as

$$Q = \overline{A.B + \overline{B}.C}$$

Note that the line above the expression, often called a bar, means that the whole expression is inverted. The solution to the problem is shown in Fig. 7.1.12.

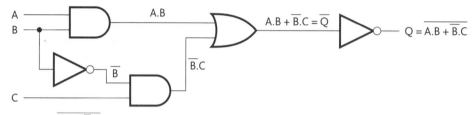

Fig. 7.1.12 *Solution to* $Q = \overline{A.B + \overline{B}.C}$

Input A	Input B	Output
0	0	0
0	1	1
1	0	1
1	1	0

a

Input A	Input B	Output
0	0	0
0	1	1
1	0	1
1	1	1

b

Fig. 7.1.13 *Truth tables for (a) the XOR function and (b) the OR function*

Fig. 7.1.14 *XOR function: symbol*

Exclusive OR function

The **exclusive OR function**, also known as the EX-OR or XOR function, is a Boolean function that differs slightly from the normal OR function, often called the inclusive OR function. The difference can be seen from the truth tables in Fig. 7.1.13.

Notice that the inclusive OR function gives an output of 1 if any input is 1 but the exclusive OR function gives an output of 1 if only one of the inputs is 1 and not if both inputs are 1. A gate which performs this function is called an exclusive OR, EX-OR or XOR gate. The XOR gate is sometimes known as a non-equivalence gate as its output is 1 if the inputs are not equivalent. Fig. 7.1.14 shows the symbol for the exclusive OR gate.

The exclusive OR truth table in Fig. 7.1.13 shows that the Boolean expression for the condition $A = 1$, $B = 0$ is $A.\overline{B}$, i.e. A AND (NOT B) and the Boolean expression for the condition $A = 0$, $B = 1$ is $\overline{A}.B$ i.e. (NOT A) AND B. Therefore, $Q = 1$ for $A.\overline{B}$ OR $\overline{A}.B$, so

$$Q = A.\overline{B} + \overline{A}.B$$

This is the Boolean algebra representation of the exclusive OR function.

NAND function

The **NAND function** is a Boolean function which is simply a combination of the AND function and the NOT function (inverter); NOT AND is abbreviated to NAND. Consequently, the NAND function may be represented by the logic circuit in Fig. 7.1.15. The NAND of two variables A and B is represented in Boolean algebra as $\overline{A.B}$, the inversion of $A.B$.

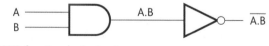

Fig. 7.1.15 *NAND function: logic circuit*

Fig. 7.1.16 shows the symbol for a single gate which performs the NAND function, along with its truth table. The small circle on the output indicates an inverted output.

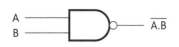

Input A	Input B	Output
0	0	1
0	1	1
1	0	1
1	1	0

Fig. 7.1.16 *NAND function: symbol and truth table*

NOR function

The **NOR function** is the NOT OR function; it may be implemented as in Fig. 7.1.17.

Fig. 7.1.17 *NOR function: logic circuit*

The NOR function of two variables A and B is represented in Boolean algebra as $\overline{A + B}$, the inversion of $A + B$. Fig. 7.1.18 shows the symbol for a single gate which performs the NOR function, along with its truth table.

NOR truth table

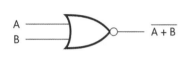

Input A	Input B	Output
0	0	1
0	1	0
1	0	0
1	1	0

Fig. 7.1.18 *NOR function: symbol and truth table*

> **Key terms**
>
> **NOR function:** the output is true only when all inputs are false.

Questions

5 Draw truth tables for the NAND, NOR and XOR logic gates.

6 Draw the circuit symbols for the AND, OR, NOT, NAND, NOR and XOR logic gates.

7 Express Q in terms of Boolean variables A, B and C for the arrangements of logic gates in Fig. 7.1.19.

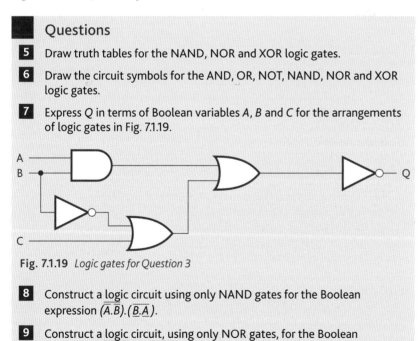

Fig. 7.1.19 *Logic gates for Question 3*

8 Construct a logic circuit using only NAND gates for the Boolean expression $(\overline{A.B}).(\overline{B.A})$.

9 Construct a logic circuit, using only NOR gates, for the Boolean expression $(\overline{A + B}) + (A + \overline{B})$.

> **Key point**
>
> Wire gate inputs of NAND gate together to produce a NOT gate.

💡 De Morgan's laws

De Morgan's laws enable Boolean expressions to be converted to forms requiring only the OR and NOT functions or only the AND and NOT functions. This means that any Boolean expression may be implemented using only OR gates and NOT gates (NOR gates) or using only AND gates and NOT gates (NAND gates). NAND and NOR gates may be used as NOT gates by connecting all the gate inputs together. Therefore, NOR gates alone or NAND gates alone can implement any Boolean function. The fabrication on a single chip of many NOR gates or many NAND gates is possible with integrated circuit technology. In general, **De Morgan's laws** may be written as follows:

$$A_1 + A_2 + A_3 + \ldots + A_n = \overline{\overline{A_1}.\overline{A_2}.\overline{A_3}. \ldots .\overline{A_n}}$$

$$A_1.A_2.A_3. \ldots .A_n = \overline{\overline{A_1} + \overline{A_2} + \overline{A_3} + \ldots + \overline{A_n}}$$

where any finite number n of Boolean variables may be included.

In their simplest form the laws become

$$A + B = \overline{\overline{A}.\overline{B}}$$

$$A.B = \overline{\overline{A} + \overline{B}}$$

The laws are easily remembered as everything associated with an expression must be changed:

- The logical connectives must be changed: AND to OR and OR to AND.
- The logical state of each variable must be changed: A to $\overline{A}$, $\overline{A}$ to A.
- The logical state of the complete expression must be changed: expression to expression, expression to expression.

Worked example _____

De Morgan's laws enable $\overline{A} + \overline{B}$ and $\overline{A}.\overline{B}$ to be implemented with a single logic gate using the inputs A and B rather than $\overline{A}$ and $\overline{B}$.

$$\overline{A} + \overline{B} = \overline{\overline{\overline{A}}.\overline{\overline{B}}} = \overline{A.B}, \text{ the Boolean expression for a NAND gate}$$

$$\overline{A}.\overline{B} = \overline{\overline{\overline{A}} + \overline{\overline{B}}} = \overline{A + B}, \text{ the Boolean expression for a NOR gate}$$

_____

Worked example _____

Table 5 shows a truth table for output Q in terms of inputs A and B. Select the rows of the table where $Q = 1$ (row 2 and row 3). Using the values for row 2, $A.\overline{B}$ makes 1 ($A = 1$ and $B = 0$). Using the values for row 3, $\overline{A}.B$ makes 1 ($A = 0$ and $B = 1$).

Therefore, the Boolean expression is

$$Q = A.\overline{B} + \overline{A}.B$$

Table 5 *Truth table*

Row	A	B	Q
1	0	0	0
2	1	0	1
3	0	1	1
4	1	1	0

_____

Table 6 *Truth table*

Row	A	B	Q
1	0	0	1
2	1	0	0
3	0	1	0
4	1	1	1

Worked example _____

To create the truth table for $Q = (\overline{A} + B).(A + \overline{B})$, begin by simplifying it:

$$Q = (\overline{A} + B).(A + \overline{B}) = \overline{A}.A + \overline{A}.\overline{B} + B.A + B.\overline{B}$$
$$= \overline{A}.\overline{B} + B.A \quad (\overline{A}.A = B.\overline{B} = 0)$$

$Q = 1$ when $\overline{A}.\overline{B} = 1$ or $B.A = 1$, i.e. when $A = B = 0$ and $A = B = 1$. Table 6 shows the finished truth table.

_____

The following identities apply for the Boolean variables A, B and C:

$$A.A = A$$
$$A.\bar{A} = 0$$
$$1 + A = 1$$
$$0 + A = A$$
$$A + A = A$$
$$A + \bar{A} = 1$$
$$0.A = 0$$
$$1.A = A$$
$$A + AB = A(1 + B) = A.1 = A$$
$$A.(A + B) = A.A + A.B = A.(1 + B) = A.1 = A$$
$$A.B = B.A$$
$$A + B = B + A$$
$$(A + B) + C = A + (B + C)$$

Questions

10 Show that $A.\bar{B} + \bar{A}.B = \overline{(A + B).(A + \bar{B})}$, where A and B are Boolean variables.

11 Show that $\overline{(A + B).(A + \bar{B})} = (A + B).(\overline{A} + \overline{B})$ by using $\bar{A}.A = B.\bar{B} = 0$.

12 Simplify $\overline{1}.B$ where B is a Boolean variable and 1 is a Boolean constant.

13 Show that $\overline{(A.\overline{A.B}).(B.\overline{A.B})} = A.\bar{B} + B.\bar{A}$.

14 Output $Q = \bar{A}.(C + \bar{D}) + \bar{B}.(C + \bar{D})$ where A, B, C and D are Boolean inputs. Show how it is possible to use just four NAND gates to produce output Q from A, B, C and D. One of the NAND gates is used as a NOT gate.

In this topic you have covered:.

- Boolean variables may have two discrete possible values, e.g. true or false, 1 or 0

- a truth table shows the result of applying a logical function to all possible input combinations

- OR function (+): output is true if either or both inputs are true

- AND function (.): the output is true if all inputs are true

- NOT function ($^-$): the output is the inversion of the input

- XOR function ($\oplus$): the output is true if either input is true but not if both are true

- NAND function (NOT AND): the output is true if any input is false

- NOR function (NOT OR): the output is true only when all inputs are false

- logic gates perform Boolean functions such as AND, OR and NOT

- output Q is expressed in terms of Boolean inputs X, Y, Z, etc., and Boolean functions

- De Morgan's laws: $A + B = \overline{\bar{A}.\bar{B}}$ and $A.B = \overline{\bar{A} + \bar{B}}$

- to simplify a logical expression, use a truth table to write down input combinations that make the output 1 then use De Morgan's laws to produce a solution in NAND or NOR

- the logic gate symbols:

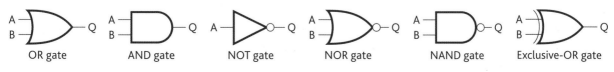

| OR gate | AND gate | NOT gate | NOR gate | NAND gate | Exclusive-OR gate |

7.2 Computer architecture

Internal hardware and external components of a computer

Three-box model

A computer system can be considered as consisting of three boxes:

- the processor, commonly known as the central processing unit (CPU), e.g. Pentium 4
- storage, known as main memory or simply memory
- input and output (I/O) electronics for communication with other devices.

การเชื่อมต่อภายใน.

These three boxes need interconnecting. This is usually done by wiring known as a bus (Fig. 7.2.1).

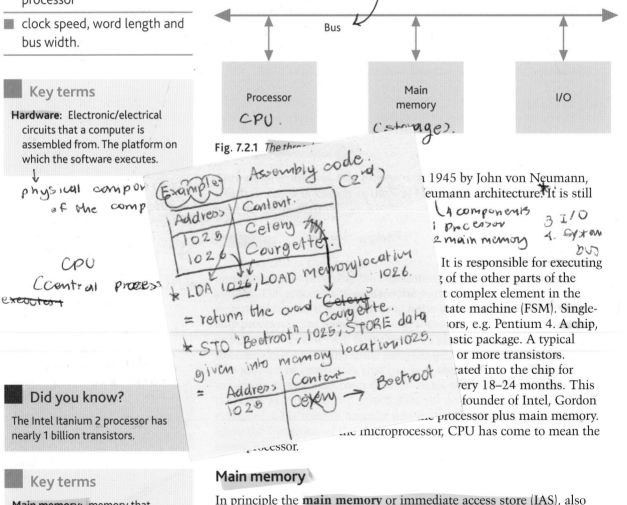

Bus

Processor

CPU.

Main memory

(storage).

I/O

Fig. 7.2.1 *The thr...*

physical compon... of the comp...

CPU
(Central process... executes)

... in 1945 by John von Neumann, ... eumann architecture. It is still

4 components
1 processor   3 I/O
2 main memory   4. system
                    bus

It is responsible for executing ... of the other parts of the ... t complex element in the ... ate machine (FSM). Single-... ors, e.g. Pentium 4. A chip, ... stic package. A typical ... or more transistors. ... rated into the chip for ... very 18–24 months. This ... founder of Intel, Gordon ... processor plus main memory. ... microprocessor, CPU has come to mean the ...ocessor.

Example — Assembly code. (2nd)

Address	Content
1025	Celery ~~Courgette~~
1026	Courgette

* LDA 1026; LOAD memory location 1026.
= return the word "Celery" Courgette.
* STO "Beetroot", 1025; STORE data given into memory location 1025.

Address	Content
1025	~~Celery~~ → Beetroot

Main memory

In principle the **main memory** or immediate access store (IAS), also known simply as store, is the simplest part of the computer. In a von Neumann computer it is used as a store for program instructions and data. Main memory is available in one or more integrated circuits, or

using the system bus to communicate with CPU.

using RAM / ROM

memory chips. Memory chips with the capacity to store 512 KB (512 × 1024 bytes) are often used in PC systems. Each byte goes into a separate area of the chip, called a **memory location**. Main memory is made up of RAM chips but can also include one or more ROM chips.

RAM

* The more main memory = you have the larger the number of programs you can run at once

Random access memory (RAM) is used for memory that is readable and writable. It can be implemented in many technologies (e.g. SRAM and SDRAM). **RAM** is used by the processor to store (write) data and load (read) it back. The contents of RAM are volatile – they are forgotten when the power is turned off.

might be several GB ** RAM is much larger and stores the code to run the operating system and programs that you run on your computer*

ROM

Read-only memory (ROM) doesn't forget when the power is turned off – the contents are non-volatile. **ROM** provides random access like RAM but it cannot be written to once it is set up. It is used to hold fixed programs such as the bootstrap program in a PC. *few KB*

EEPROM

Electrically erasable programmable read-only memory (EEPROM) does allow the contents to be altered. **EEPROM** chips require considerable time to alter a location – writing takes over 100 times longer than reading. Flash memory is faster at writing than other types of EEPROM because blocks of bytes are written in one go rather than single bytes. Flash memory EEPROM chips are widely used for non-volatile storage in consumer applications such as SIM cards in mobile phones, memory cards in digital cameras and memory in MP3 players, memory sticks and PDAs.

Bus

processor
main memory
I/O

The three boxes are connected by a bus called the **system bus or external bus**, which acts as a connecting tube between the three components. This connecting tube can transmit a single binary word between the processor and the store or I/O component, and send an address to the store or I/O component.

In reality, a **computer bus** is a set of parallel wires that connect independent components of a computer system in order to pass signals between them. Some signals represent data, some represent an address and others control information. For this reason, the system bus is split into three separate buses:

1. **Data bus:** a bidirectional bus, typically consisting of 32 wires, used to transport data between the three components of the three-box model.
2. **Address bus:** a unidirectional bus, typically consisting of 32 wires, used to address memory and I/O locations. *(single - direction)*
3. **Control bus:** a bidirectional bus, typically consisting of 8 wires, used to transport control signals between the three components of the three-box model.

I/O

To be useful, the CPU needs to communicate with devices known as peripherals. The expanded three-box model in Figure 2 shows peripherals connected to the CPU through **I/O** controllers. Figure 3 shows a more detailed view. The control bus carries control signals such as these:

Key point

A binary word is a binary number formed in a fixed number of bits, typically 8, 16, 32 or 64. Often the word size is determined by the number of bus lines in the data bus or the size of registers in the processor.

- **Clock signal:** for timing purposes.
- **Reset signal:** used to initialise components.
- **Memory read:** used to assert that the memory location currently in use is being read from.
- **Memory write:** used to assert that the memory location currently in use is being written to.
- **I/O:** used to indicate that the processor wishes to use an I/O controller not main memory when I/O and main memory share memory addresses.

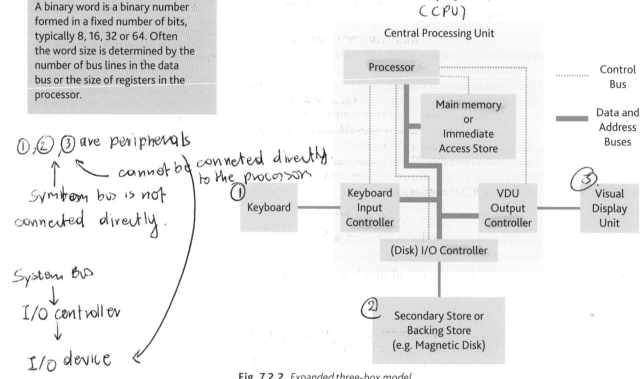

Fig. 7.2.2 *Expanded three-box model*

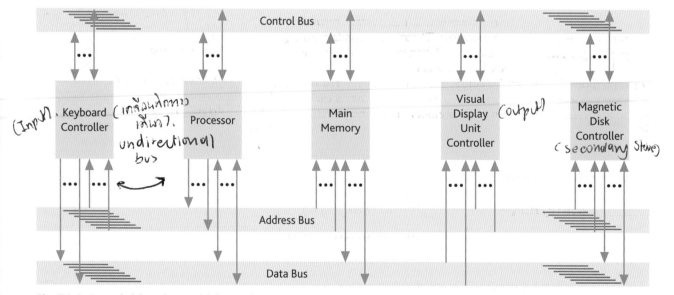

Fig. 7.2.3 *Expanded three-box model showing bus structure*

Periplerals = I/O devices.

A computer device that is not part of the CPU (processor and main memory) is called a **peripheral** or peripheral device. The system bus is not connected directly to I/O devices; it is connected to an I/O controller then the I/O controller is connected to the I/O device.

I/O controllers and I/O devices

The processor communicates through mechanisms and devices that are grouped into **I/O controllers** and **I/O devices**. I/O devices are peripherals, such as keyboards, visual display units, magnetic disks, CD-R and DVD-R drives, network cards and speakers.

I/O controllers include the keyboard controller and the magnetic disk controller. Peripheral devices cannot be connected directly to the processor. Each peripheral operates in a different way and it would not be sensible to design processors to directly control every possible peripheral. If processors controlled peripherals directly, the invention of a new type of peripheral would require the processor to be redesigned. Instead, the processor controls and communicates with a peripheral device through an I/O controller or device controller. Some I/O controllers can input and output bits, e.g. a floppy disk controller. Other controllers operate in one direction only, either as an input controller, e.g. a keyboard controller, or as an output controller, e.g. a VDU controller.

connect device - system bus.

The controller is an electronic circuit consisting of three parts:

- electronics that interface the controller to the system bus
- a set of data, command and status registers
- electronics appropriate for sending control signals to the device connected to the computer. = allows I/O devices to be connected to the CPU without.

I/O device - processor. having to have specials hardware for each one

I/O port

The processor exchanges data with a peripheral device through a part of an I/O controller called an I/O port. An I/O port is simply a set of data, command and status registers. Registers are storage locations that can be written to and read from.

Secondary storage = peripheral

Secondary storage or backing store is permanent storage memory, not directly connected to the processor. Therefore **secondary storage** is a type of peripheral. A magnetic hard disk is a typical example of secondary storage. Secondary storage is connected to the processor and main memory through an I/O controller. Data is transferred from the secondary storage device to the I/O controller then across the system bus to the main memory or from main memory across the system bus to the I/O controller then to secondary storage. Table 1 shows some examples of secondary storage. will store data permanently, without the need for the electricity to remain always on

Table 1 *Types of secondary storage*

Secondary storage	Removable medium
Magnetic hard disk	No (if internal in a PC system)
CD-ROM, CD-R, CD-RW	Yes
DVD-ROM, DVD-R, DVD-RW	Yes
Memory stick	Yes

■ Functional characteristics of a processor

The processor controls the system bus, and the system bus communicates between the boxes in the three-box model. A processor performs operations on data by executing program instructions. A program changes the contents of main memory by sending single binary words back and forth through the system bus. Program instructions and data are fetched from main memory and the results are written to main memory. Only one operation happens at a time, so the control signals and the data bus can be shared over the whole memory. The processor places a numeric code on the address bus to specify which location is currently being used, or addressed. A processor spends a lot of time calculating addresses, fetching addresses from memory along the data bus and sending addresses to memory along the address bus. This is just so that useful data can be fetched or stored in memory.

In the von Neumann computer, a large proportion of traffic on the system bus is not useful data but merely the addresses of this data.

Addressable memory

The processor needs to be able to distinguish the parts of main memory that store individual bytes, so each main memory location has a **main memory address**, like a house address. It is a unique numeric code. When a processor needs to select a main memory location, it puts the unique address corresponding to this location onto the address bus. The processor then asserts, over the control bus, whether it wishes to read from this location or write to this location. Finally, the processor uses the data bus to transfer a byte or bytes between itself and the addressed memory location. All three components of the system bus – address bus, control bus and data bus – are needed when the processor uses a single memory location. A given memory location gains exclusive access of the system bus at a particular instant but it must share access with all the other memory locations at all other times, so the system bus is a shared bus.

💡 Stored program concept

The **stored program concept** was proposed by John von Neumann and Alan Turing in separate publications in 1945:

■ A program must be resident in main memory to be executed.

■ Machine code instructions are fetched, one after another, from main memory in sequence and are executed, one at a time, in the processor.

The processor is instructed to perform arithmetic and logical operations such as ADD, SUBTRACT, AND and OR. These computer instructions are represented by numbers called machine code instructions and are stored in the same way as data. Thus a bit pattern such as 01000110

■ Did you know?

A large proportion of the traffic in the connecting tube between a processor and main memory is not useful data. This is known as the von Neumann bottleneck.

■ Key terms

Main memory address: a unique numeric code corresponding to a location in memory.

Stored program concept: a program must be resident in main memory to be executed; it is processed by fetching machine code instructions in sequence from main memory and executing them, one at a time, in the processor.

○ The program must be in main memory in order for it to be executed

○ The instructions are fetched, decoded and executed one at a time

■ Did you know?

The Manchester Small Scale Experimental Machine (SSEM), known as Baby, was the world's first stored program computer. It was built in 1948 specifically as a test for the memory devices.

might represent the number 46_{16} or the letter F as data but it could also be used to tell a processor to perform an addition. Thus a single memory location holds values which can be interpreted as data or as instructions by the processor in a von Neumann computer.

Types of stored program computer

Von Neumann stored program computer

The von Neumann stored program computer is a serial machine. Serial means that instructions and data are fetched one after another, one at a time. The von Neumann computer has a single memory shared between program instructions and data. Data and instructions travel along a shared data bus (Fig. 7.2.4).

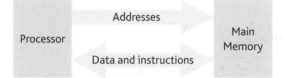

Fig. 7.2.4 *Von Neumann architecture*

Harvard stored program computer

The Harvard stored program computer has separate instruction and data memories (Fig. 7.2.5). The term 'Harvard architecture' is normally used for stored program computers that use separate instruction and data buses. Instructions are fetched serially from instruction memory and executed in the processor. When an instruction needs data, it is fetched from data memory.

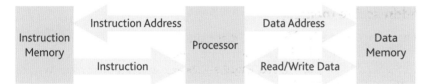

Fig. 7.2.5 *Harvard architecture*

Von Neumann versus Harvard

In the von Neumann architecture, instruction fetches and data references share the same bus, so they compete for resources. In a Harvard architecture there is no competition, so instruction fetches and reading and writing of data can take place in parallel. This increases the overall processing speed.

Microcontroller

A microcontroller is a complete computer (processor, memory and I/O) on a single chip. The most common high-end (32-bit) microcontroller computers on a chip are ARM microcontrollers. Microcontrollers are typically used as embedded computers where a cheap, compact yet programmable system is needed. An embedded computer is a special-purpose computer system built into another device, e.g. an MP3 player, a car or a router, and designed to perform a few dedicated functions. In contrast, a general-purpose computer, such as a personal computer, can be programmed and reprogrammed to do many different tasks. Microcontrollers often use the Harvard architecture.

> **Key point**
>
> The term 'von Neumann architecture' is normally used for stored program computers that have a single main memory shared between program instructions and data.

> **Key point**
>
> The Harvard stored program computer has separate instruction and data memories.

🖳 PC activity

Use Digital Works examples of buses, ALU and registers to understand the internal hardware of a computer.

inside CPU
coordinate
I+O devices of
a computer
system.

Questions

6 What is meant by addressable memory?

7 Describe the role of each of the following buses when the processor uses a main memory location for a reading operation: (a) address bus, (b) control bus, (c) data bus.

8 Explain the stored program concept.

9 Give a definition for (a) von Neumann architecture, (b) Harvard architecture, (c) microcontroller and (d) embedded computer.

💡 Structure and role of the processor

A processor consists of the following components (Fig. 7.2.6):

■ **Program control unit:** fetches program instructions from memory, decodes them and executes them one at a time. *CU* *IWM*

■ **Arithmetic and logic unit:** the ALU performs arithmetic and logical operations on data such as addition and subtraction; fixed-point and floating-point arithmetic; Boolean logic such as AND, OR, XOR; and a range of shift operations. *(ALU)* *digital circuit.*

■ **Registers:** fast memory locations inside the processor (or an I/O controller) that may be dedicated or general-purpose. *A small amount of fast storage which is part of the processor for calculating*

■ **Internal clock:** derived directly or indirectly from the system clock.

■ **Internal buses:** several internal buses link the control unit, the ALU and the registers.

■ **Logic gates:** used for flow control.

General-purpose and dedicated registers

Registers are very fast memory locations inside the processor. **General-purpose registers** (R0, R1, etc.) are available for the programmer to use in programs to store data temporarily. They have not been assigned a specific role by the processor designer. R1 is register store having address 1; do not confuse it with memory location having address 1. General-purpose registers are accessed with instructions such as LOAD, STORE and ADD. **Dedicated registers** are registers that have been assigned a specific role by the processor designer. They have names such as SP, PC, SR and ACC, MAR, MBR and CIR. Programmers may read or manipulate some but not all of these registers. Here are some dedicated registers:

Key terms

Register: a very fast memory location inside the processor or I/O controller.

General-purpose register: a register not assigned a specific role by the processor designer. Programmers may use general-purpose registers.

Dedicated register: a register assigned a specific role by the processor designer. Programmers may use some but not all dedicated registers.

■ **Stack pointer (SP):** points to a stack holding return addresses, procedure or function parameters, and local variables; it is accessed when a procedure or function is called or an interrupt is serviced.

■ **Program counter (PC):** points to the next instruction to be fetched and executed. *hold the memory address for the next instruction*

■ **Status register (SR):** holds condition codes to indicate the outcome of operations. For example, an arithmetic operation may produce a positive, negative, zero or overflow result, so a flag is set accordingly. Also status information, such as whether interrupts are enabled or disabled, is indicated in the status register.

■ **Accumulator (ACC):** holds the result of the current set of calculations, e.g. ADD #36 means add the number 36 to the current contents of the accumulator register and store the result in the accumulator.

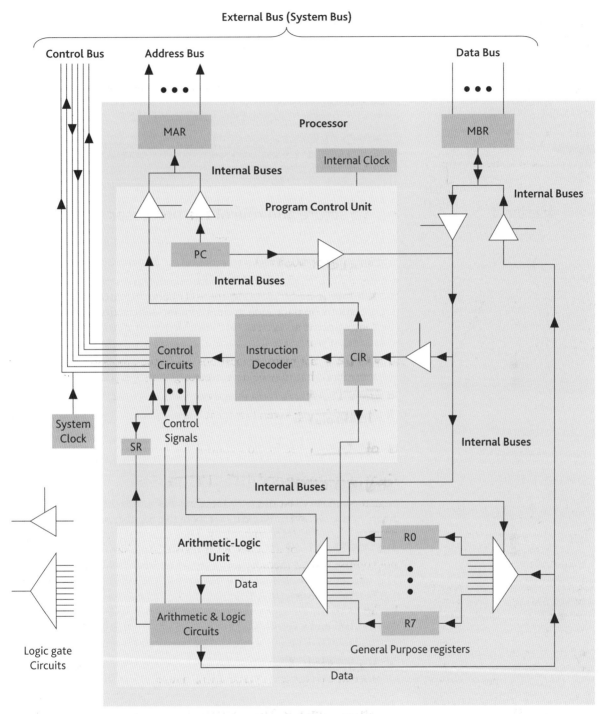

Fig. 7.2.6 *Simplified internal structure of a processor*

▓ **Current instruction register (CIR):** holds the current instruction to be executed while it is decoded and executed.

▓ **Memory address register (MAR):** holds the address of the memory location currently being accessed by the processor.

▓ **Memory buffer register (MBR):** holds the data item being transferred to or from the memory location currently being accessed by the processor.

▓ **Did you know?**

Edge-triggered D-type flip-flops are often used for registers. A D-type flip-flop is a kind of logic circuit designed to store one bit. It is too expensive to use D-type flip-flops for main memory, which has millions of locations.

System clock and clock speed

Every computer has its own system clock, a quartz-controlled oscillator that supplies a timing signal at a fixed rate. Other timing signals are derived from this oscillator. These timing signals are used to regulate the rate at which instructions are executed and to synchronise the operation of various computer components. Clock rates, frequencies or speed are expressed in megahertz (MHz) or gigahertz (GHz).

Processors are designed to execute instructions at a given frequency, e.g. 1 GHz. This is known as the **clock speed** or clock frequency of the processor. A processor executes a particular instruction in a fixed number of clock ticks, or clock cycles. Some instructions require more clock ticks than others. The system clock supplies the clock ticks that a processor requires to execute instructions. The system clock's frequency is raised to the rate that the processor requires by frequency-multiplying circuits. This is done inside the processor, so this clock is called an internal clock.

The operation of the system bus also requires clock ticks when a binary word is transferred between the processor and main memory or an I/O controller. Ideally, the tick rate of the bus should match the tick rate of the processor but often it is lower. Clock ticks derived from the system clock are supplied to the electronics of the system bus. Similarly, clock ticks are distributed to main memory to support its operation.

Computer clock speed has been doubling roughly every year. The Intel 8088, found in many computers around 1990, ran at 4.77 MHz. The 1 GHz mark was passed in 2000.

Word length

The language of the computer is binary. The computer works with binary words which are codes for instructions, memory addresses, characters, integer numbers, colours of pixels and digitised sound samples. Each binary word consists of binary digits. An example of a binary word is 10101111_2. The subscript 2 means that the pattern of 1s and 0s is a binary word. The **word length** is simply the number of digits in the word.

Bus width

Bus width refers to the number of signal wires or lines allocated to a bus. The signal on an individual line represents one binary digit, i.e. a 1 or a 0. Therefore, more wires mean more binary digits, e.g. six wires means a word of six binary digits such as 101010_2. Thus the word size or word length that can be accommodated on a bus increases with increasing bus width (Table 2). The number of binary digits in a word transferred over a bus is the same as the number of wires in the bus.

Table 2 *The effect of bus width on binary word size*

No. of wires in bus, n	No. of bits in a word on the bus	No. of different binary words, 2^n	No. of different binary words as a power of 2	Example of a binary word on the bus	The largest word counting in denary $2^n - 1$
1	1	2	2^1	1	1
2	2	4	2^2	10	3
3	3	8	2^3	101	7
4	4	16	2^4	1100	15
8	8	256	2^8	11110001	255
16	16	65,536	2^{16}	1101101111110000	65,535
20	20	1,048,576	2^{20}	......	1,048,575
24	24	16,777,216	2^{24}	......	16,777,215

Questions

10 Name three internal components of a processor.

11 What is meant by (a) register, (b) a general-purpose register and (c) a dedicated register?

12 Name two dedicated registers.

13 What is meant by (a) clock speed, (b) word length and (c) bus width?

14 How many signal wires make up an address bus that can address 2^{16} memory locations?

15 What is the largest denary number that can be transferred across a data bus with 16 wires?

16 A particular computer has 256 MB of RAM. How many bus wires are needed to address every byte of this memory?

Effect of clock speed, word length and bus width on performance

For a processor or microprocessor, performance means how quickly a task can be completed, all other things being equal. It can be measured approximately by running some standard programs on the processor and assessing how many machine operations are completed per unit time. The unit that is used is giga-ops per second (GOPS) or mega-ops per second (MOPS); here giga means 10^9 and mega means 10^6.

Increasing clock speed

All other things being equal, a processor with clock speed or frequency of 2 GHz should execute the same machine code program twice as fast as a processor from the same family with clock speed 1 GHz. This makes sense if we assume that each machine code instruction is executed in one clock cycle, or tick, in both processors. As the 2 GHz processor's clock cycle is half the duration of the 1 GHz processor's clock cycle, it will take half the time to execute an instruction. Fig. 7.2.7 shows how processor clock speed has increased since 1986.

Did you know?

A simple hand-held calculator operates at about 10 operations per second, because each calculation request to a typical calculator requires only a single operation and there is rarely any need for its response time to exceed the operator's response time of about 0.1 second. This gives one operation in 0.1 second.

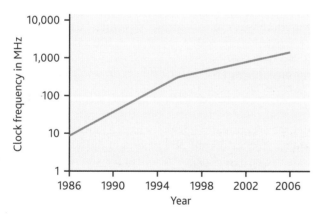

Fig. 7.2.7 *Increase in processor clock frequency since 1986*

Limits on clock speed

A limit has to be set on clock frequency, because the heat generated in the chip by higher clock frequencies cannot be removed quickly enough. The problem is made worse when more transistors are packed into the

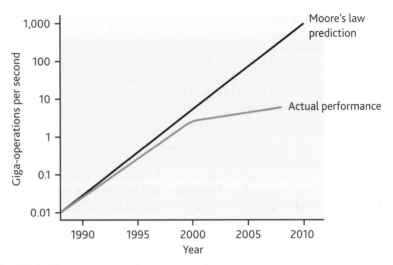

Fig. 7.2.8 *Microprocessor performance over time*

same space. Fig. 7.2.8 shows Moore's law as a performance curve for a single processor on a chip and the actual achieved performance.

The reason for the deviation from Moore's law is that packing more transistors into the same area increases the power consumption, which results in more heat. A similar consequence occurs when the clock frequency is increased. If transistor density and clock frequency continued to increase, it would eventually generate more heat per square centimetre than is generated on the surface of the sun.

Multicore microprocessors

The strategy now is to use the increase in transistor density to put more than one processor onto the microprocessor chip. These processors are called cores and operate at lower frequencies than single-core processors to overcome the heating problem caused by clock frequency. With more than one processor per chip, multiple tasks can be run at the same time or a single task can be split across several processors. Multicore processors are ideal for multimedia work. Microsoft Windows Movie Maker 2.0 and Adobe Photoshop CS are examples of widely used applications that show significant performance improvement on multicore systems.

Increasing word length

The word length of its registers affects the processor's speed performance. The registers that can do arithmetic operations – the general-purpose registers and the accumulator – usually have a similar word length. Typical word lengths are 32 bits and 64 bits in modern processors. The bigger the word length, the bigger the operands and results they can accommodate. When operands and results exceed the word length of the registers, extra processing must be done to split operands and results across several registers. This reduces speed performance.

Registers used to store the binary codes for main memory addresses affect the number of bytes or locations of main memory that can be used. A longer word means more binary codes and therefore more memory bytes that can be used, i.e. addressed. The main registers used for addressing main memory are the program counter and the memory address register.

> ### ▮ Key point
>
> To use a memory location, the address code must first be sent along the address bus then a binary signal must be sent along a control wire to assert a read or write operation. Next a word must be sent along the data bus.

> ### ▮ Key point
>
> An instruction comprises an operation code part and one or more operand code parts.

Increasing bus width

The worst time penalty occurs in the system bus between the processor and main memory. If the current instruction register's word length is not big enough to hold a complete instruction, the system bus must be used again to transfer one or more operand words into other registers, which slows down the performance of the processor.

The system bus is the bottleneck. The larger the data word or instruction word that can pass along its length in one go, the fewer the number of times it needs to be used. In a von Neumann computer, a data or instruction word passes over the data bus. A wider data bus should improve a computer's speed performance. Address words pass along the address bus. A wider address bus allows longer address words, so more memory can be addressed.

Questions

17 What is the effect on processor performance of increasing (a) clock speed, (b) word length and (c) bus width?

18 Why is there a limit on clock speed?

19 Why are microprocessors being designed with multiple cores?

In this topic you have covered:

- the three-box model consists of a processor, main memory and I/O connected by a system bus
- a system bus is made up of a data bus, an address bus and a control bus
- a system bus is a shared bus
- an I/O controller is the interface between the system bus and an I/O device. It contains I/O ports
- secondary storage is permanent storage, e.g. a magnetic disk
- peripherals are not part of the processor and main memory
- memory locations are uniquely identified by address codes
- in the stored program concept, a program must be resident in main memory to be executed
- a program is processed by fetching machine code instructions in sequence from main memory then decoding and executing them, one at a time, in the processor
- a processor consists of an ALU, a control unit and instruction decoder, registers, an internal clock, internal buses and logic gates
- a system clock provides timing signals so the system can run properly
- increasing the clock frequency or the word length increases the processor speed of operation
- increasing the address bus width allows more memory to be addressed
- increasing the data bus width increases the speed of operation.

7.3 Basic machine code operations and the fetch–execute cycle

Key terms

Machine code instruction: a binary code that a machine can understand and execute.

Compiled high-level language program: a program translated into machine code before it is executed on a digital computer.

Op-code: the part of a machine code instruction that denotes the basic machine operation, e.g. ADD.

Operand: the part of a machine code instruction that represents a single item of binary data or the address of a single item of binary data.

Machine code instructions

The language used by digital computers is binary, expressed as voltage levels. Typically, 5 volts is used for binary digit 1 and 0 volts is used for binary digit 0. A digital computer is instructed to carry out operations such as ADD with instructions coded in binary. These instructions are known as **machine code instructions**. An example of a machine code instruction that performs addition is

```
0001 0001 0000 1111
```

Expressed in assembly language, a mnemonic form of machine code, this machine code instruction is

```
ADD R1, #15
```

Compiled high-level language programs are translated into machine code before they are executed on a digital computer. The executable form of compiled high-level language programs is therefore in machine code. The processor decodes and executes the machine code instructions.

A machine code instruction consists of a number of binary digits, known as bits. A machine code instruction is typically 32 bits, subdivided into an operation code, or **op-code**, and an **operand** (Fig. 7.3.1).

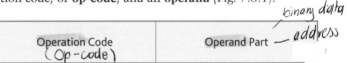

Operation Code (Op-code)	Operand Part — *address*

Fig. 7.3.1 *Typical format for machine code instructions*

The op-code denotes the basic machine operation, e.g. ADD. The operand, if present, represents one item of data or the address of one item of data. In fact, an operand can be further divided so that it represents not just one operand but several. We consider a simplified machine with one register for arithmetic, called the accumulator, and 16 bits for each machine code instruction. The operations ADD, LOAD and STORE all use the accumulator, so the accumulator does not need to be specified as it is always implied. Some machine code instructions are shown in Table 1 along with their more user-friendly mnemonics.

Table 1 *A section of a machine code program*

MC instruction: 16 bits	Mnemonic	Explanation
0001 0000 0000 0011	LOAD #3	Place 3 into the accumulator
1000 0000 0000 1101	STORE 13	Place a copy of the accumulator contents into the memory location with address 13
0001 0000 0000 0110	LOAD #6	Place 6 into the accumulator
0100 0000 0000 1101	ADD 13	Sum the contents of the accumulator and memory location 13; place the result into the accumulator
1000 0000 0000 1110	STORE 14	Place a copy of the accumulator contents into the memory location with address 14

Lists of binary numbers are hard for humans to comprehend, so assembly language was invented. Assembly language is a form of machine code that uses mnemonics for op-codes and register references. Data and addresses are expressed in decimal or hexadecimal in assembly language.

Table 2 shows how binary codes can be chosen for a simplified machine that uses 4 bits for the op-code.

Table 2 *Some op-codes and their meaning*

Op-code: 4 bits	Basic machine operation	Interpretation
0000	Load involving main memory	Load the accumulator register with a value fetched from the main memory location specified in operand part of the instruction
0001	Load involving operand part	Load the accumulator register with the value in the operand part of the instruction
0100	Add involving main memory	Add to the contents of the accumulator a value fetched from the main memory location specified in the operand part of the instruction
0101	Add involving operand part	Add to the contents of the accumulator the value in the operand part of the instruction
1000	Store involving main memory	Store the contents of the accumulator in the main memory location specified in the operand part of the instruction

The 12-bit operand can be interpreted in various ways: 0000 0000 1111 is 15 in decimal and may represent a value; 0000 1111 1111 is 255 in decimal and represents an address of a main memory location.

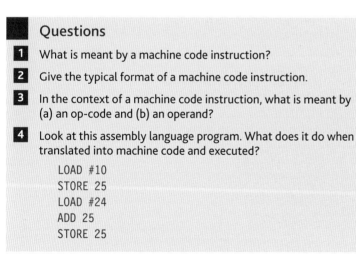

Questions

1 What is meant by a machine code instruction?

2 Give the typical format of a machine code instruction.

3 In the context of a machine code instruction, what is meant by (a) an op-code and (b) an operand?

4 Look at this assembly language program. What does it do when translated into machine code and executed?

```
LOAD #10
STORE 25
LOAD #24
ADD 25
STORE 25
```

Machine code representation in hexadecimal

People who have to work directly with machine code prefer to display it in hexadecimal. The hexadecimal form of a machine code program takes up less space than the binary form. Table 3 shows the hexadecimal equivalent of the program in Table 1. It is easier to work with, so that makes it less prone to errors. Op-codes are easier to recognise, which makes the hexadecimal form easier to understand than its machine code equivalent.

Table 3 *Machine code and its hexadecimal equivalent*

MC instruction	Hexadecimal
0001 0000 0000 0011	1003
1000 0000 0000 1101	800D
0001 0000 0000 0110	1006
0100 0000 0000 1101	400D
1000 0000 0000 1110	800E

(2ⁿᵃ)   (1ˢᵗ)

Table 4 *Memory dump*

Memory address	Memory contents
500	1003
501	800D
502	1006

People who write in low-level languages – assembly language or machine code – often get a memory dump of the area of main memory used by their programs when they go wrong. They look at the memory dump to discover the cause of the error. A memory dump is just a copy of the memory contents. Memory dumps are normally viewed in hexadecimal not binary as hexadecimal is easier on the eye. Table 4 shows a typical memory dump. The memory address is followed by the memory contents.

■ **Did you know?**

Intel's 32-bit x86 processors, first introduced in 1985, all have the same basic instruction set of over 100 basic machine operations. Intel's Itanium processor has a different instruction set; it supports extended parallel instruction computing (EPIC). Besides the operation to be executed, an EPIC instruction contains information about how to execute that operation in parallel with others.

■ **Questions**

5 Translate the following machine code instructions into their hexadecimal equivalents: 1000 0101 1100 0011 and 0101 1111 0111 1100.

6 Give two reasons for translating machine code instructions into hexadecimal.

■ **Key terms**

Instruction set: the set of bit patterns or binary codes for the machine operations that a processor has been designed to perform.

💡 **Instruction sets**

The code in Table 2 reserves 4 bits for the op-code part. Sixteen different codes can be coded in 4 bits. This means the codes can represent 16 different machine operations; some are shown in Table 2. These 16 different operations are called an **instruction set**.

A processor is designed to understand and execute a particular instruction set. If a designer requires a processor to have 64 different operations, the format of a machine code instruction must use 6 bits for the op-code part because $2^6 = 64$. An op-code can be subdivided into a part that denotes the basic operation, e.g. ADD, and a part called the addressing mode that denotes how the operands should be interpreted. Table 5 shows some general addressing modes and Fig. 7.3.2 shows some possible codes for them.

Table 5 *Some addressing modes*

General addressing mode	Explanation
Register transfer involving main memory	The main memory address is specified in the operand part
Operand to register transfer	A value is specified in the operand part
Operand part not used	Some instructions do not require an operand; an example is HALT, which halts an executing program

Op-code	
Operation	Addressing Mode
00	00
01	01
10	10
11	11

Fig. 7.3.2 *Op-code: some possible codes for operation and addressing mode*

Fetch–execute cycle

Instructions are fetched one at a time from main memory, decoded and executed. Fig. 7.3.3 shows an instruction being fetched, decoded and executed. The result is that the operand part of the instruction is added to the current contents of the accumulator register, overwriting the accumulator contents. A stored program computer is designed to repeat the sequence fetch, decode and execute in a cycle called the fetch–execute cycle. The following registers are always involved in this cycle:

- The program counter (PC) points to the next instruction to be fetched and executed.
- The memory address register (MAR) holds the address of the currently addressed memory location.
- The memory buffer register (MBR), also known as the memory data register (MDR), holds the code read from the currently addressed memory location.
- The current instruction register (CIR), often just IR, holds the most recently fetched machine code instruction.

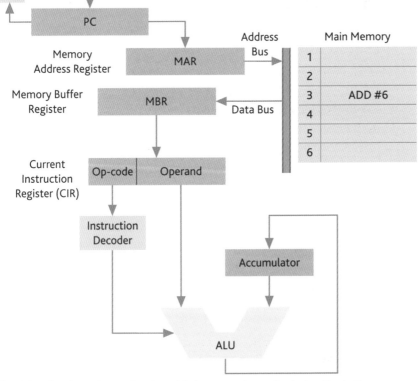

Fig. 7.3.3 *Tracing an instruction that adds the operand part of an instruction to the accumulator*

The fetch–execute cycle can be broken into steps that are synchronised by the system clock and controlled by the control unit. The fetch phase has four steps:

1 The address of the next instruction to be executed, held in the PC, is copied to the MAR.

2 The instruction held at that address is placed in the MBR.

3 Simultaneously, the contents of the PC are incremented by 1 to get ready for the next instruction.

4 The contents of the MBR are copied to the CIR. This frees up the MBR for the execute phase.

The execute phase has two steps:

1 The instruction held in the CIR is decoded.

2 The instruction is executed.

In register transfer notation the fetch–execute cycle is described as follows:

the contents of (handwritten annotation)

$$MAR \leftarrow [PC]$$

$$PC \leftarrow [PC] + 1; MBR \leftarrow [Memory]_{addressed}$$

$$CIR \leftarrow [MBR]$$

$$[CIR] \text{ decoded and executed}$$

where [PC] means the contents of PC, MAR← means assigned to MAR and $x; y$ means operation x and operation y are executed at the same time.

Questions

10 Name three registers that are essential to the fetch–execute cycle.

11 Explain the role of the essential registers in the fetch–execute cycle.

12 Describe the fetch–execute cycle (a) in your own words and (b) in register transfer notation.

13 Describe with the aid of a diagram the execution of the machine code instruction ADD #23.

☑ *In this topic you have covered:*

- machine code instructions are binary codes that a machine can understand and execute

- compiled high-level languages are translated into machine code

- a machine code instruction consists of an op-code and zero or more operands

- the op-code denotes the basic machine operation, e.g. ADD

- the operand represents a single item of binary data or its address

- the mnemonic form of a machine code instruction is often used. It is called assembly language

- a fixed number of bits is allocated to op-code; this fixes the number of basic machine operations the processor supports

- people find it easier and less error-prone to work with machine code in hexadecimal form

- a processor's instruction set is the set of machine operations it is designed to perform

- in the fetch–execute cycle, instructions are fetched one at a time, decoded and executed

- the essential registers involved in the fetch–execute cycle are the PC, MAR, MBR and CIR.

8 Computer systems

8.1 Hardware devices

💡 Input methods and devices

Mouse

In 1964 the first prototype computer mouse was made by Douglas Engelbart using a wooden shell with two metal wheels. Engelbart had made the mouse for his graphical user interface (GUI) called 'windows'. In 1970 Engelbart received US Patent 3,541,541 for the wooden shell with two metal wheels; the patent application described it as an 'X-Y position indicator for a display system'. Engelbart said, 'It was nicknamed the mouse because the tail came out the end.' Today the mouse is indispensable. It still works by detecting the movement in two axes, X and Y, of a hand-held mouse or, in the case of a trackpad or touchpad, a finger moving over the pad. The mouse also has two or three buttons – left, right and middle – to click on a component and control the GUI. The wireless mouse communicates by a wireless signal instead of down a wire.

Keyboard

The standard computer keyboard is used to enter text into a computer system. The electronic components in the keyboard continually scan the rows of keys to detect the pressing of a key or key combination. They identify which key/key combination has been pressed and send the key's scan code to the computer. Software in the computer interprets the scan code and converts it into an ASCII code or Unicode code.

Bar code reader

A bar code reader, or bar code scanner, is an electronic device for reading bar codes printed on items such as cans, cardboard and plastic packaging, and the covers of books or magazines. A bar code is a sequence of white and black bars (Fig. 8.1.1) that encodes information such as a product identifier. The product identifier is usually printed in human-readable form beneath the bar code.

198-11926167-2420-4

Fig. 8.1.1 *Bar code*

A bar code reader consists of a light source, a lens, photoelectric detectors (photodiodes) and decoder circuitry to analyse the bar code's image data and generate character codes. The scanner uses the light source to illuminate the black and white bands. More light is reflected from a white band than from a dark band. The pattern of reflection is converted from optical form to electrical form by photoelectric detectors in the bar code reader. The electrical form of the reflection data is analysed and the bar code is decoded into character form. The scanner outputs the character codes, e.g. ASCII codes, as a sequence of binary digits for processing by a computer.

Scanners

In computing, a scanner is a device that captures an electrical equivalent of a picture, printed text, handwriting or a solid object such as an ornament. It produces a digital representation suitable for storing in a computer system.

Flatbed scanner

A flatbed scanner usually has a glass pane, or platen, illuminated from beneath by a bright light, often xenon or cold-cathode fluorescent. An array of light-detecting sensors spanning the width of the glass pane is moved slowly with the light source along the length of the glass pane to pick up light reflected from anything placed on top of the pane. The reflected light is converted into an equivalent electrical signal. Colour scanners typically contain three rows, or arrays, of sensors with red, green and blue filters that measure the intensity of the primary colours in the reflected light. A digitised image of the entire scanned area is created; it can be stored and processed by the computer attached to the scanner.

An item to be scanned is placed face down on the glass, an opaque cover is lowered over it to exclude ambient light, and the sensor array and light source move across the pane to read the intensity of the reflected light from the entire area.

Fingerprint scanner

A fingerprint reader is a security device that takes a 'picture' of a finger so that the pattern of ridges and valleys in the image can be analysed. It consists of a sensor and decoder circuitry to analyse the captured image data and output it in electrical form for processing by computer against stored fingerprint data. Some fingerprint scanners are optical devices that use light sensors; others use electrical currents to map the skin contours of a finger. Fingerprint readers that attach to the USB or PCMIA port of a PC are now used in place of passwords to authenticate user logins.

Retina scanner

A retina scanner consists of a low-energy infrared light source that is directed onto the retina of the eye. Photoelectric detectors convert the reflected light into an electrical signal and decoding circuitry outputs an encoded form of the retinal pattern for storage or comparison by a computer. Each person's retina is unique and remains virtually unchanged from birth to death. The blood vessels in the retina absorb light more readily than the surrounding tissue.

Iris scanner

The iris is a flat, circular, coloured membrane suspended vertically in the aqueous humour of the eye. An iris scanner uses a camera sensitive to infrared light and placed no more than 3 ft (0.9 m) from the subject to capture an image of their iris and store it electronically. A complex algorithm is applied to the electronic image to create a code of typically 512 bytes. This code is then compared with a database of iris codes to see if there is a match. There is sufficient random variation in iris pattern in the general population for iris recognition to identify a person reliably.

Optical mark reader

An optical mark reader optically senses marks placed in predefined positions on a form (Fig. 8.1.2). The form is passed under a light source and the intensity of reflected light from each row of the form is measured and converted by photoelectric sensors into an electrical equivalent. Pencil marks do not reflect as much light as the background colour of the form and this is used to detect the presence of the marks. Registration marks placed at regular fixed positions along the edge of the form enable the rows to be identified. Optical mark recognition is used for processing multiple-choice answer grids, national lottery tickets and some customer response forms.

National Lottery Entry Form

Which draw?	– 1 –	– 2 –	– 3 –	– 4 –	– 5 –
Wed – –	– 6 –	– 7 –	– 8 –	– 9 –	– 10 –
	– 11 –	– 12 –	– 13 –	– 14 –	– 15 –
Sat – –	– 16 –	– 17 –	– 18 –	– 19 –	– 20 –
	– 21 –	– 22 –	– 23 –	– 24 –	– 25 –
Both – –	– 26 –	– 27 –	– 28 –	– 29 –	– 30 –
	– 31 –	– 32 –	– 33 –	– 34 –	– 35 –
	– 36 –	– 37 –	– 38 –	– 39 –	– 40 –
	– 41 –	– 42 –	– 43 –	– 44 –	– 45 –
	– 46 –	– 47 –	– 48 –	– 49 –	

Fig. 8.1.2 *A form designed for optical mark recognition*

Optical character reader

All optical character recognition (OCR) systems use an optical scanner to input images of text then analyse the resulting digital images to recognise the characters. Some forms, such as gas bills, are preprinted with the relevant customer details in a special font that is good for OCR (Fig. 8.1.3). Then they can be processed automatically when they are returned by the customer.

OCR systems are used to automate postal sorting. They capture an image of the address on the envelope, extract the postcode then print the postcode in a machine-readable code of phosphor dots. The phosphor dots are used in the rest of the automatic sorting process. It takes a fraction of a second as the letter passes through the machine.

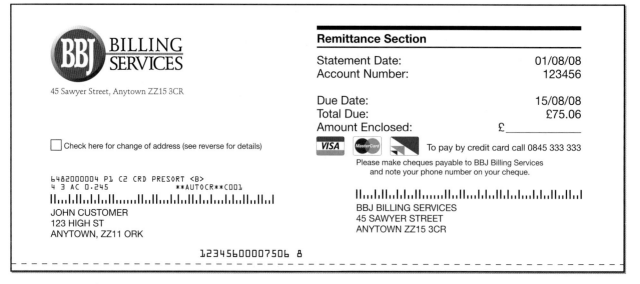

Fig. 8.1.3 *OCR billing form preprinted in a machine-readable font*

Magnetic stripe reader

Magnetic stripe readers read information encoded magnetically in a stripe on the back of a plastic or cardboard card about 8.5 cm × 6.5 cm (Fig. 8.1.4). The stripe on the back of the card is composed of magnetic particles encased in tape made of plastic. The orientation of the particles in the stripe is used to encode binary data. Most stripes can store up to 2 KB of information. They are used in applications such as credit and debit cards, library membership cards, railway tickets, bus tickets, phone cards and hotel keys. They have to be slowly and steadily swiped through the magnetic stripe reader to induce a current in the reader. Magnetic stripe cards are gradually being replaced by smart cards.

Magnetic stripe

Signature:

Dingley Dell Town Lending Library Borrower's card

Fig. 8.1.4 *Magnetic stripe on a library card*

Smart card reader

A smart card is a plastic card the size of a credit card that holds an integrated circuit chip. The chip contains a microprocessor, a small amount of ROM, a small amount of EEPROM, a small amount of RAM and a computer bus system. The smart card reader provides power when the smart card is inserted into the reader. Applications are stored in ROM and EEPROM. The EEPROM is mainly used to store persistent data and the RAM is used as a scratch pad for temporary data when the stored applications are executed. The microprocessor executes the stored applications. Smart cards are used in many applications, such as credit and debit cards, mobile phone cards, railway tickets such as the Oyster card (see also p168) and electronic cash. Smart cards have enough processing power to encrypt and decrypt data, so they are used in transactions that require a degree of security against fraud.

Fig. 8.1.5 shows a Mondex smart card supplied to students at Exeter University. It is used to store a digital representation of cash, access codes to buildings on the campus, the university enrolment number and data required for sitting exams. To pay by Mondex in shops on the university campus, the card is inserted into the shop's smart card reader. The smart card reader reduces the amount of electronic cash recorded on the card and increases the amount stored in the shop's smart card. The shop connects to a Mondex bank at the end of the day to upload the electronic cash to its Mondex account. The Mondex card was developed jointly by British Telecom, National Westminster Bank and Midland Bank, which is now HSBC. It was first piloted in Swindon, Wiltshire.

Fig. 8.1.5 *A smart card used for electronic cash, identification and access to premises*

RFID reader

Radio frequency identification (RFID) uses radio frequencies (RF) to transmit data, a timing signal and energy between a reader and an RFID device (Fig. 8.1.6). RFID devices do not need a physical electrical contact to transfer data. An RFID system has a transponder and a reader. The transponder is located on the object to be identified. The reader, or interrogator, may be able to read data or to read and write data, but it is always called a reader.

The RFID transponder can be powered by RF energy from the reader or it may use an internal battery. It has a small RF antenna and circuitry for

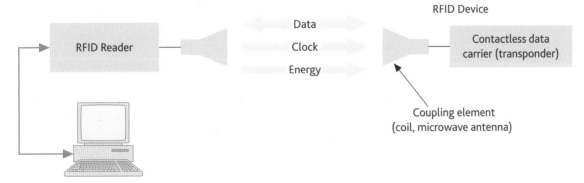

Fig. 8.1.6 *RFID reader and transponder*

transmitting and receiving data. The data capacity of RFID transponders is normally a few bytes to several kilobytes, but a transponder with a data capacity of just 1 bit can distinguish between transponder present and transponder not present. Most 1-bit transponders are used in electronic article surveillance (EAS) systems to protect goods in shops and businesses. They are removed or deactivated at the till when the goods are paid for. A reader installed at the shop's exit raises an alarm if goods are removed before the transponder has been deactivated.

RFID smart cards, such as Transport for London's Oyster card, are used as tickets for short journeys on public transport. RFID devices are attached to products to respond with the product's serial number when interrogated. They can be used as contactless security badges to give access to protected premises. Electronic immobilisers for cars use RFID; the ignition key is combined with a transponder. An RFID device placed under an animal's skin can be used for tracking and identification. RFID devices are put in the stomach of cattle and remain there for life.

Touch-sensitive screen

A touch-sensitive screen is a type of visual display unit that allows a user to interact with an application. The user touches regions of the screen associated with the application. In one arrangement, the screen has been specially adapted so that the region just in front of the screen is criss-crossed by horizontal and vertical beams of infrared light, invisible to the naked eye. The breaking of these beams by a finger or other passive pointing object, e.g. a pencil, is detected at the receiving end of each beam by a series of photoelectric sensors, one per beam. An electronic circuit connected to these sensors correlates broken horizontal and vertical beams and tells the computer the coordinates. The executing application then maps the coordinates to an action.

Graphics tablet

A graphics tablet allows graphics to be drawn into a computer by hand rather like drawing with pencil and paper. A flat board, the tablet, is connected to the computer. A wired or wireless pen device, called the stylus, is moved across the surface of the tablet. Pressing the tip of the stylus against the surface operates a microswitch, which causes the movement to be recorded by the computer. The stylus may also be used as a pointing device to select commands by pointing and clicking on an area of the tablet. These commands may be operating system commands or application commands such as drawing commands in a drawing package. The board contains electronics to detect the position of the stylus tip. A graphics tablet is used with a drawing package to create line drawings.

In a variation on the graphics tablet, the stylus is replaced by a puck with control buttons and a lens containing cross hairs. The puck is moved across the surface and aligned with a line drawing using the cross hairs. The left or right button is then pressed to record the position of the cross hairs. The graphics tablet may be used to digitise line drawings. The tablet contains electronics to detect the position of the cross hairs.

Voice recognition

A computer can be trained to recognise a person's voice and to turn speech into text using a microphone, sound card and appropriate software. This system can be used to issue commands to the computer and to dictate sentences directly into applications.

Digital still camera

A digital camera is an electronic device used to capture and store photographs digitally on a memory card before uploading to a computer via a USB connection. Typical compact digital cameras are multifunctional and some can record sound and video as well as photographs. All use either a charge-coupled device (CCD) or a CMOS image sensor to sense the light intensities across the focal plane.

Questions

1. Name four input devices other than mouse and keyboard.
2. Explain the operation of a bar code scanner.
3. Explain the operation of a flatbed scanner.
4. Explain the operation of an RFID reader.
5. Explain the operation of a touch-sensitive screen.

Output methods and devices

Visual display unit

Computers require some form of visual display unit (VDU) or monitor to show entered data and the results of processing.

Cathode-ray tube

A cathode-ray tube (CRT) is a vacuum tube with a narrow neck and a flat rectangular base. The screen is coated on the inside with a phosphor that emits light when struck by an electron beam. The neck is surrounded by electromagnets and inside the neck is an electron gun. In a raster-driven VDU, the electron beam produced by the electron gun in the neck is dragged across the screen a line at a time so it covers every horizontal line of the screen, starting at the top of the screen and finishing at the bottom. This action is repeated many times per second so the displayed image does not flicker noticeably. The retinal image from each phosphor dot persists in the human brain for about 0.05 second. As long as the whole screen is swept in a shorter time than 0.05 second, the sensation of flicker is avoided.

Colour CRT VDUs use three independent electron guns: a red gun, a green gun and a blue gun. The screen is made up of lines of phosphor dots arranged in triplets and each triplet consists of one red phosphor, one green phosphor and one blue phosphor. Three independent electron beams are arranged to strike their corresponding phosphor in each triplet. The effect produced in the eye is a combination of the received intensities of red, green and blue light. The eye additively mixes these primary colours to produce the colour. The three electron beams are dragged across the screen to produce a colour image.

Flat screen

Liquid crystals can change the polarisation state of light when an electric field is applied to them. They can be used with a light source and polarising filters, similar to Polaroid sunglasses, to control the amount of light that reaches a screen. A liquid crystal display (LCD) flat screen is a matrix of liquid crystal cells and each cell constitutes one pixel when the screen is used at full resolution. For colour displays, each pixel is divided into three or four subpixels covered with colour filters for additive mixing of red, green and blue. Four-subpixel arrangements have a neutral greyscale pixel to improve brightness control.

Some flat screen LCD displays are made using tiny thin film transistors (TFTs). Each pixel consists of a TFT, a capacitor and the liquid crystal. The transistor acts as a switch and the capacitor as a reservoir for the electrical charge needed to create the electric field that changes the polarisation of the light passing through the liquid crystal. The capacitor can hold the charge until the next refresh cycle. Unlike CRT monitors, LCD flat screens display information well only at the resolution for which they are designed, known as the native resolution.

Besides a thinner display, flat screens have lower power consumption, normally 30 per cent lower, and eliminate the electrical spikes associated with CRTs. LCD screens do not need to be redrawn to remain visible, so there is no flicker. Screen geometry is always perfect as there is no projection system, unlike with CRT monitors, which can lead to distortion, especially at the screen's corners.

Plasma screen

Plasma screens are ideal for large displays. Each pixel is controlled by a miniature fluorescent light. When the control voltage is applied, the gas becomes plasma and releases ultraviolet light, which strikes phosphors on the front of the screen to emit visible light. Unlike LCD screens, plasma screens have a wide viewing angle and produce colours similar to conventional CRTs. Plasma screens have traditionally suffered from low contrast caused by the need to apply a constant low voltage to each pixel. Without this priming, plasma cells would suffer from poor response times similar to fluorescent light bulbs. One consequence is that pixels in the off state still emit some light, which reduces contrast. The greatest limitation of plasma screens is pixel size, typically 0.81 mm. This is unsuitable for smaller monitors viewed at close range because the pixels are too blocky. Plasma screens generate a lot of heat, enough to injure people that touch them.

Speech output

Words in electronic documents can be output as spoken words using specialist speech synthesis software, a sound card and speakers.

Electronic paper

E Ink and Xerox are two US companies that have developed flexible, paper-thin displays which create images using tiny coloured beads that move or rotate in response to an electric field. An electrically charged pencil can be used to write on the display, and it can be fed through a device that erases the image and writes a new page.

Impact printer

Impact printers are used in applications that require multi-part stationery or printing through carbonised envelopes, perhaps to print payslips or credit card PINs sent by a bank to a customer. Impact printers use an inked ribbon to mark paper with an impression of a character. In a dot-matrix printer, the ribbon is struck hard by up to 24 metal pins that form the outline of the character. It is this action that marks the paper. Dot-matrix printers are very noisy.

In an application that prints to multi-part stationery, the stationery consists of several layers of paper and each layer except the bottom layer is carbonised on the reverse side so that the marks made on the top copy appear on all the copies beneath. Multi-part stationery is used when multiple copies of an invoice or receipt are required, one for the customer, one for the local office and one for headquarters.

In an application printing payslips or PINs, the ribbon is removed so that the pins hit the outside of a sealed envelope containing a slip of paper. The inside of the envelope is carbonised and acts just like carbon paper. When the pins hit the envelope, the carbon makes marks on paper inside the envelope.

Non-impact printer

Inkjet printer

Non-impact printers transfer ink to paper using electrostatics or some other non-impact technique. Inkjet printers can print high-quality text, graphics and photographic images in colour. An inkjet printer produces coloured output by printing a line of colour at a time. Printing a line of characters involves printing several lines of colour before the whole line of characters emerges.

Colour inkjet printers use four cartridges containing cyan, magenta, yellow and black (CMYK) ink. Printed colours are produced by subtractive mixing, whereas VDU colours are produced by additive mixing. Cyan is a mixture of blue and green, magenta is a mixture of red and blue, and yellow is a mixture of red and green. When layered on top of each other and viewed in white light, the white light passing through the ink pigments is reflected back to the eye. To produce a blue image, cyan must be combined with magenta. The red component in the white light is absorbed by the cyan and the green component is absorbed by the magenta; this leaves the blue component, which is seen by the eye.

A mixture of all three pigments absorbs nearly all visible colours, appearing nearly black but not black enough for quality printing. That is why a fourth cartridge is filled with black pigment. It is used for black and white printing and for printing black in coloured images. Inkjet printers can be slow when printing in the highest resolution and the ink can smudge. For the very best quality, special paper is required. Cartridges for colour inkjet printers are still relatively expensive.

Laser printer

A laser printer prints a whole page at a time. It prints high-quality text and graphics on plain paper. A page description language usually describes the page to be printed as lines, arcs and polygons. A processor in the laser printer generates a bitmap of the page in raster memory from the page description. A negative charge is applied to the photosensitive drum at the heart of the laser printer. One or more laser beams are directed onto the rotating drum's surface. The lasers are turned on or off at positions determined by the bitmap data stored in the raster memory. This causes the negative charge to be neutralised or reversed at positions corresponding to the black parts of the page to be printed.

The resulting pattern of charges on the drum's surface is an image of the page to be printed. The charged surface of the drum is exposed to toner, fine particles of dry plastic powder mixed with carbon black or colouring agents. The charged toner particles are given a negative charge so they attach to the uncharged or positively charged regions of the drum and not to the negatively charged regions. Darker areas are achieved by depositing thicker layers of toner. A higher voltage applied to the gap between toner cartridge and drum surface forces more toner onto the drum.

The raster memory stores the greyscale data for each area of the page and this is used to set the appropriate voltage level. By rolling and pressing the rotating drum over a sheet of paper, the toner is transferred onto the paper. Transfer may be assisted by using a positively charged transfer roller on the back of the paper to pull the toner from the surface of the drum to the paper. The paper is passed through heated rollers that squeeze the paper and fuse the toner to the paper.

Bitmap and TrueType fonts

Computers represent characters as numeric codes in ASCII, Unicode, etc. The shape of a character depends on its font. Fig. 8.1.7 shows the character A in the font Book Antiqua. A character font may be printed by bitmap or from a description of its straight lines and curves. Bitmap fonts become blocky when they are scaled.

TrueType and PostScript fonts use the descriptive method. This method allows character fonts to be scaled accurately because the computer uses the geometric description of the font to simply draw an outline shape at a specific size, and then fills it with ink to create the character. The ability to scale to any size means that TrueType fonts are independent of the resolution of the screen or printer.

Fig. 8.1.7 *The letter A in font Book Antiqua*

Plotter

A plotter is an output device that moves a pen across paper in a continuous movement so that a two-dimensional drawing can be made. The pen is lifted when not drawing on the paper and lowered to draw on the paper. Pens of different colours are parked in holders on one side of the plotter and may be picked up or parked by the drawing arm under program control. For high-quality work, special drawing paper is used to reduce ink spreading or bleeding over the paper's surface. In a flatbed plotter, the paper is placed flat on a platen. The pen may move in the X direction and the Y direction at the same time.

In a drum plotter, a roll of paper at least 1 m wide is fed over a drum so the perforated edges of the paper engage with sprockets on the drum. The paper can be rolled forwards and backwards over the drum under program control. The pen is located above the paper and constrained to move the length of the drum in a straight line in both directions. To draw a circle, the paper and the pen must be moved back and forth. A drum plotter can be used to produce engineering drawings at a very large scale.

Questions

6   Explain the operation of an LCD TFT flat screen.

7   Give two reasons why dot-matrix printers are still used.

8   Explain the operation of a black and white laser printer.

9   What output device would be used to produce large engineering drawings?

💡 Secondary storage devices

To avoid having to re-enter data and programs every time some processing is required, storage devices keep permanent copies of data and programs in a form that can be readily accessed in a computer system.

Magnetic media

💡 *Hard disk*

IBM developed magnetic disk drives in the late 1950s. The disk drive allows rapid random (direct) access to large amounts of data. All disk drives use a thin circular platter made of non-ferrous metal or plastic and rotate it at up to 10,000 revolutions per minute beneath a read–write head that moves radially across the surface of the platter. Fig. 8.1.8 shows the basic design.

> ### ■ Did you know?
> IBM obtained the technology for making magnetic disks from Manchester University where a one kilobyte magnetic disk had been made on a one metre-wide platter.

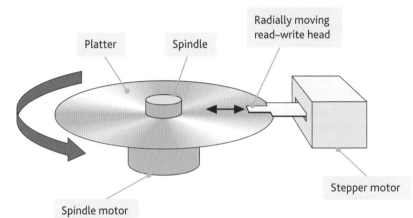

Fig. 8.1.8 *Magnetic disk drive*

The platter is coated with an emulsion of iron or cobalt oxide particles that act as tiny magnets. Binary data is recorded by aligning these tiny magnets in one direction to represent a binary 0 and in the opposite direction to represent a binary 1. Binary data is recorded in concentric rings, or **tracks**, subdivided into **sectors** that hold a fixed number of bytes, such as 512 (Fig. 8.1.9 on p174). A hard disk can store and retrieve a large volume of data.

To read data stored on the hard disk, the read–write head is moved to the desired track and waits for the relevant sector to pass beneath it. When data is passed from the hard disk to the computer and vice versa, a whole sector is read or written each time. A disk sector is often called a **disk block** or a block.

The top and bottom surfaces of a platter may be used to store data. A block address for a single-platter system is composed of a surface address, a track address and a sector address. Typically, the surfaces are numbered 0 and 1, the tracks 0 to 7,000 and the sectors 0 to 63.

Modern hard disks for a PC system are sealed units, called Winchester disks, containing several platters mounted on a common spindle. The platters are sealed inside an assembly which allows the disk to operate with minimal risk of damage from contaminants. The read–write heads are built into the assembly. The greater the number of platters, the greater the storage capacity.

> ### ■ Key terms
> **Track:** one of the concentric rings on a platter of a hard disk.
>
> **Sector:** a subdivision of a track.
>
> **Disk block:** the smallest unit of transfer between a computer and a disk; a disk sector.

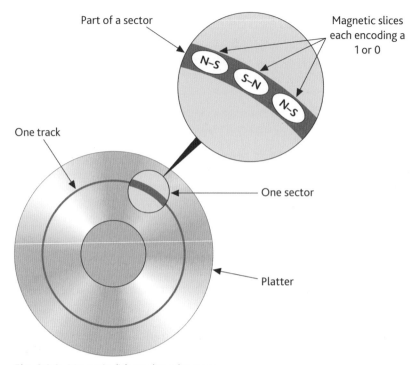

Fig. 8.1.9 *Magnetic disk: tracks and sectors*

Magnetic tape

Early computers needed a cheap way to store large quantities of data. In 1927 in Germany, Fritz Pfleumer developed a way of recording speech onto plastic tape coated with a magnetic oxide. AEG acquired the commercial development rights to Pfleumer's ideas in 1932 and, with BASF's help on plastic film technology, it produced a modern reel-to-reel tape recorder in 1935. Magnetic tape readers and writers based on the reel-to-reel tape recorder were included in the early computers of the 1950s as they were more reliable than earlier paper tape systems. They persisted until the early 1990s.

Magnetic tape consists of a thin ribbon of plastic. The tape is coated on one side with a material that can be magnetised to record the bit patterns that represent data. Open-reel tape systems have given way to data cartridge and cassette closed systems in which the tape is wound around one or two reels inside the cartridge or cassette. The cartridge is completely sealed except for an access door to put the tape in contact with the recording heads in the tape drive. A mechanism moves the tape between the supply and take-up reels. The cartridge technologies in general use are digital linear tape (DLT) and digital audio tape (DAT). Capacities range from 10 GB up to 800 GB and data transfer speeds range from 200 KB per second to 20 MB per second.

Magnetic tape is robust, so it can be used to transfer large amounts of data from one system to another. Data can only be written or read serially. Finding a particular item of data on a magnetic tape can take a long time, because the tape has to be searched from the beginning and items have to be read in the order they were written. Nevertheless, it is a cost-effective way to store data that does not have to be accessed immediately. Today much smaller, sealed versions of the early reel-to-reel devices are used for backup and archiving.

Did you know?

Backing up data means taking a copy of data and storing it somewhere safe, e.g. in a fireproof safe or off-site. Archiving data means removing it from the online storage medium, usually to free up space. Data qualifies for archiving if it has not been accessed recently and will not be accessed regularly in the future. Programs and data may be backed up and archived.

Optical media

The earliest commercial optical discs were plastic read-only discs that stored television programmes. Introduced in 1978 as consumer products, they were based on a standard called LaserVision and stored up to an hour of broadcast-quality video on each side of the 12 inch (30 cm) disc.

LaserVision records the video image as a frequency modulated (FM) signal on a tight spiral track that makes 54,000 turns in covering a disc surface. The turns of the spiral are 1.6 μm apart (1 μm = 10^{-6} m), corresponding to a track density of almost 16,000 tracks per inch (630 tracks per millimetre). The FM signal is recorded by making pits or trenches in the disc's surface; a pit is a physical depression.

Because of their high storage capacity and easy interchangeability, people wondered whether LaserVision discs could store digital data. Sony produced its Compact Disc, a read-only optical audio disc on which audio information was encoded digitally. Compact discs (CDs) store up to 74 minutes of very high quality audio on one surface of a 120 mm plastic disc; they can be considered as miniature versions of LaserVision discs.

CD-ROM

The success of CDs led to a new format, CD read-only memory (CD-ROM). Introduced early in 1985, this format was initially used to publish encyclopedias, reference works, professional directories and other large databases. CD-ROMs were ideal for this because they had a high storage capacity of 600–700 MB, offered fast data access and were portable, rugged and read-only. Today's CD-ROMs are also used for software distribution.

The data is written on the discs using disc-mastering machinery that impresses pits into a continuous spiral track. The silvery data surface contains pits in a single track 3.5 miles (5.6 km) long. The disc spins at

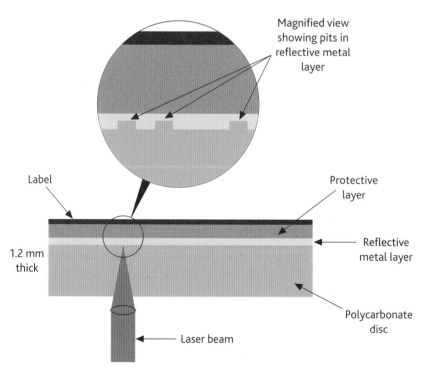

Fig. 8.1.10 *CD-ROM: cross-section through its layers*

200–500 revolutions per minute depending on which radius is being read. A data bit is read by focusing a laser beam onto a point in the reflective metal layer where the pits are impressed (Fig. 8.1.10).

CD-R

Commercial write once, read many (WORM) times optical disc drives emerged in 1983. The first generation of optical disc drives used 12-inch (30 cm) discs that stored about 1,000 MB per surface. The discs can be written only once. Any region can be written on but then it cannot be altered. Data bits are recorded by burning a pit in a thin film of metal using a high-power laser. A laser with a much lower power is used to read the data bits. Their first use was in systems that store document images.

Today CD-Recordable (CD-R) discs that support WORM operation are readily available in the standard size of 120 mm; they are also known as writable CDs. They can record about 600–700 MB of data or 74 minutes of music. The recording beam creates a spot of less reflective disc by inducing a chemical reaction between a reflective gold layer and its dye coating.

CD-RW

A CD-Rewritable (CD-RW) or CD-Erasable (CD-E) disc can be read and written to over and over again. CD-RW drives have a magnet and a laser. The laser is similar to the laser in a CD-ROM drive. The write operation uses the magnet and the laser. The read operation uses only the laser. The data tracks are arranged in sectors. To record or change data, the laser heats a precise spot on the disc to a temperature of 200 °C. The magnet is then used to set the state of the data bit at this spot. The disc cools and fixes the data bit.

The data is fixed regardless of any external magnetic fields, which makes the data far more secure than in traditional magnetic media, where the data can easily be affected by a small magnet. CD-RW drives can keep their read–write heads a safe distance from the disc surface, so they do not suffer the head crashes and wear problems of floppy disk drives. When the laser reads the disc, it uses much less power to avoid heating the disc. The laser light is polarised as it reflects off the surface and the degree of polarisation indicates the value of the data bit.

DVD-ROM

Digital versatile disc or digital video disc (DVD) is an optical standard that offers much greater storage capacity than CDs. CDs and DVDs store data in the form of microscopic pits that represent binary ones and zeros. On a CD the minimum length of a pit is $0.834\ \mu m$; on a DVD it is $0.4\ \mu m$. This lets the disc-mastering machinery squeeze the pits more closely together. On a DVD the data track's spiral spacing is $0.74\ \mu m$, whereas on a CD it is $1.6\ \mu m$.

To read the smaller pits, DVD drives use a laser with a shorter wavelength. The red laser diodes used in DVD drives are identical to those in bar code readers. Reducing the pit size and track separation increases the disc's capacity by a factor of about 7: 4.7 GB for a DVD compared with 682 MB for a CD. Some manufacturers have two layers and use both sides, which further increases the capacity of DVDs. It is possible to store several hours of full-motion video on a single-sided disc.

DVD-R

DVD-R is a WORM format similar to CD-R. It replaces the data layer of read-only polycarbonate with an organic dye. DVD-R drives record data by burning spots in the dye to alter the amount of laser light reflected. The discs have a capacity of 4.7 GB. DVD-R discs may be used for archiving data. The archival life is claimed to be 70–100 years. It is possible to store about 4 hours of full-motion video on a single-sided disc.

DVD-RW

The DVD-RW format provides a rewritable optical disc with a typical capacity of 4.7 GB. The format was developed by Pioneer in November 1999. A DVD-RW disc may be written to about 1,000 times before it needs replacement. DVD-RW discs are commonly used for backing up data and home DVD recorders. One benefit of using a rewritable disc is that if there are writing errors when recording data, the disc is not ruined and it can still store data by erasing the faulty data.

A competing rewritable format is DVD+RW. Hybrid drives that can handle both, often labelled DVD±RW, are very popular as there is not yet a single standard for recordable DVDs. The recording layer in DVD-RW and DVD+RW is not an organic dye, but a special phase-change metal alloy. By adjusting the power of a laser beam, the alloy can be switched back and forth between a crystalline phase and an amorphous phase. Data can be written, erased and rewritten.

DVD-RAM

DVD-RAM is a rewritable format that has built-in error control and a defect management system, so it is considered to be better than the other DVD technologies for tasks such as data storage, backup and archiving. DVD-RAM is used in camcorders and set-top boxes because it is very easily written to and erased, which is useful for in-camera editing. DVD-RAM stores data in concentric tracks and can be accessed in a similar way to magnetic disks, usually without any special software. DVD-RW and DVD+RW discs store data in one spiral track and require special software for reading and writing. DVD-RAM is a pure phase-change medium, similar to CD-RW and DVD-RW. Capacities range from 2.58 to 9.4 GB.

Blu-ray disc

A Blu-ray disc (BD) is a high-density optical disc that stores digital information, including high-definition video. Its name derives from the blue-violet laser used for reading and writing. It uses a wavelength of 405 nm, shorter than the 650 nm red laser used to read and write DVDs. This allows it to store more data. A single-layer Blu-ray disc can store 25 GB, whereas a single-layer DVD can store 4.7 GB. A dual-layer Blu-ray disc can store 50 GB, whereas a dual-layer DVD can store 8.5 GB. Blu-ray disc format is similar to Professional Disc for Data (PDD) format, developed by Sony and available since 2004, but it offers higher data transfer speeds. PDD was not intended for home video use and was aimed at business data archiving and backup.

HD DVD

High-definition DVD (HD DVD) aimed to be the successor to standard DVD and was derived from the same underlying technologies. It could store about 30 GB, 3.5 times as much data as a dual-layer DVD. It was a rival to Blu-ray until recently, when the number of major Hollywood film studios supporting Blu-ray increased, causing HD DVD's demise. The HD DVD standard was jointly developed by Toshiba and NEC. The first HD DVD-ROM drives were released in early 2006 and the first HD DVD recorders were released in mid-2007 in Japan.

Solid-state memory

NAND-type flash memory is a type of EEPROM which supports erasure of an individual block of memory cells. To alter the contents of a particular memory location, it copies the entire block into an off-chip buffer memory, erases the block, then rewrites the data back into the same block, making the necessary alteration to the relevant memory location. It requires a dedicated microprocessor with RAM buffer, and this is included in a USB flash memory drive. It can also be used as a music codec to turn a flash drive into an MP3 player.

USB flash drive

A USB flash drive, or memory stick, is a NAND-type flash-memory device plus a **USB** interface. Typically drives are small, lightweight, removable and rewritable. PC manufacturers are increasingly shipping computers without floppy disk drives because USB flash drives are more compact, faster, hold more data and are more reliable due to their lack of moving parts and more robust design. A drawback is their small size, which makes them easy to misplace, leave behind or lose.

A flash drive consists of a small printed circuit board typically in a plastic or metal casing, making the drive sturdy enough to be carried about in a pocket. Only the USB connector protrudes from this protection and it is usually covered by a removable cap. Most flash drives use a standard, type-A USB connection, which allows them to be connected directly to a port on a personal computer. A NAND-type flash memory chip is mounted on the printed circuit board.

Their most common use is to transport and store personal files, such as documents, pictures and video. A person can store their medical alert information on MedicTag flash drives for use in emergencies. Flash drives can also be used to carry applications that run on the host computer without requiring installation. Flash drives are a relatively dense form of storage; even the cheapest flash drive can store all the data on dozens of floppy disks. Current capacities range from 64 MB to 32 GB. Mid-range flash drives under normal conditions support several hundred thousand cycles, although write operations gradually become slower as the device ages.

Some manufacturers are beginning to ship laptops with flash memory secondary storage in place of magnetic hard disk storage. The attraction is lower power consumption and faster booting of the operating system. Other manufacturers intend using flash memory as cache memory for hard drives to save on hard drive activity.

Memory card

A memory card, or flash memory card, is a solid-state flash-memory device used for data storage in digital cameras, hand-held and laptop computers, telephones, music players and games consoles. Memory cards offer high capability for re-recording, power-free storage, a small form factor and rugged environmental specifications.

Comparison of types of storage media

Hard disk drive manufacturers specify disk capacity using the SI prefixes mega (10^6), giga (10^9), and tera (10^{12}), abbreviated to M, G and T, respectively. Byte is abbreviated to B. Operating systems frequently report capacity using the same abbreviations but with a binary interpretation. Under this interpretation, the prefix mega means $2^{20} = 1,048,576$;

Table 1 *Storage media: capacity, speed of transfer and speed of access*

Storage medium	Capacity	Transfer speed	Access time (ms)
Magnetic hard disk	19.3 GB to 1.2 TB	5–110 MB/s	Under 10
Magnetic floppy disk	737,280 to 1,474,560 bytes	250–500 kbit/s	94
Magnetic tape cartridge or cassette	10–800 GB	200 KB/s to 20 MB/s	Long
CD-ROM, CD-R, CD-RW	600–700 MB	153,600 to 7,372,800 B/s, 1× to 48×	~100
DVD-ROM, DVD-R, DVD±RW, DVD-RAM	2.8–17.1 GB	1,385,000 to 22,160,000 B/s, 1× to 16×	~100
Blu-ray	25–50 GB	36–288 Mbit/s, 1× to 8×	110
PDD	25–50 GB	10 MB/s	100
HD DVD	15–51 GB	36 Mbit/s	500
USB flash drive	32 MB to 5 GB	1–60 MB/s	0.8 to 10
Memory card	128 MB to 4 GB	900 KB/s to 22.5 MB/s	0.8 to 10

Table 2 *Storage media and their applications*

Storage medium	Applications
Magnetic hard disk	Online storage of programs and data files
Magnetic floppy disk	Backing up and transferring small files; boot disk for an operating system
Magnetic tape	Backing up and archiving large volumes of data
CD-ROM	Distributing software
CD-R	Transferring files, distributing software, storing photographs, backing up data, archiving data
CD-RW	Backing up data, transferring files
DVD-ROM	Distributing software or videos
DVD-R	Transferring files, distributing software or videos, storing photographs, backing up data, archiving data
DVD±RW	Backing up data, transferring files
DVD-RAM	Backing up data
Blu-ray	Distributing videos
PDD	Backing up and archiving data
HD DVD	Recording high-density video
USB flash drive	Transferring files, running applications
Memory card	Storing photographs in a digital camera; storing music in audio devices; storing data in a mobile phone

similar usage is applied to prefixes of greater magnitude. This results in a discrepancy between the disk manufacturer's stated capacity and what the operating system reports. The difference becomes much more noticeable in the multi-gigabyte range.

For example, a disk manufacturer may use the SI definition of giga to arrive at a size of 30 GB. However, the utilities provided by Windows define a gigabyte as $2^{30} = 1{,}073{,}741{,}824$ bytes, so the operating system reports the capacity of the disk drive as 28.0 GB. A new unit called the gibibyte (GiB) is beginning to be used. This is equivalent to the binary interpretation. The capacities expressed in Table 1 use the SI units. Table 1 compares the different types of storage media on their capacity, transfer speed and **access time**. Access time consists of latency – the overhead of getting to the right place on the device and preparing to access it – and transfer time. Table 2 compares the uses for the different types of storage media.

Key terms

Access time: the time from the start of one storage device access to the time when the next access can be started.

Questions

10 In the context of a magnetic disk, what is (a) a track, (b) a sector, (c) a disk block and (d) block address?

11 Explain how data is recorded and then read from a CD-ROM.

12 What is (a) CD-R, (b) CD-RW and (c) DVD-RAM?

13 What is flash memory?

In this topic you have covered:

- input methods and devices
- output methods and devices
- storage media: magnetic, optical, solid-state
- capacity and speed of access for various storage media.

8.2 Classification of software

Key terms

Software: consists of sequences of instructions called programs that can be understood and executed by hardware.

System software

System **software** performs the tasks needed to operate the hardware. Fig. 8.2.1 shows the families of software.

Operating systems

Every computer needs operating system software to run the hardware. Operating systems act as an interface between user and hardware and provide the user with a virtual machine. This means that the machine is much easier to use than it would be if the user had to manipulate the hardware directly. The operating system hides the complexity of the hardware from the user. Operating systems provide a software platform on which other programs can run. Application programs are usually written to run on a specific platform. For example, a program written to run on a PC using MS Windows may not run on an Apple Mac using MacOS. See the A2 book for more information about operating systems.

Library programs

A program library is a collection of compiled routines that other programs can use. For example, in Pascal the StrUtils library makes available many

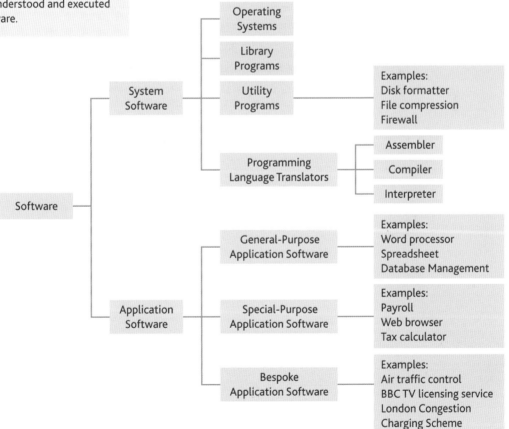

Fig. 8.2.1 *Types of software*

functions and procedures that you can use when you write a program, such as the function MidStr. Different software applications may share run-time libraries. The same print routine may be used by a word processor and by a spreadsheet program.

Utility programs

Utilities are programs that perform a very specific task related to working with computers. For example, you may wish to compress a file or format a disk. Some utility programs come bundled with the operating system, others you can install on your computer at a later time.

Language translators

Computers can run only machine code programs. When you write a program in a second-generation or higher-generation language (p185), this program must be translated before it can be executed. A program written in assembly code needs to be translated with an assembler. When you program in a high-level language such as Java or Delphi you need a compiler for the language you are using. You also need to consider the platform you wish to run your program on. For example, you need a different compiler for a Delphi program to be used on a PC running MS Windows than for a PC running Linux.

Assembler

An **assembler** is a program that translates an assembly language program into machine code. There are many different assembly languages (p184). The assembler takes an assembly language program and converts each mnemonic instruction into its binary equivalent.

Compiler

A **compiler** is a program that takes a program in a high-level language, the source code, and translates it into object code. It looks at the entire source code to translate and optimise the instructions. If the program is long, it may take some time to compile. The resulting object code will run much faster than interpreted code (p182) as no translation needs to take place at run-time. No compiler needs to be available during run-time. This means that, once the software has been developed, the object code can be distributed to users who do not need the development environment on their computers.

Interpreter

An **interpreter** analyses and executes each line of a high-level language program without looking at the entire program. Execution will be slower than for the equivalent compiled code as the source code is analysed statement by statement during execution. As each statement is analysed, the interpreter calls routines to carry out each instruction. No object code is generated. This means the program has to be interpreted each time it is run.

The advantage of interpreters over compilers is that a program can be executed immediately without having to wait for it to be compiled. If a compiler and an interpreter exist for a high-level language, a programmer may use the interpreter to test sections during program development. When development is complete, the program is compiled and only the object code is distributed to users. This gives some protection against copying of source code. However, there are programs that can turn object code back into source code.

There are some interesting hybrids. Programs written in the programming language Java are usually compiled into bytecode, which is interpreted at run-time. This makes the bytecode form of the Java program platform-independent, i.e. it will run on different machines and different operating systems without needing to be changed.

Questions

1. Which one of the following is system software: word processor, disk formatter, database?
2. Give an example of a type of language translator.
3. Explain what an assembler is used for.
4. What type of language translator is required for a high-level programming language such as C#?
5. What is the code the compiler reads? What is the code the compiler creates?

Application software

Application software allows users to perform non-computer tasks such as writing a letter or processing orders.

Bespoke software

Many software suppliers sell off-the-shelf applications that can be installed and used by many customers. This means the software will cost less to buy as a large customer base will pay for the development. **Bespoke software** is written and optimised for one customer's specific needs; one customer will pay all the development costs, so bespoke software is usually expensive. Sometimes bespoke software is the only way the customer can get software that does what they want. Some organisations have their own software development departments to produce and maintain bespoke software, whereas other organisations contract out their software requirements. The UK government commissions big software houses to produce systems for Her Majesty's Revenue and Customs (HMRC) and the Home Office. Some big department stores have an in-house software development department to produce and maintain stock control systems and online ordering systems.

General-purpose software

General-purpose software is often called generic software. It can be used for many different tasks. For example, a word processor can be used to write letters, sales brochures, books, etc. It is usually bought off the shelf and the most common way is in office suites that contain a word processor, spreadsheet, database and presentation software.

Special-purpose software

Special-purpose software supports one specific task. For example, a supermarket chain will have a stock control system for its stock control. A motoring organisation may offer its customers a route-planning application. A web browser will allow you to surf the web. It may have various advanced features but its purpose is to be a web browser and nothing else.

Questions

6. Why is bespoke software more expensive to buy than off-the-shelf software?
7. Which of the following is general-purpose software and which is special-purpose software: a spreadsheet, an accounting package, a presentation package, a photo editor?
8. What is meant by application software?

🔆 Generations of programming language

First-generation languages

Machine code is the only program code that the computer can execute directly. It is extremely tedious for humans to write programs in machine code as it consists entirely of 0s and 1s. You may be able to use hexadecimal instead of binary when inputting a machine code program, but this is still very laborious. Each family of processors has its own machine language – the instruction set and the codes that represent these instructions.

Second-generation languages

Assembly language was invented to make programming slightly easier than using machine code. An assembly language uses the same structure and instruction set as the machine language it is based on, but it uses mnemonics instead of numbers. An assembly language program must be translated into machine code using an assembler before it can be executed. Generally one assembly language instruction will translate into one machine code instruction. Fig. 8.2.2 shows that at memory address 00407947 there is the assembly language instruction MOV edi,ecx. Its equivalent in hex is 8BF9 and in binary it is 1000101111111001.

```
00407944 53              push ebx
00407945 56              push esi
00407946 57              push edi
00407947 8BF9            mov edi,ecx
00407949 8BF2            mov esi,edx
0040794B 8BD8            mov ebx,eax
0040794D 56              push esi
0040794E 57              push edi
0040794F 8BCB            mov exc,ebx
00407951 B201            mov dl,$01
00407953 A190734000      mov eax,[$00407390]
00407958 E88B3A0000      call Exception.CreateResFmt
0040795D E87ABFFFFF      call @RaiseExcept
00407962 5F              pop edi
00407963 5E              pop esi
00407964 5B              pop ebx
00407965 C3              ret
```

Memory addresses → 00407962
Machine code represented in hex → 5E
Assembly code → pop ebx

Fig. 8.2.2 *Part of a compiled Delphi program as seen in the debugger*

Programmers still use assembly language when fast execution of the program is essential or when they need to perform an operation that isn't possible in a high-level language, such as directly addressing registers. Good assembly language programmers can write code which takes up less memory space than even an optimising compiler can produce from a high-level language program. For example, the software for a mobile phone or device drivers may well have been developed using assembly language.

First- and second-generation languages are known as low-level languages because the instruction sets they use reflect the processor architecture. They are also called machine-oriented languages. Third-generation languages and higher are developed to aid problem solving, so they are called problem-oriented languages.

Activity

Find out the type of processor in your computer. What instruction set is used to program it?

Third-generation languages

Low-level languages are imperative. This means the instructions are executed in a programmer-defined sequence. Third-generation languages are also imperative. They are sometimes known as procedural languages. One statement in a third-generation language is translated into several machine code statements.

A great many third-generation languages have been developed since the 1950s. As computers were used to solve more and more types of problem, new languages were invented to make it easier to solve these problems:

- Fortran was developed for scientific and engineering applications.
- COBOL was designed to produce solutions to business problems.
- C was mainly used to write system software.
- PHP was designed for server-side scripting.

Fourth-generation languages   – HTML, CSS, SQL

Fourth-generation languages, known as declarative programming languages, such as Prolog and SQL, define what is to be computed rather than how the computation is to be done. In a declarative program you write, or declare, facts that are processed by a standard algorithm for that language to produce the desired result.

For example, the following SQL code creates a table, inserts a row into the table then processes some of the columns:

```
CREATE TABLE Employee(EmployeeID INT, EmployeeName VARCHAR)
INSERT INTO Employee VALUES ('1234', 'Fred Bloggs')
SELECT EmployeeID FROM Employee WHERE EmployeeName = "Bloggs";
```

See the A2 book for more information about SQL.

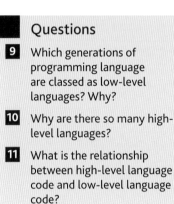

Activity

1. Find 10 third-generation languages. Why were they invented?

2. Which third-generation language do you use the most? Does an interpreter exist for your language? For which platforms can you get a compiler for your programming language?

Questions

9. Which generations of programming language are classed as low-level languages? Why?

10. Why are there so many high-level languages?

11. What is the relationship between high-level language code and low-level language code?

✔ *In this topic you have covered:*

- system software: operating systems, library programs, utility programs, language translators
- application software: general-purpose, special-purpose and bespoke
- assemblers translate assembly code into machine code
- a high-level language program is called source code
- a compiler translates source code into object code
- an interpreter analyses each statement of the source code as it executes the statement
- machine code, assembly languages, imperative languages and declarative languages.

9.1 Structure of the Internet

What is the Internet?

The term 'internet' can best be understood by breaking it up into 'inter' and 'net'. Then 'net' refers to a computer network and 'inter' refers to interconnections between two or more computer networks and computers on these networks. This is how the Internet began back in the 1970s. The problem was how to connect packet-switched networks in North America and Europe. It was solved by Robert Kahn, Vint Cerf and others, and the Internet was born.

Any network of computer networks is an internet or internetwork. NHS workers will use a secure private internet to access patient records stored on computer. The network used by the general public for e-mail and web page access is a special internet called the **Internet**. The Internet is a network of interconnected computer networks – wide area and local area – and computers using a globally unique address space based on Internet Protocol (IP) and Transmission Control Protocol (TCP) to support public access to e-mail and web pages, among other things. Fig. 9.1.1 shows how computer networks and computers are connected by the Internet.

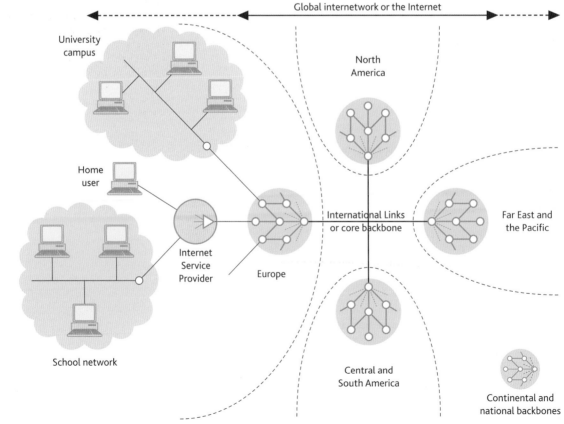

Fig. 9.1.1 *General architecture of part of the Internet*

Europe, North America, Central and South America, the Far East and the Pacific are linked by very high-speed connections which form the core backbone of the Internet. Each continent has a backbone of very high-speed links which interconnect routers located in each country. Routers are special switches that receive incoming packets of data along one link and send them as outgoing packets on another link.

Each packet contains the address of its destination; the router uses the destination address to choose the right outgoing link. Within national boundaries, networks belonging to large businesses and organisations such as universities are connected directly to the national backbone using special **routers** called router gateways. Smaller organisations and home users of the Internet connect to an Internet Service Provider (ISP), which connects to the national backbone through a router gateway. Fig. 9.1.2 shows three networks connected by a router gateway and a router.

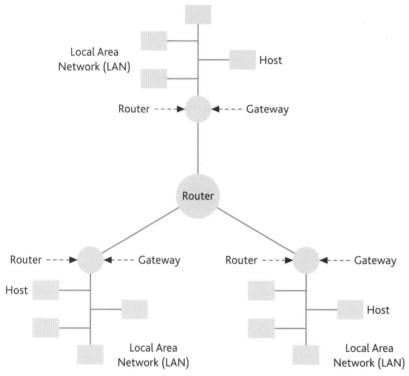

Fig. 9.1.2 *Router gateway and router joining three dissimilar networks*

A **gateway** allows one network to be connected to another so that packets from one network can be translated into a form that is compatible with the other. Strictly speaking, a gateway is only necessary when the communication channels on either side of it use different link layer protocols. If the channels use the same link layer protocol, the machine is just a router.

Case study

History of the Internet

Log on to **www.nelsonthornes.com/aqaqce/computing.htm** and download the extension reading materials.

Design of the Internet

The design of the Internet is based on the Catenet concept of a network of networks proposed by Vint Cerf in 1978. This concept described data packets flowing essentially unaltered throughout the Internet with their source and destination addresses used as unique labels for the end systems. In 1961 Leonard Kleinrock showed that packet switching was a better switching method than circuit switching, which connects two points with a complete end-to-end electrical circuit for communication. The Internet uses packet switching.

Rules of packet transmission

The packet or datagram is the unit of communication in the Internet. In its simplest form, a packet consists of three parts:

Source address	Destination address	Payload (the data)

When computer X, connected to the Internet, wishes to send a message or a document to computer Y, also connected to the Internet, computer X splits the message or document into chunks; Fig. 9.1.3 shows five chunks: A, B, C, D and E. Computer X then generates as many packets as there are chunks, placing each chunk in the payload part of the next available packet. The unique address of the sending computer is placed in the source address part of each packet and the unique address of the receiving computer is placed in the destination address part of each packet.

Each packet is then dispatched to the Internet through a router gateway. The packets are sent independently through a series of interconnected routers until they reach their destination. Each router examines the destination address of a packet to determine what to do with it. Packets traverse the Internet unaltered in this simple model. Computer Y could reply to computer X by a similar process.

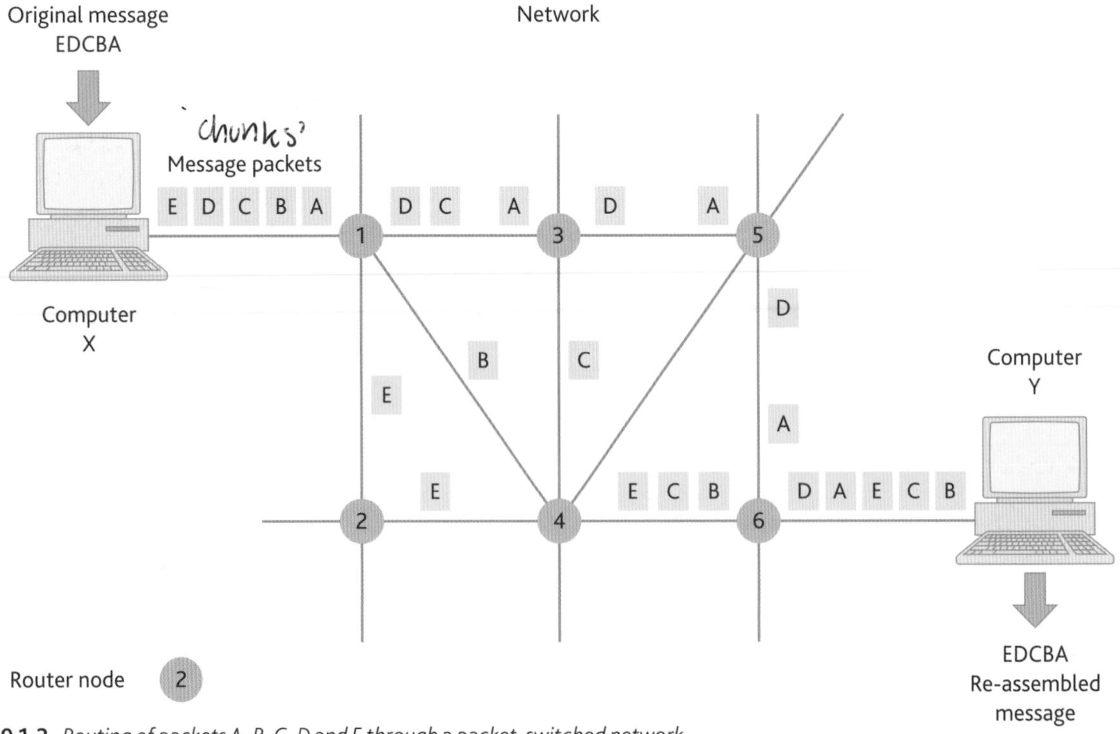

Did you know?

Sir Tim Berners-Lee said, 'There's a freedom about the Internet: as long as we accept the rules of sending packets around, we can send packets containing anything to anywhere.'

Fig. 9.1.3 *Routing of packets A, B, C, D and E through a packet-switched network*

The end-to-end principle

Cerf and Kahn proposed that the two communicating computers, X and Y in our example, should be the endpoints of the communication. The end-to-end principle states that the two end computers should be in control of the communication. The Internet's role is to move packets between these two endpoints. This has several advantages:

■ The sending application in computer X and the receiving application in computer Y are able to survive a partial network failure. Computer X detects the failure and simply resends the packets that did not get through.

■ Packets can be rerouted around failures very quickly and sent along alternative paths.

■ The Internet can grow easily because control resides in the endpoints not in the Internet.

■ There is no requirement for Internet routers to notify each other as endpoint connections are formed or dropped; this simplifies the design of routers.

■ The integrity and security of each packet sent is handled by the endpoints, which simplifies the role of the Internet.

■ Each endpoint need only be aware of the router to which it is directly connected and, optionally, a name resolution service.

Open architecture networking

The Internet uses open architecture networking. Designers are free to design networks however they want, but all these different networks can communicate over the Internet. Each network is connected to the Internet through a router gateway.

Single logical address space

The end-to-end principle requires that each computer using the Internet should be uniquely identified. Cerf and Kahn proposed that each computer be labelled with a globally unique address known as an **IP address**. Their numbering system, called IPv4, is used today and allows 2^{32} different addresses. All these unique addresses make up a single logical address space. At the binary level, an IPv4 address consists of 32 bits (4 bytes). Cerf and Kahn split an IP address into two parts (Fig. 4): bits that identify the network connected to the Internet and bits that identify a host (e.g. computer) connected to the network.

31	0
NetID	HostID

Fig. 9.1.4 *IPv4 address structure*

The thinking behind this was that since the Internet is made up of networks, being able to identify each network would help routers enormously in the task of routing packets to the correct destination network. An Internet address can be expressed like this, where a dot separates each byte of the 32-bit address:

196.100.11.4

The network ID in this case is 196.100.11 and the host ID is 4.

Routers

Routers are used because it is not practical to connect every host directly to every other host. Instead a few hosts connect to a router, which connects to other routers, and so on, to form a network.

A router receives packets or datagrams from one host or router and uses the destination IP address that they contain to pass on the packets, correctly formatted, to another host or router. It is vital that hosts and routers can identify the network part of the destination IP address, because this part features largely in routing.

Fig. 9.1.5 shows the hierarchy of routers for a single country. Each router in this hierarchy maintains a table of other routers, computers and networks it is directly connected to and enough information about the hierarchical structure of the Internet to route a packet to the desired destination.

For example, the IP address range 202.0.0.0. to 203.255.255.255 has been allocated to the Asia-Pacific region. A host on a school network in England wishing to communicate with a host on a network in Malaysia will send packets to the gateway router on the school network. This router will pass the packets onto the local router it is connected to. The local router will pass these packets on to the regional router it is connected to. The regional router will pass packets on to the national router it is connected to, and so on, until the gateway router of the destination network is reached. Each router in the path uses the NetID part of the IP address to make the routing decision. In this example the decision is to route packets up the national hierarchy because 202/203 addresses are outside England.

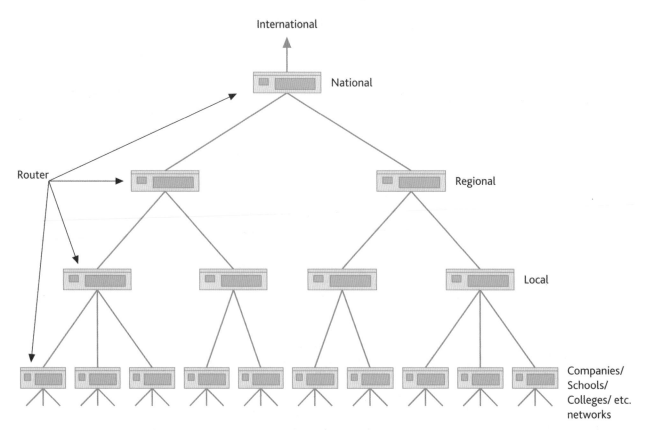

Fig. 9.1.5 *Routing hierarchy for one country*

🗗 The World Wide Web

The World Wide Web (**WWW**), commonly known as the Web, is a system of interlinked hypertext documents accessed via the Internet. Using a web browser, users view web pages that may contain text, images and other multimedia and navigate between them using hyperlinks. The WWW began in 1989 when researchers at the CERN particle physics laboratory in Geneva devised a way to link and exchange reports, images and other material. The initial proposal came from UK physicist Sir Tim Berners-Lee and Robert Cailliau of Belgium. To demonstrate the capabilities of the proposal, Sir Tim wrote the world's first web browser in the programming language Pascal.

What is an intranet?

An **intranet** is a private computer network that uses Internet protocols to securely share part of an organisation's information or operations with its employees. Some~~times intranet refers to an internal web site.~~ The concepts and techno~~logies of the Internet, such as clients and serv~~ running the TCP/IP ~~protocols, are used to build an intranet with~~ application-level pro~~tocols such as HTTP, FTP, POP3 and SMTP.~~

■ Questions

1. What is the Inte~~rnet~~
2. What is the Wor~~ld Wide Web~~
3. What role does ~~
4. What is a router~~
5. Describe (a) the ~~
   networking prin~~

■ Domain nam~~es and IP addresses~~

In the early days of the Internet, users of Internet applications such as e-mail were required to enter IP addresses when they wanted to set the destination and source addresses of an e-mail they were sending. This wasn't a problem while the number of IP addresses in use was very small. However, as the number of networks began to grow, it became a lot harder to use IP addressing directly. The Domain Name System (DNS) was invented so that users could use a memorable name to refer to a network and a host on that network. The DNS, part of which is shown in Fig. 6, is a hierarchical system of names and abbreviations. *ลักษณะนิอ*

The root is abbreviated to a full stop. Using this domain name hierarchy, an example of a **domain name** is ags.bucks.sch.uk. This domain name identifies a network of computers located at a school in Buckinghamshire in the UK. The part of the IP address which identifies this network is 195.112.56. A particular host on this network is mail.ags.bucks.sch.uk. This name is an example of a fully qualified domain name (**FQDN**) that uniquely identifies a host. When the host ID of this computer, 124, is added to the network ID, the IP address becomes 195.112.56.124.

For convenience, people often use 'domain name' when they mean fully qualified domain name. The domain .uk includes all hosts that use the top-level domain name suffix 'uk'. The second-level domain .sch includes all the hosts that use 'sch', the third-level domain .bucks includes all the

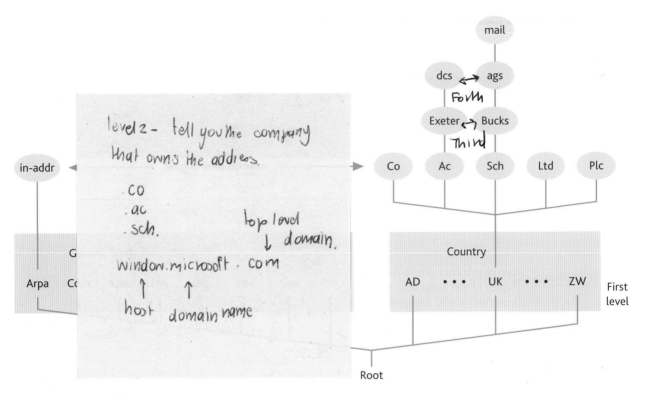

Fig. 9.1.6 *DNS hierarchy*

Table 1 *Some level 1 domain names*

Domain name	Type of organisation
com	Commercial
edu	Educational
org	Non-commercial
uk	Located in UK

hosts in Buckinghamshire, and the fourth-level domain .ags includes all the hosts in the organisation AGS with a globally unique IP address. Finally, mail is the public name of the host.

DNS servers translate FQDNs into IP addresses. Hosts use **DNS servers** to resolve domain names into IP addresses before connecting to other hosts on the Internet. Table 1 shows the interpretation of some top-level domain names.

Table 2 shows the interpretation of some second-level domain names.

Table 2 *Some level 2 domain names*

Domain name	Type of organisation
co	Commercial
ac	Academic, higher education or further education
sch	School

Uniform resource locator

A uniform resource locator (URL) is a short string that represents the target of a hyperlink; it was introduced in early 1990 in Tim Berners-Lee's proposals for hypertext. A **URL** specifies which server to access, the access method and the location in the server. Fig. 9.1.7 shows that a URL consists of several parts. The simplest version contains three parts:

■ **How:** defines which protocol is to be used.

■ **Where:** defines the host.

What: specifies the name of the requested object and the complete path to it.

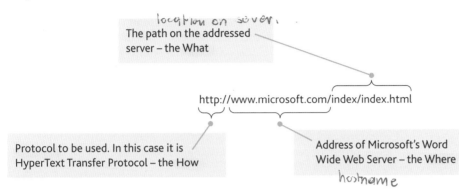

location on server.

The path on the addressed server – the What

http://www.microsoft.com/index/index.html

Protocol to be used. In this case it is HyperText Transfer Protocol – the How

Address of Microsoft's Word Wide Web Server – the Where

hostname

Fig. 9.1.7 *Structure of a URL*

Uniform resource identifier

The World Wide Web Consortium (W3C) and the Internet Engineering Task Force (IETF) say that a URL is a type of URI, so its use should be discouraged in favour of the term **URI**. Uniform resource identifiers (URIs) include URLs and uniform resource names (URNs). A URL identifies a resource by its network location whereas a URN identifies it by name. Table 3 shows examples of URLs and URNs.

Table 3 *Examples of URIs*

Resource	Type
http://somehost/path/resource.txt	URL
ftp://somehost/resource.txt	URL
urn:isbn:0-06-251587-X	URN

Internet registries and registrars

Internet registries store registered domain names. These registries track the associations between Internet addresses such as 196.100.11.4 and domain names, such as educational-computing.co.uk. Each major domain, such as .com, has its own separate registry. Registries make it possible to map domain names to IP addresses.

Private companies called Internet registrars are responsible for registering Internet domains to people and organisations, domains such as educational-computing.co.uk. Until recently, a quasi-public company called InterNIC had sole responsibility for doing this, but it has been replaced by other registrars. Internet registrars are overseen by boards of people from private and public institutions.

Internet Service Provider

An Internet Service Provider (ISP) or Internet Access Provider (IAP) is a business or organisation that sells people Internet access (Fig. 9.1.1 p186).

Key terms

URI: uniform resource identifier; specifies how to access a resource on the Internet.

Did you know?

In technical publications, especially standards produced by the IETF and the W3C, the term URL has long been deprecated as it is rarely necessary to distinguish between URLs and URIs.

Questions

6 When was DNS invented?

7 Name three top-level domain names other than country names.

8 Explain the difference between a domain name and a fully qualified domain name.

9 What is the purpose of a DNS server?

10 Give an example of a URL.

11 What is the difference between a URL and a URI?

Key terms

Server: a software process that provides a service requested by a client.

Client: a software process that requests and uses the services provided by a server.

Client–server model: a client software process initiates a request for a service from a server software process, and the server responds to that request.

Protocol: a set of agreed signals, codes and rules for data exchange between systems.

Protocol stack: a collection of protocol layers; each layer is responsible for part of the process governed by the stack.

TCP/IP protocol stack: a protocol stack for TCP/IP; it has an application layer, a transport layer, a network layer and a link layer.

Port: an address for a software process.

The client–server model

In the client–server model, the client and the server are software processes. A **server** waits for a request from a **client**. The request may be to read information or write information. The client initiates the communication. The server responds. In the **client–server model**, the server has to exist and be known about before a client can successfully connect to its services.

Protocol

All communication needs protocols so it goes smoothly and without errors. A **protocol** is a set of agreed signals, codes and rules for data exchange between systems.

TCP/IP protocol stack

Networking protocols are usually developed in layers. Each layer is responsible for a different part of the communication process. The **TCP/IP protocol stack** is normally considered as four-layers (Fig. 9.1.8). The collection of layers is known as a **protocol stack**. Each layer has a different responsibility.

Application	Telnet, FTP, e-mail (SMTP, POP3), Web Browsing (HTTP)
Transport	TCP
Network	IP
Link	Device driver and interface card

Fig. 9.1.8 *The four layers of the TCP/IP protocol stack*

Transport layer

The end-to-end principle of the Internet requires that the two endpoints, the hosts, are responsible for establishing, supervising and maintaining a connection between two communicating processes, one on each host. To do this, each host must have a piece of software called Transmission Control Protocol (TCP). TCP ensures a reliable flow of data and relieves applications from having to deal with the problems of connecting the hosts, detecting when errors occur, retransmitting packets and detecting when a connection is broken. It also splits data that the applications wish to send into chunks that fit packets and reassembles received packets into data for applications.

TCP enables applications executing on two hosts to establish a connection and exchange streams of data. TCP guarantees delivery of data and also guarantees that packets will be delivered in the order they were sent. TCP is responsible for dividing the data passed to it from the application into chunks for the network layer.

TCP ports

A typical host on a TCP/IP internetwork runs many processes at the same time. Each process generates data that it sends to TCP, which in turn passes it to the IP software layer for transmission. This means that TCP must work out which process to send the data to, and this requires an additional address element called a **port**.

Fig. 9.1.9 shows two application-to-application connections made by TCP: the web browser on host 195.112.56.7 connects to the web server on host 210.34.56.78, and the Telnet client on host 195.112.56.7 connects to the Telnet server on host 210.34.56.78.

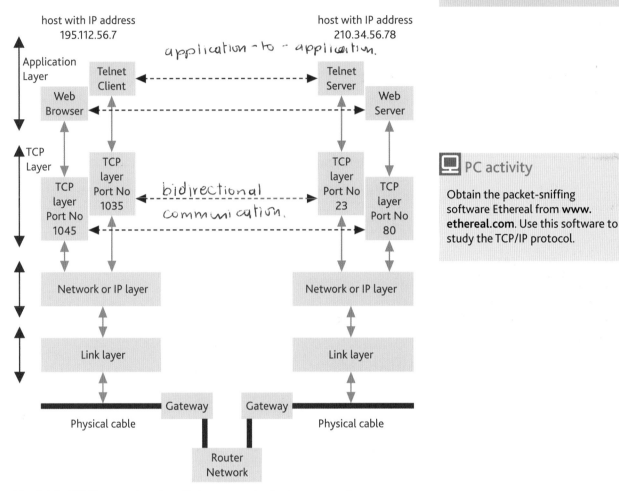

Fig. 9.1.9 *TCP/IP protocol stack applied to communication between two hosts*

The TCP program keeps track of the client application connections running on 195.112.56.7 by assigning each a different port number chosen in the range 1024 to 4095. In this case it has allocated port 1045 to the web browser and port 1035 to the Telnet client.

Servers accept multiple simultaneous connections from clients. Each executing server needs only one port number but no two servers may use the same port at the same time on the same machine. In Fig. 9.1.9 port 80 is for the web server and port 23 is for a Telnet server.

Sockets

The combination of host IP address and port number is known as a **socket**. Fig. 9.1.9 shows two sockets on the client side: 195.112.56.7:1045 and 195.112.56.7:1035. The connection between two sockets provides a **bidirectional** communication path between the end processes or applications, e.g. 195.112.56.7:1045 connects to 210.34.56.78:80.

Network layer

The **network layer**, or IP layer, addresses the packets handed to it from the transport layer with source and destination IP addresses then hands them on to the link layer. The network layer also receives packets from the link layer, removes the source and destination addresses then passes them to the transport layer. The transport layer uses the destination port number to pass the payload data on to the corresponding application.

Link layer

The **link layer** adds source and destination hardware addresses to packets that it receives from the network layer then despatches the packets onto the local cable. The destination address is the gateway's hardware address. In an Ethernet local area network (LAN) these hardware addresses are Ethernet card addresses, or MAC addresses. In Fig. 9.1.9 a packet despatched by the link layer of 195.112.56.7 onto the cable would assign Ethernet addresses as follows: Ethernet card address of 195.112.56.7, Ethernet card address of the gateway connected to the cable joined to 195.112.56.7. The gateway is the host to which the sending host is directly connected and which is also connected to the Internet.

Application layer

The **application layer** handles the details of the particular networking application. The application layer uses different protocols for different applications. One protocol it uses is File Transfer Protocol (FTP).

Encapsulation

Fig. 9.1.10 shows a complete packet produced by a web client application as the packet emerges from 195.112.56.7 onto the cable. It has the

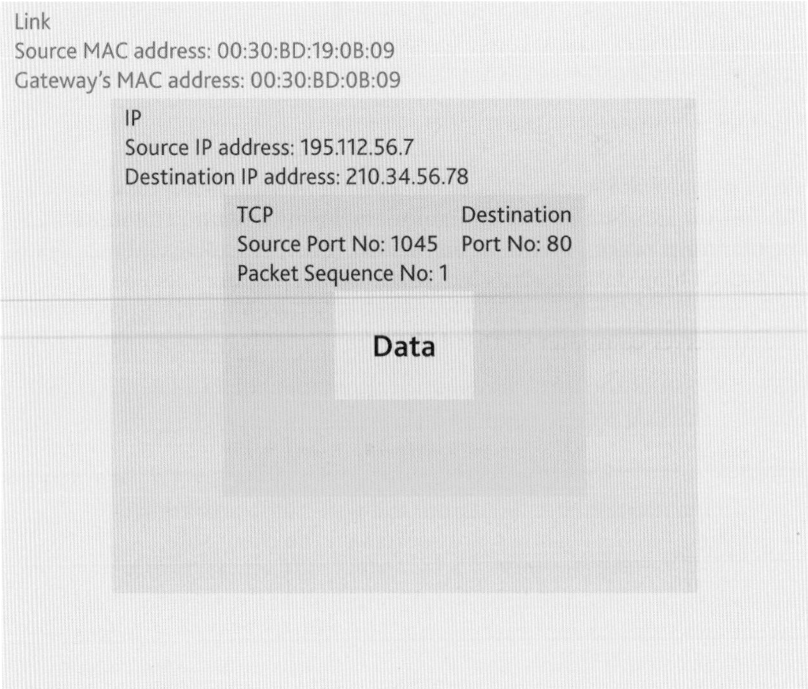

Link
Source MAC address: 00:30:BD:19:0B:09
Gateway's MAC address: 00:30:BD:0B:09

IP
Source IP address: 195.112.56.7
Destination IP address: 210.34.56.78

TCP   Destination
Source Port No: 1045   Port No: 80
Packet Sequence No: 1

Data

Fig. 9.1.10 *An Ethernet frame contains an IP packet, which contains a TCP packet, which contains the payload data*

payload, the TCP port numbers of source and destination, the IP addresses of source and destination, and the MAC addresses of source and gateway network cards.

Client port numbers

Each client process is assigned a temporary port number called a **client port number**. Client port numbers lie in the range 1024 to 4095. They are allocated incrementally, beginning at 1024.

Well-known port numbers

Clients initiate application data transfers using TCP, so they need to know the port number of the server process. Consequently, servers are required to use universally known port numbers. These are the **well-known port numbers**, which lie in the range 0 to 1023, and the registered port numbers, which lie in the range 1024 to 4095. Table 4 shows some well-known port numbers and their associated server.

Table 4 *Some well-known port numbers and their servers*

Port	Server
20	FTP server, file transfer data
21	FTP server, file transfer control
80 and 8080	Web server
25	SMTP server
110	POP3 server
23	Telnet server

Application-level protocols

HTTP

Hypertext Transfer Protocol (HTTP) is a very simple application-level protocol. In this protocol, a client machine sends a request message to the server and the server responds with a response message (Fig. 9.1.11). The response message may contain many forms of data. The most popular form of data is text formatted using Hypertext Markup Language (HTML). Other data, such as images or audio files, may also be transmitted. TCP establishes a connection between the client computer and the server computer so that HTTP has a pathway for its request and response messages.

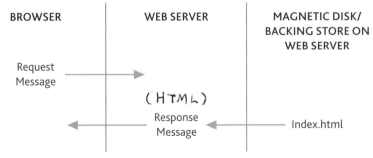

Fig. 9.1.11 *HTTP request–response messages*

The simplest request message is

```
GET / <Return key pressed>
<Return key pressed>
```

This gets the default web page, index.html, for the given site. HTTP finishes with the connection after the response message is sent; the TCP connection is broken unless specifically requested to stay connected.

A web page returned by an HTTP GET request is a text file containing content to be displayed together with instructions on how to style and structure this content when displayed. Here is what a web browser does:

1 It accepts a URI from a user.

2 It extracts the FQDN and uses a DNS server to translate it into an IP address.

3 It sends a GET request for the web resource specified in the URI; the request is sent to a web server at this IP address – port 80 unless another port number is specified.

4 It receives the file returned by the web server.

5 It renders this file's contents in a web browser window; that means it uses the style and structure instructions to display the content appropriately.

6 If this file contains other URIs, e.g. a reference to a graphic, then the browser should issue a GET to obtain this resource from the web server and, when received, display it according to the instructions on style and structure.

 **PC activity**

Use packet-sniffing software to study HTTP.

FTP

File Transfer Protocol (FTP) is an application-layer protocol that enables files on one host, computer B, to be copied to another host, computer A (Fig. 9.1.12). One host runs an FTP client and the other an FTP server. FTP servers use two ports: port 21 for commands and port 20 for data.

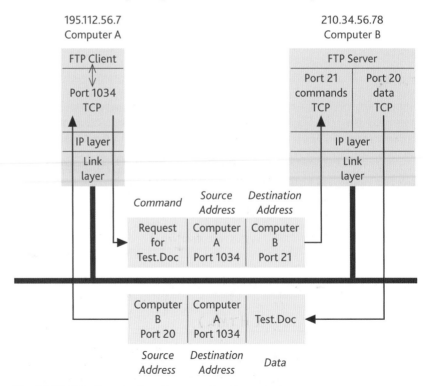

Fig. 9.1.12 *FTP of Test.doc from Computer B to Computer A*

Microsoft has an FTP server with the name ftp://ftp.microsoft.com. Fig. 9.1.13 shows the user interface screen for computer A running an FTP client connected to computer B.

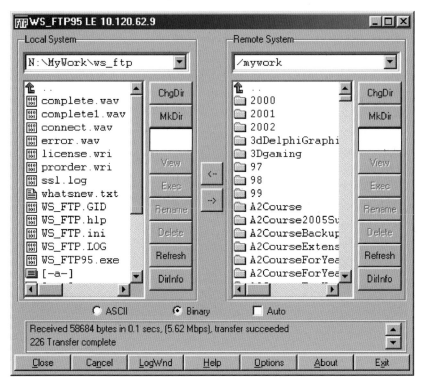

Fig. 9.1.13 *FTP client connected to an FTP server*

Some FTP servers restrict access to their service and require users to use a registered user name and password. Other FTP servers do not restrict access but may prompt users for a user name; then the user name is normally 'anonymous'. The user may be prompted for a password too. If the user name is 'anonymous', it is sufficient to supply an e-mail address as the password.

Telnet

Telnet is a text-based protocol that can be used to manage a remote machine, read the HTML text of a web page, and send and retrieve e-mail. Fig. 9.1.14 shows Microsoft's command-line Telnet client being

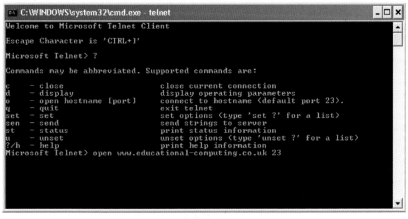

Fig. 9.1.14 *Using Microsoft's Telnet client to open a connection to a Telnet server on a remote machine*

Key point

To use the File Transfer Protocol through a web browser, the protocol ftp:// must be used in the address bar.

PC activity

Enter ftp://ftp.microsoft.com into the address bar of a web browser to go to Microsoft's FTP site.

PC activity

Open a Telnet connection to a remote server.

used to open a TCP/IP connection to the Telnet server on the site **www. educational-computing.co.uk** listening on port 23. Port 23 is the well-known listening port number of Telnet servers. Use of this port number enables the Telnet client to manage the remote machine, i.e. to create files or folders, to delete files or folders, to open files for viewing, etc., as if the remote machine were the user's own local machine.

Fig. 9.1.15 shows the client's console after the connection is opened. The user is invited to log in to an area on the remote machine. The site **www. educational-computing.co.uk** is hosted on a remote machine with the name scratchy.nildram.co.uk. After logging in, the Telnet client accepts operating system commands.

Fig. 9.1.15 *Screen for logging into a remote machine using a Telnet connection*

 PC activity

Using a Telnet connection to a remote server hosting web pages, open a connection to the web server then retrieve a web page using the GET command.

If the Telnet client were to use command

```
open www.educational-computing.co.uk 80
```

the Telnet client would open a TCP/IP connection to the site's web server listening on port 80. Sending the command

```
GET /
```

followed by a line break should retrieve the web site's default web page.

If the client were to use the command

```
open mail.ags.bucks.sch.uk 110
```

the Telnet client would open a TCP/IP connection to the site's mail server listening on port 110, the port for the well-known POP3 mail server. Two mail commands are LIST and RETR n. RETR n retrieves the nth e-mail message and displays it in full on the client's console. It is also possible to send an e-mail using a Telnet client.

POP3 and SMTP

Simple Mail Transfer Protocol (SMTP) is used by e-mail clients to send e-mail. It is a relatively simple text-based protocol. One or more recipients of a message are specified then the message text is transferred to a mail server listening on port 25. The mail server takes care of delivering the mail to the ultimate destination using SMTP. The user who retrieves the message from the destination mail server uses the application-layer protocol POP3 to retrieve the stored mail. POP3 is Post Office Protocol version 3. E-mail is stored in a mailbox and a user does not need to be connected for mail to be sent to them. The server holds incoming mail until the user connects and requests the mail.

 PC activity

Using a Telnet connection to a remote server hosting a mail server, access an email account and send/retrieve e-mail.

HTTPS

Hypertext Transfer Protocol over Secure Sockets Layer (HTTPS) is a web protocol developed by Netscape that encrypts and decrypts user page requests as well as the pages that are returned by the web server. HTTPS uses Secure Sockets Layer (SSL) beneath the HTTP application layer. HTTPS uses port 443 instead of port 80 in its interactions with TCP/IP. HTTPS is widely used on the web for security-sensitive communication, such as payment transactions and corporate logons.

In this topic you have covered:

- the Internet is a network of networks and computers that use unique IP addresses and TCP/IP

- messages are split into packets, which are routed independently by packet switching

- routers are used because it is not practical to connect every host directly to every other host

- an intranet is a private computer network that uses Internet protocols

- the world wide web is a system of interlinked hypertext documents accessed via the Internet

- in the client–server model, a client process requests a service from a server process

- a protocol provides agreed signals, codes and rules for data exchange between systems

- the TCP/IP protocol stack consists of four layers: application, transport, network and link

- some application protocols are HTTP, FTP, Telnet, POP3, SMTP and HTTPS

- domain names are registered in Internet registries

- domain names are organised hierarchically into a Domain Name System (DNS).

- DNS servers translate domain names into IP addresses

- a URI specifies how to access a resource on the Internet

- a URL is a URI that identifies a resource by its network location.

Questions

18 Explain the protocol HTTP.

19 Describe the role of (a) FTP, (b) POP3 (c) SMTP, (d) Telnet and (e) HTTPS.

9.2 Web site design

In this topic you will cover:

- web page construction and HTML
- style sheets.

Key terms

Home page: the starting page for a web site; it often has links to other parts of the site.

HTML: Hypertext Markup Language; the language used to write web pages. It consists of text that defines the content of the page and tags that define how the content should be structured.

Hyperlink: a link from one web page to another; a hypertext link.

Hypertext: a body of text, graphics, etc., stored in a machine-readable form and structured so that a reader can cross-refer between related items of information.

Source: the HTML code to create a web page.

Web browser: software that displays a web page by rendering the HTML elements.

Web page: a document on the world wide web written in HTML and displayed in a web browser.

Web site: a set of linked documents associated with a particular person, organisation or topic that is held on a computer system and can be accessed as part of the world wide web.

A **web page** is a document containing text; graphics (images) and other embedded media, e.g. sound; and links (pointers) to other web pages. The links are called **hyperlinks** and a special markup language called **HTML** was created so that these links could be written as strings of text. A web page that points to other web pages is said to use **hypertext**. By convention, when a web page is displayed in a browser, the hyperlinks are underlined. A **web site** consists of one or more linked web pages. One of the pages of a web site is denoted the **home page**. Hypertext navigation is a major component of web page design.

Figure 1 shows an example of a web page containing text, graphics and hyperlinks after it is rendered in a **web browser**. The **source** for this web page was created in a text editor, Microsoft's WordPad, and saved with the extension .html.

Fig. 9.2.1 *This web page contains text, graphics and hyperlinks*

Text in a web page can be two kinds of information: content for display and formatting. A web browser needs formatting information so that it can present the content as intended. Content is placed between start and end tags:

```
<something> information content </something>
```

where <something> is the start tag and </something> is the end tag. The start tag, the content and the end tag form an element. Tags mainly mark areas of the web page that are to be formatted. This is why HTML is called a markup language.

Since 1996 there has been a move away from using HTML to control formatting. This information is now put in a cascading style sheet (CSS). A CSS is usually an external file with the extension .css.

💡 Web page construction

Here is the skeletal structure for any web page:

```
<html>
  <head>
    <title>Title of the Web Page goes here </title>
  </head>
  <body>
     Content of the Web Page goes here
  </body>
</html>
```

All tags should be written in lower case to conform to the latest standard defined by the World Wide Web Consortium (W3C). Extensible Hypertext Markup Language (XHTML) is the latest version of HTML. XHTML will gradually replace HTML. XHTML is compatible with HTML 4.01. XHTML is a combination of HTML and Extensible Markup Language (XML). The web page should be saved with file extension .html.

The html tag

The markup part of every web page must begin with `<html>` and end with `</html>`. These two tags tell the browser that the document is written in HTML and that it should translate every tag it finds between them into the proper effect. Everything you put into the markup part of your web page must go between these two tags.

The head and title tags

There are two separate parts to the markup part of your web page, the head and the body. The head comes first, is surrounded by the `<head>` and `</head>` tags and usually contains information about the web page enclosed in the `<meta />` tag that is not displayed as normal text but may be used by search engines and other programs to categorise or list the page. This information is optional. Here is an example:

```
<head>
  <title>HTML Example</title>
  <meta name="generator" content="TextPad 4.6" />
  <meta name="author" content="Fred Bloggs" />
  <meta name="keywords" content="example, html" />
  <meta name="description" content="Example of simple HTML" />
</head>
```

In this example, `name` and `content` are **attributes** of the HTML tag `<meta />`. The head section also contains the title of the page, enclosed between the tags `<title>` and `</title>`. The title appears in the title bar of the browser window. The title is used by search engines, browser history lists, favourites lists and bookmark facilities.

The body tag

Everything that you place in the body of your web page will be displayed in the main window of a browser. This section is structured with the tags `<body>` and `</body>`.

Regular text and paragraphs

Most web pages contain just plain text, typed as text into the body section of the web page. However, there are some key differences

> **Key terms**
>
> **Attribute:** a named field that appears inside an HTML tag.

between plain text and body text. Firstly, line breaks have to be explicitly marked with the `<br />` tag. Text can also be separated with the `<p>` tag, or paragraph tag. The `<p>` tag is paired with the `</p>` tag. When the combination `<p>` `</p>` is used, not only is a new line started but also an empty line is put before the paragraph text and after it. Web browsers also ignore multiple spaces and tabs in normal text. Multiple spaces and tabs are reduced to a single space. Fig. 9.2.2 shows how the following HTML code appears in a browser.

```
a) The  cat  sat
on  the
 mat.
b) The cat sat <p>on the mat.</p>
c) The cat sat <p>on</p>the mat.
```

Notice that the browser ignores the spaces and new lines and that `<p>` `</p>` forces text onto a new line.

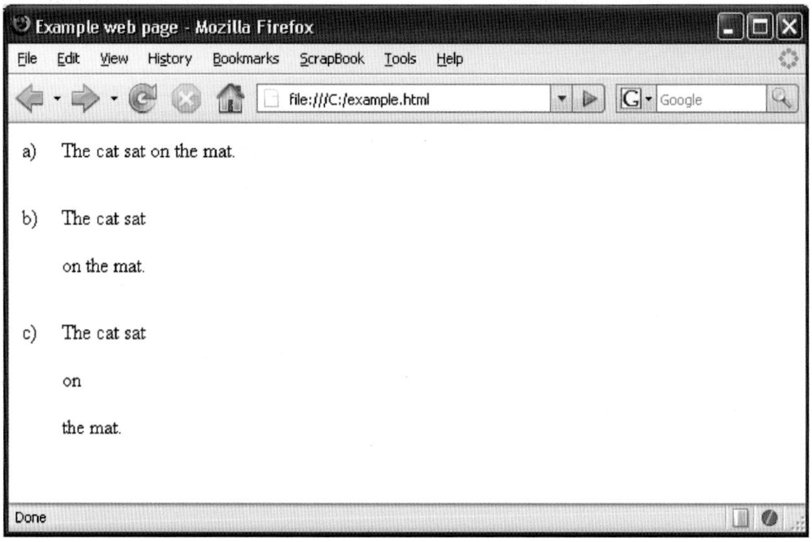

Fig. 9.2.2 *How the HTML code examples appear in a browser*

Headings

Often a web page needs to include headings in larger, bolder text that stands out. To create headings, use `<h#>Heading text</h#>` and replace # with a number from 1 to 6. The text inside will be bold and usually larger – h1 gives the largest headings – and surrounded by empty lines. Fig. 9.2.3 shows how the following lines of HTML code appear in a browser:

h 1~6

Big

```
<h1>This is an h1 heading.</h1>
<h2>This is an h2 heading.</h2>
<h3>This is an h3 heading.</h3>
<h4>This is an h4 heading.</h4>
<h5>This is an h5 heading.</h5>
```
Small
```
<h6>This is an h6 heading.</h6>
```

Typography

The main purpose of all web design is communication, so choose an appropriate font for text in a web page. As a rule of thumb, paragraph text should use a sans serif font such as Arial and headlines should use a serif

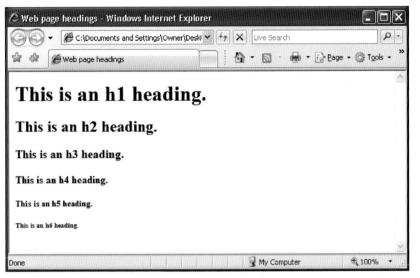

Fig. 9.2.3 *Headings tags*

font such as Times New Roman – the opposite of what is used for printed text. The number of font families supported across modern operating systems is very small and the number shared is even smaller.
A web browser relies on the fonts installed in the operating system. Choose from the safe list of fonts that are guaranteed to be supported (Fig. 9.2.4).

Explore font settings at **www.typetester.maratz.com**. Anything from 45 to 75 characters is widely regarded as a satisfactory line length, and 66 characters – letters and spaces – is widely considered ideal.

Colour in web pages

Choose colours that work together. Three colour schemes are worth mentioning:

- **Monochromatic:** use a single base colour and any number of tints or shades of that colour.
- **Analogous:** use any three colours that are side by side on a 12-part colour wheel, such as yellow-green, yellow and yellow-orange. Usually one of the three colours predominates.
- **Complementary:** use colours that are located opposite each other on the colour wheel, such as green and red, yellow and violet, or orange and blue.

Fig. 9.2.5 (overleaf) shows the colour wheel being used for analogous and complementary colour schemes.

Colour may be expressed as a six-digit hexadecimal number, two digits per primary colour. For example, #FFFFFF corresponds to white, #0000FF to blue, #00FF00 to green and #FF0000 to red, the additive primary colours.

Images

To include an image on a web page use `<img src="image1.gif" alt="first image" width="70" height="70"/>`. The attribute `alt` allows a text description of the image to be used in place of the image in text-only browsers. The width and height attributes set the image's display size in pixels.

Arial
Arial Black
Comic Sans MS
Courier New
Georgia Impact
Times New Roman
Trebuchet MS
Verdana

Fig. 9.2.4 *Web-safe fonts*

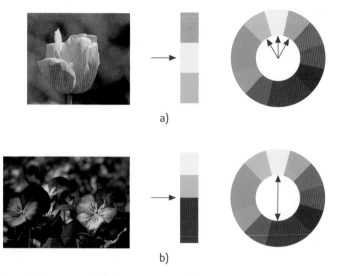

Fig. 9.2.5 *Colour wheel for (a) analogous and (b) complementary colour schemes*

สีกลืนกลังกัน   สีตรงข้าม

Links

Links, or hyperlinks, are the hooks that make it possible to navigate to information without knowing the precise details of its location or identity. For example, you may not know the name of a file on **www. educational-computing.co.uk** that contains an article you want to read, but you can still get to it by clicking on the appropriate link.

Text links to other pages

A URI is a string of text that tells the browser where to go. It consists of a protocol (e.g. HTTP) plus an FQDN such as **www.educational-computing.co.uk**, sometimes followed by the path name of a file. The text string 'educational-computing.co.uk' is a domain name and www identifies a specific host server. To create a link in a web page, use tags `<a> </a>` and the attribute `href`:

```
<a href="http://domain name/path name">Caption for link</a>
```

Any text typed between `<a href ... >` and `</a>` will be displayed in blue and underlined. If the user clicks on this text, they will be taken to the specified URI. To make a link to www.educational-computing.co.uk, the HTML

```
<a href="http://www.educational-computing.co.uk">Click here
for ECS!</a>
```

will display in a web browser as

Click here for ECS!   ← have line.

Text links in a page

To make separate sections of a web page directly accessible, perhaps to create an index of web page contents with links, you must first mark the target of any links by creating an anchor. An anchor is an HTML tag that gives a specific place in your web page a name. Anchors use the same `<a></a>` tag pair as regular links. To create an anchor, simply write `<a name="anchorname"></a>` immediately in front of the place you want your link to point to. For example, the top of a page could have an anchor called `top`:

```
<a name="top"></a>
```

To link to a named anchor, use href plus # and the anchor name. This HTML

```
<a href="#top">Click here for the top of this page</a>
```

produces

Click here for the top of this page

If you click on the link, it will take you to the anchor named top.

Lists

Lists come in two kinds: ordered and unordered. The list is enclosed by tags and each list item is enclosed by tags.

Ordered lists (1,2,3, A, ··)

A web browser automatically numbers and indents each list item in an ordered list. An ordered list is enclosed by the tags <ol> and </ol> and each list item by <li> .. </li>. The HTML

```
<ol>
  <li> Task 1 </li>
  <li> Task 2 </li>
  <li> Task 3 </li>
  <li> Task 4 </li>
</ol>
```

produces

1. Task 1
2. Task 2
3. Task 3
4. Task 4

Unordered lists (• , ° , ° , °••)

Unordered lists are the same as ordered lists but the browser does not automatically number the list items. Instead each item starts with a symbol, or dingbat, such as filled square or filled circle. An unordered list is created in the same way as an ordered list, but the list is enclosed by <ul> and </ul> instead of <ol> and </ol>.

Questions

1 Write the HTML anchor element for a link to **www.educational-computing.co.uk**. The link text should be 'Click me to link to ECS Ltd'.

2 Using an example, explain how to use links in a document so users can jump to different places in the document.

3 Write the HTML element that will display an ordered list of the following three items: Pascal Programming, Databases and Binary Arithmetic.

4 Name and describe three colour schemes that are used in web design.

5 Show the result of the following HTML fragment when rendered in a web browser:

The cat sat <p>on the mat</p> so the story goes.

6 Show the result of the following HTML fragment when rendered in a web browser:

The cat sat <h3>on the mat</h3> so the story goes.

not replace but supplement → HTML.

Key terms

Structure: headings, paragraphs, line breaks, hypertext links, lists and embedded media.

Style: a visual effect such as text colour, font size or background colour.

Type selector: a selector that is an HTML tag; it targets every instance of an element.

(in HTML)
can be both internal or external (.CSS).
✓ define how to display HTML element

Key point

The original HTML specifications contained logical tags almost exclusively, logical meaning how a page is structured into headings, paragraphs and sections. Using HTML in this way allows a page to be read in any number of browser types, e.g. aural browsers, text-only browsers and Braille displays, and still be presented appropriately.

Cascading style sheets (CSS).

Until recently, HTML was used to specify the structure and style of web pages. Every piece of text has **structure**. Unfortunately, HTML started to be used for **style** (presentational effects) – basic formatting to create visual effects such as text colour and font size.

This was not the original intention of HTML's creators. Using HTML for visual effects made web pages difficult to understand and edit. The solution was cascading style sheets (CSS). CSS allows designers to control how a web page will display in a web browser and separates this presentational information from the web page content and its logical structure. Presentational tags, such as the font tag, could be ditched and layout could be controlled using CSS instead of tables. One CSS may be written and applied to all the pages in a web site; this is an external style sheet. The same information may be put in the head of an HTML document; this is an embedded style sheet. The formatting in the head is still kept separate from the content in the body.

Selectors

Elements of an HTML page such as the paragraph element p must be selected to follow a style rule. A style rule consists of three parts: a type selector, a property and a value:

```
selector {property : value}
```

The selector is normally the HTML tag you wish to style, the property is the attribute you wish to change, and each property can take a value. The property and value are separated by a colon and surrounded by curly brackets, or braces:

selector → h1 {color : red} *property* *value*

If the value is two or more words, put double quotes around it:

```
p {font-family : "sans serif"}
```

To specify more than one property, separate each property with a semicolon. The style rule

```
p {text-align: center; color: blue}
```

defines a centre-aligned paragraph with a blue text colour. Selectors may be grouped by separating each selector with a comma. This is the way to group all header elements and make them appear in red text:

```
h1, h2, h3, h4, h5, h6 {color : red}
```

A selector that is an HTML tag is known as a **type selector**. Type selectors target every instance of an element.

Embedded style sheet

The following HTML shows the use of an embedded style sheet which contains the style rule for the paragraph containing the text 'Hello World!':

```
<head>
  <title>HTML Example</title>
  <style type="text/css">
    p { color : navy;
        font-family : "courier new";
        font-weight : bold;
        font-size : 24pt;
        background-color : yellow;
    }
  </style>
</head>

<body>
  <p>Hello World!</p>
</body>
```

An embedded style sheet is placed in the head section of the web page source and the style rules are enclosed between the tags `<style type="text/css">` and `</style>`. The element selector is p in this example.

External style sheet

An external style sheet is by far the best way of styling a web site. A single external style sheet may be linked to each web page on a web site so that the styling is consistent throughout the site. Any changes that are made to the external style sheet apply to the whole web site. Here are some style rules stored in the file MyStyles.css; note the extension .css:

```
h1 { font-size : 16pt;
     color : orange;
   }
h2 { margin : 1in;
     color : red;
     font-family : arial;
     font-size : 10pt;
   }
h3 { margin-left : 2in;
     color : navy;
     font-size : 2em;
   }
```

The HTML file CSSEx1.html uses the external style sheet MyStyles.css, which is linked or imported into the web page (Fig. 9.2.6). MyStyles.css uses type selectors.

▣ PC activity

Examine the effect of using different embedded style sheets on a given web page. Now edit the embedded style sheet to see its effect on the appearance of the web page.

```
<!doctype html public "~//W3C/DTD xhtml 1.0 Strict//en"
"http://www.w3.org/TR/xhtml1/DTD/xhtml1-strict.dtd">

<html>
  <head>
    <title>CSS Sample</title>
    <link rel="stylesheet" type="text/css"
        href="MyStyles.css" />
  </head>
  <body>
    <h1>This is going to be a headline.</h1>
    <h2>Hello World!</h2>
    <h3>This will be another headline.</h3>
    <h4>Hello World Again!</h4>
  </body>
</html>
```

To apply MyStyles.css to a web page, the web page must contain a link reference in the `<head>` section. A link reference uses the tag `<link />` with attributes `rel, type and href`. Attribute `rel` specifies that the relationship is of type stylesheet; attribute `type` specifies that the style sheet has format CSS text, and attribute `href` is the hypertext reference to MyStyles.css.

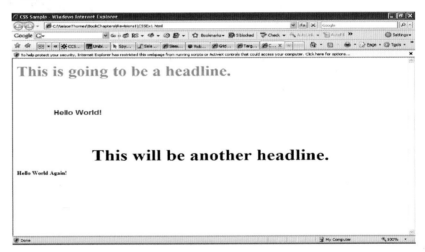

Fig. 9.2.6 *Appearance of web page CSSEx1.html in a web browser*

Class selector

Class selectors can be used to select any HTML element that has a class attribute. Here is the declaration for a class selector to embolden and colour text red:

```
.boldRed {color : red; font-weight : bold}
```

It can be applied in a web page to tags <h1> and <p>:

```
<h1 class = boldRed>Hello World!</h1>
<p class = boldRed>Hello World!</p>
```

If you want to be more restrictive, you can use class and type selectors together. Any type selector can be used. The class **boldRed** can be made to apply inside paragraphs only by changing the declaration as follows:

```
p.boldRed {color : red; font-weight : bold}
```

Block-level elements

The element `<div></div>` is a block-level element. Block-level elements mark divisions in page structure. The elements `<p></p>`, `<h#></h#>`, `<ol></ol>`, `<ul></ul>` and `<li></li>` are also block-level elements. Block-level elements generally add a blank line before and after their content (`<li></li>` is an exception). Good web page design uses the `<div>` element to divide a web page into distinct sections. It is used in conjunction with the CSS class attribute to create new elements (Fig. 9.2.7). It can also be used very effectively to create layouts using the rule of thirds.

```html
<html>
  <head>
    <title>Styles in context </title>
    <style type ="text/css">
      .german {font-family : fantasy;
               font-size : 32pt;color : green}
      .french {font-family : cursive;
               font-size : 36pt; color: blue}
    </style>
  </head>
  <body>
    <p> Hello World </p>
    <div class="german">
      <p> Hallo Welt </p>
    </div>
    <div class="french">
      <p>Bonjour Monde</p>
    </div>
  </body>
</html>
```

Fig. 9.2.7 *Appearance of a class-controlled div in a web browser*

ID selectors

An ID selector is an alternative to a class selector. In a style sheet it is declared with a # as follows:

```
#header {font : bold 130% Verdana}
```

The key difference between IDs and classes is that IDs identify a specific element and therefore must be unique on the page – a specific ID can be used only once per document. Classes mark elements as members of a group and can be used multiple times; a defined style may be applied to multiple elements. An ID selector is used as follows with the attribute id: `<div id = "header">`. There is just one header section per web page containing the logo and basic site-wide information, so it makes sense to use an ID selector labelled `"header"` rather than a class selector.

A typical web page is divided into several sections. Where more than one section serves a similar purpose, it makes sense to use a common class selector for each, e.g. `<div class = "warning">`. Class selectors can be combined together in elements; for example, `<div class ="redBold underlineAll"` has two rules: the selector class `redBold` and the selector class `underlineAll`. ID selectors cannot be combined this way. There may be times when a declaration conflicts with another declaration. These conflicts are resolved using the cascade rules. If a class selector and an ID selector are in conflict, the ID selector is chosen.

🖥 PC activity

Examine the use of `<div>` with class and ID selectors.

Layout

Always plan the layout of your web pages. The artists of the Renaissance used divine proportion, or the golden ratio, to design their paintings, sculptures and architecture. Observed in nature by the early Greeks, it is a way of dividing up a line or scene into the ratio 1:1.62. Use this ratio or an approximation of this ratio for your web pages. A simplified version is the rule of thirds. The area of the web page is divided into thirds, horizontally and vertically, which creates nine squares. Fig. 9.2.8 shows a design that relies on the rule of thirds. Other possibilities are created by dividing each vertical third in half.

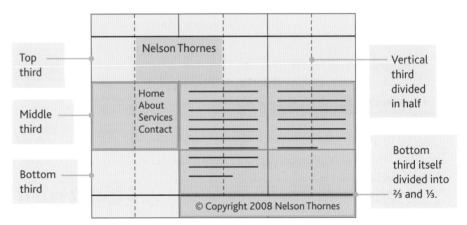

Fig. 9.2.8 *A grid created using the rule of thirds*

Inline elements

Inline elements fit in with the flow of the document. Three examples are `<span></span>`, `<strong></strong>` and `<em></em>`. The HTML

```
<span style="color : red; font-size : 14pt">You can add
coloured text</span>
```

produces

> You can add coloured text

The HTML

```
<strong>Bold text</strong>
```

produces

> **Bold text**

And the HTML

```
<em>Italicised text</em>
```

produces

> *Italicised text*

Other inline elements are `<a></a>`, the tag combination for inserting an anchor into a web page and `<img />`, the tag for inserting an image.

Comments

The comment tag is used to insert a comment into the source of a web page. A comment is ignored by the browser. You can use comments to explain your web page source, which can help you when you edit the source code at a later date. In external style sheets, comments are set between /* and */. In HTML code, a comment is written like this:

```
<!-This text is a comment->
<p>This is a regular paragraph</p>
```

And the browser displays this:

```
This is a regular paragraph
```

Questions

7 What is a style sheet?

8 Explain why style sheets are used and name two ways they can be incorporated into a web page.

9 What is the structure of a style rule?

10 Write the style rules for an external style sheet that will

   a centre and colour the text red in all paragraphs and

   b set heading h1 to colour blue, font size 32 points and font family serif.

11 (a) List four block-level HTML elements. (b) List three inline HTML elements.

12 Explain the CSS style rule `.redBold {color : red}`.

13 Describe two differences between a class selector and an ID selector.

 PC activity

Choose a set of web pages and examine how each web page looks in IE 7, Firefox 2.0.0.x, Opera 7, Netscape Navigator 9 and Safari 3.

Did you know?

W3C offers a web page validation service. This service checks the markup validity of Web documents in HTML and XHTML.

 **PC activity**

Go to **http://validator.w3.org** and use the validation service.

In this topic you have covered:

- web pages are written in HTML. The HTML for a web page is called its source

- text in a web page can be content for display, or formatting that describes structure and presentation

- a hyperlink is a way to link text or graphics in a web page to another location on the web

- page structure: `<html> <head> <title> ... </title> </head> <body> ... </body> </html>`

- block-level tags: `<div></div> <p></p> <hr /> <h#></h#> <ol></ol> <ul></ul> <li></li>`

- use `<div></div>` to divide a web page into sections

- inline tags: `<span></span> <strong></strong> <em></em> <br /> <a></a> <img />`

- all tags should be written in lower case

- a style sheet is a collection of rules about presentation; it may be embedded or external

- a style rule is expressed like this: `selector {property : value}`

- there are three kinds of selector: type, class, and ID that you need to be aware of

- a selector selects the elements on an HTML page that are affected by the style rules

- CSS is a way to separate a web page's formatting from its content

- a good rule for page layout is the rule of thirds

- three web-page colour schemes: monochromatic, analogous, complementary.

10 Consequences of uses of computers

10.1 Legal and ethical issues

In this topic you will cover:

- current laws that refer to computerised data and programs

- codes of conduct

- the potential impact on society of emerging technologies.

Key terms

Copyright: protects material, such as literature, art, music, sound recordings, films and broadcasts.

Design right: protects how something looks.

Patent: protects how an invention works or what it does.

Trademark: protects the name or logo used to identify a business or product.

Cracking: illegally breaking into a computer system.

Hacking: illegally breaking into a computer system; programming in an unstructured way.

Activity

1. Summarise an interesting case of hacking.

2. What is the difference between white hat, grey hat and black hat hackers?

Current laws

1 Copyright, Designs and Patents Act 1988

Intellectual property means you own what you create. This can be music, art, films, broadcasts, sound recordings or literature. Literature also covers computer programs. You may wish to use your intellectual property to gain financial reward. Many people earn their living from creating intellectual property. The Copyright, Designs and Patents Act 1988 was passed to protect intellectual property.

Copyright means that you should only copy or use copyrighted work with the copyright owner's permission. Copyright applies to any medium. This means you are not allowed to make a copy of copyrighted material in another medium without permission. There is an exception if you are using it for educational purposes, such as research or private study. You must always acknowledge your sources. If you create music, films, photography or written material, you receive automatic protection from copyright laws. **Design right** gives you protection from copying of your original design. You can register your design to protect it from being copied for up to 25 years.

If you invent something new that can be made or used, you may wish to **patent** it. This will protect your idea for up to 20 years. Your invention must have an inventive step that is not obvious to someone with knowledge and experience in the subject. Scientific and mathematical discoveries are excluded, as are some computer programs. An organisation can register a **trademark** so customers can tell it apart from other organisations. A trademark can be a name, logo, domain name, slogan, shape or sound. For more information, visit the web site of the Intellectual Property Office (**www.ipo.gov.uk**).

2 Computer Misuse Act 1990

The maximum penalty for an offence under the Computer Misuse Act 1990 is a fine or prison sentence. The act distinguishes between three offences in order of increasing severity:

- unauthorised access to computer material, i.e. data or programs
- unauthorised access with intent to commit or facilitate commission of further offences
- unauthorised modification of computer material.

Sections 35–38 of the Police and Justice Act 2006 amend the Computer Misuse Act 1990. Unauthorised access is sometimes known as **cracking** or **hacking**.

(3) Data Protection Act 1984 and 1998

EU laws on privacy of information have influenced the Data Protection Act (DPA). Here are the eight principles that govern **personal data** and **data processors**:

1 ▦ **Data gathering:** personal data shall be processed fairly and lawfully and under certain conditions. These conditions include that the data subject has given consent, that they know what data is being gathered and what the data is used for.

2 ▦ **Data purpose:** personal data shall be obtained only for one or more specified and lawful purposes, and shall not be further processed in any manner incompatible with that purpose.

3 ▦ **Data quantity:** personal data shall be adequate, relevant and not excessive in relation to the purpose for which they are processed.

4 ▦ **Data quality:** personal data shall be accurate and, where necessary, kept up to date.

5 ▦ **Data lifetime:** personal data processed for any purpose shall not be kept for longer than is necessary for that purpose.

6 ▦ **Data subject's rights:** personal data shall be processed in accordance with the rights of **data subjects** under the Data Protection Act. The rights include that the data subject is told what data is held about them, for what purposes and to whom it may be disclosed. The data subject also has the right to have inaccurate data destroyed or corrected and the right to compensation for damage or distress resulting from contravention of the act.

7 ▦ **Internal data security:** appropriate technical and organisational measures shall be taken against unauthorised or unlawful processing of personal data and against accidental loss or destruction of, or damage to, personal data.

8 ▦ **External data security:** personal data shall not be transferred to a country or territory outside the EU, unless that country or territory ensures an adequate level of protection for the rights and freedoms of data subjects in relation to the processing of personal data.

Under this act, every **data controller** must register with the Information Commissioner. There are important exemptions to the act. The main ones are national security, crime prevention and detection, taxation, and domestic purposes such as your personal address book. For more information, visit the website of the Information Commissioner's Office (**www.ico.gov.uk**).

(4) Health and Safety (Display Screen Equipment) Regulations 1992

If display screen equipment use is a significant part of their work activity, employees must have training and information on how to use the equipment safely. Employees can request an eye test. They should have breaks or changes in activity. They should have a suitable workstation with adjustable chair, a footrest if required, and a detachable keyboard if a keyboard is required for operation (Figure 1).

Students are not classed as employees under the act, but it still makes sense to follows these recommendations on the website of the Health and Safety Executive (**www.hse.gov.uk**):

215

- Your forearms should be approximately horizontal and your eyes the same height as the top of the VDU.

- You should have enough work space to accept whatever documents or other equipment you need.

- Try different arrangements of keyboard, screen, mouse and documents to find the best arrangement for you. A document holder may help you avoid awkward neck and eye movements.

- Arrange your desk and VDU to avoid glare, or bright reflections on the screen. This will be easiest if neither you nor the screen is directly facing windows or bright lights. Adjust curtains or blinds to prevent unwanted light.

- Adjust the brightness and contrast controls on the screen to suit lighting conditions in the room. Make sure the screen surface is clean. Individual characters on the screen should be sharply focused and should not flicker or move.

- Make sure there is space under your desk to move your legs freely.

- Avoid excess pressure from the edge of your seat on the backs of your legs and knees. A footrest may be helpful, particularly for smaller users.

- Adjust your keyboard to get a good keying position. A space in front of the keyboard is sometimes helpful for resting the hands and wrists when not keying.

- Try to keep your wrists straight when keying. Keep a soft touch on the keys and don't overstretch your fingers. Good keyboard technique is important.

- Position the mouse within easy reach, so it can be used with the wrist straight. Sit upright and close to the desk, so you don't have to work with your mouse arm stretched. Move the keyboard out of the way if it is not being used.

- Support your forearm on the desk, and don't grip the mouse too tightly.

- Rest your fingers lightly on the buttons and do not press them hard.

- Don't sit in the same position for long periods. Make sure you change your posture as often as practicable. Some movement is desirable, but avoid repeated stretching to reach things you need.

- In setting up software, choose options giving text that is large enough to read easily on your screen, when you are sitting in a normal, comfortable working position. Select colours that are easy on the eye (avoid red text on a blue background, or vice-versa).

Fig. 10.1.1 *Health and safety regulations*

⑤ Regulation of Investigatory Powers Act 2000

Under the Regulation of Investigatory Powers Act 2000 (RIPA) it is an offence to intercept a message sent via public or private telecommunication systems (telephone calls, e-mails, etc.). The RIPA gives the security and intelligence services the right to intercept messages, and Internet Service Providers (ISPs) may be required to make this possible. Under some circumstances, the security services may also request an encryption key to an encrypted message.

The RIPA no longer applies once messages are in a mailbox, and the DPA requires ISPs and network administrators to grant privacy to users. Some organisations (schools, colleges, employers, etc.) may wish to monitor messages to ensure compliance with codes of conduct, but they must tell users that they are monitoring messages.

Questions

1 You are asked to design a user interface. Which regulations should you bear in mind and what in particular should you consider?

2 You accept your first job as a computer programmer. After a few weeks of using a workstation to type program code, you start having pains in your neck and right arm. What rights have you got under which regulations?

3 You are asked to program a new online interface for an e-commerce company. The company wants you to collect various pieces of personal information from its online customers. What laws does the company have to abide by? What does that mean for your task?

4 Imagine you are working as a network technician in a large organisation. Your friend's girlfriend also works at this organisation. Your friend asks you to intercept her e-mails as he suspects her of cheating on him. What are the regulations you need to abide by?

💡 Ethics   = หลักจริยธรรม

Code of conduct

Many organisations ask their students, employees or members to sign a code of conduct. A code of conduct is not a law. If you break an organisation's code of conduct, you cannot be criminally convicted but the organisation may follow its disciplinary procedure. The British Computer Society (BCS) has a code of conduct and a code of good practice; all BCS members must abide by them.

Ten commandments

The Computer Ethics Institute of Washington DC has proposed these 10 commandments of computer ethics:

1 Thou shalt not use a computer to harm other people.

2 Thou shalt not interfere with other people's computer work.

3 Thou shalt not snoop around in other people's computer files.

4 Thou shalt not use a computer to steal.

5 Thou shalt not use a computer to bear false witness.

6 Thou shalt not copy or use proprietary software for which you have not paid.

7 Thou shalt not use other people's computer resources without authorization or proper compensation.

8 Thou shalt not appropriate other people's intellectual output.

9 Thou shalt think about the social consequences of the program you are writing or the system you are designing.

10 Thou shalt always use a computer in ways that ensure consideration and respect for your fellow humans.

Digital rights management

The use of **digital rights management** (DRM) is controversial. Copyright holders of digital media try to limit when a user can access it. For example, you pay to download a film. DRM technology may be used to restrict when and how often you can watch this film.

Key terms

Digital rights management: application of control technologies to limit the use of digital media.

Proprietary software is usually sold under licence. A software licence lays down the terms of use, such as the number of backup copies allowed and how many users may run the software. Owners of **proprietary software** usually prohibit licence holders from making changes to the software and usually prohibit reverse engineering, selling or passing on to third parties.

[handwritten note overlapping text:] ความไม่เท่าเทียม
digital devide – the disparity between groups when acessing ICT
- age
- wealth
- education
- culture
- location

The ... Foundation (FSF) has defined free software licences ...

... the program for any purpose.

... how the program works and adapt it to your needs.

... ribute copies so you can help your neighbour.

... ve the program and release your improvements to ... the whole community benefits.

... cess to the source code is a precondition' for ... the Open Source Initiative is similarly dedicated to ... rce software. Copyleft is a form of licensing to allow ... puter software.

... the consequences if you break the code of conduct of the organisation you are working for?

6 What rules would you be breaking if you used open source software, made some changes to it then sold it as your own software?

7 When you pay for a licence for proprietary software, why should you not sell the software to third parties?

8 What technology could be used to restrict the use of digital media?

Emerging technologies

The Industrial Revolution is the term used for the accelerated technological development that started in Britain and spread through Europe and North America in the nineteenth century. It changed the lives of the population dramatically. People moved from working on the land to working in factories. The more recent technological developments are known as the digital revolution and the information age. Many people work with information and are known as knowledge workers. The gap between people with access to information technology and people without is called the digital divide.

Robotics

What is a robot?

A robot is a movable mechanical structure that can sense its surroundings and manipulate things. Its actions are controlled by computer programs. A robot may take many forms, such as a humanoid or an arm with a universal joint. A robot may have a camera so it can collect images and respond to them. A robot gets input from various sensors for light, touch, etc. Actuators start and stop motors that move parts of the robot. The control programs that process the input and produce the output can make the robot appear to be intelligent. Artificial intelligence (AI) is the area of computing that deals with robots, machine learning, expert systems and neural networks. AI is becoming more and more important.

Robots are used for repetitive tasks and tasks that require precision and decisions. For example, in car manufacturing, robots are used to spray-paint the bodywork. Welding robots produce better and more consistent welds than human welders. Robots are used extensively for tasks that are too dangerous for humans. They can be used for bomb disposal (Fig. 10.1.2).

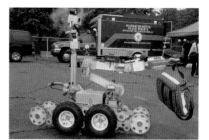

Fig. 10.1.2 *A 2004 prototype of the Carver bomb disposal robot*

Case study

Steve Grand developed a robot and called it Lucy (Fig. 10.1.3). Lucy is an orang-utan robot. She is not programmed in the conventional way of robotics. Her system consists of a synthetic nervous system. This is a theoretical model of the brain built from tens of thousands of virtual neurons that combine to form a general-purpose learning machine. This virtual brain is intended to develop and learn as Lucy 'grows up'. Lucy has learned to point at a banana. For more information, visit **www.cyberlife-research.com**.

Activity

Search for information about robots on the Internet. Describe a field where robots are used and explain why.

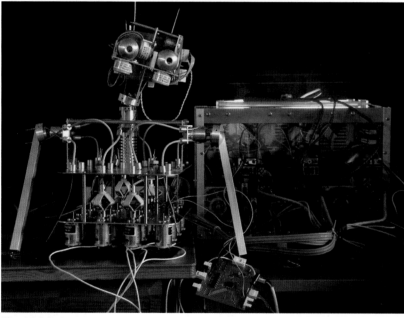

Fig. 10.1.3 *Lucy*

Questions

9 What is the digital divide?

10 The Industrial Revolution caused people to move from the countryside into towns where they found work in factories. Where do you think computer programmers will be living and working in the future?

11 Name some tasks where machines are better than humans. Name some tasks where humans are better than machines. See Topic 1.1.

12 What can Steve Grand's experiments tell us about how the human mind works?

13 What can we learn from machines?

14 What are the limitations of using machines as tools?

☑ *In this topic you covered:*

- there are many laws that refer to computerised data and programs
- personal data is data that relates to a living individual who can be identified from that data
- a data subject is an individual who is the subject of personal data
- cracking means illegally breaking into a computer system; it is also called hacking
- some organisations have codes of conduct that govern their members
- DRM applies control technologies to limit the use of digital media
- the computer developments of the twentieth century are called the digital revolution
- knowledge workers are people that work extensively with information
- the digital divide is the gap between people with IT access and people without it
- a robot is a mechanical structure whose actions are controlled by computer programs
- robots are used for repetitive tasks, precision work and jobs that are too dangerous for humans
- AI researchers develop expert systems and neural networks.

Practice questions

✓ Problem solving

1.1 Principles of computation

1   What is meant by
   (a) Computing? *(1 mark)*
   (b) Computation? *(1 mark)*
   (c) Computability? *(1 mark)*

1.2 Stages of problem solving

1   For computing coursework, a student wishes to create a system for the English department of his school that will compose poetry on any topic submitted to the system. His teacher rejects the student's proposal on the grounds that the student's problem definition is not well-defined. Give three reasons why the teacher believes this problem definition not to be well-defined. *(3 marks)*

1.3 Finite state machines

1   Fig. 1 is a state transition diagram for processing text.

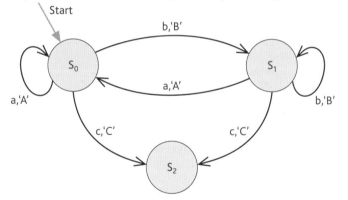

Fig. 1 *A state transition diagram for processing text*

(a) What does the input sequence abbabc produce as output? *(3 marks)*
(b) Complete this state transition table for the input sequence abac.

Input	Current state	Output	Next state
a			

(4 marks)

1.4 Algorithm design

1   An algorithm may be expressed in pseudocode or structured English using repetition statements.
(a) Name **two** other types of statement that may be used. *(2 marks)*

(b) Explain the difference between pseudocode and structured English. *(2 marks)*

(c) Dry run the following algorithm by completing a trace table, as shown below.

```
Result ← 0
y ← 0
Repeat
   Input x
   Result ← Result + x
   y ← y + 1
Until y = 4
Output Result / y
```

x	y	Result	Output
	0	0	
3			
7			
6			
8			

(4 marks)

(d) What is the purpose of this algorithm? *(1 mark)*

☑ Programming

2.5 Procedures and functions

1   In one high-level language an example of a constant definition would be CONST VatRate = 17.5; state one advantage of using a named constant, like VatRate, rather than the actual value (17.5) in a high-level language program. *(1 mark)*

AQA, 2002

2   The structured approach when writing programs uses functions and procedures.

(a) Give two reasons why procedures are used.

(b) What are parameters used for in the context of procedures and functions? *(2 marks)*

AQA, 2002

3   The following code is part of a high-level program:

```
Var Name: String;
Var Hours: Integer;
Var RateOfPay: Real;
Function CalculatePay(InHours: Integer; InRateOfPay: Real):Real;
      Var Total: Real;
```

(a) (i) Name a global variable in the above code. *(1 mark)*

   (ii) Name a local variable in the above code. *(1 mark)*

(b) Procedures and functions are often self-contained. What is meant by the term self-contained in this context? *(1 mark)*

(c) Give one reason why the use of global variables may introduce program bugs. *(1 mark)*

AQA, 2005

2.6 Arrays

1   A retail store employs 10 sales staff.

Staff try to persuade customers to take out a store card with the company when they make a purchase.

The store keeps a record of the number of new store cards issued by its sales staff over the first six months of the year.

Table 1 *StoreCards*

	[1]	[2]	[3]	[4]	[5]	[6]
[1]	12	12	6	8	3	2
[2]	12	17	7	4	5	6
[3]	2	12	0	12		
[4]	4	10	7	4		
[5]	5	0	0	0	0	0
[6]	6	1	4	6	7	8
[7]	12	19	12	**16**	17	6
[8]	13	9	7	3	4	5
[9]	12	8	4	4	5	4
[10]	14	11	12	4	5	6

The data is to be stored in a 2-dimensional array with identifier StoreCards as shown in Table 1.

The first subscript of the array represents the row number (the salesperson number), and the second subscript the column number (the month).

(a) In Table 1 the value 16 has been **emboldened**.

Explain what this value represents. *(2 marks)*

(b) Write a declaration statement for the array StoreCards. *(2 marks)*

(c) Using the data given in Table 1, write an assignment statement for the January sales for salesperson 8. *(2 marks)*

AQA, 2006

2   A company makes sofas and operates seven days a week. Each day, a record is made of the number of sofas that are rejected at the final quality control stage. An average of one reject a day is considered acceptable. This is investigated using the program below at the end of each week.

```
Program RejectReport;
Var
  DayNo: Integer;
  RejectTotal: Integer;
  DailyRejects: Array[1..7] of Integer;

Begin
  RejectTotal := 0;
  For DayNo := 1 To 7
    Do RejectTotal := RejectTotal - DailyRejects[DayNo];
  WriteLn[RejectTotal];
End.
```

(a) (i)   Write the assignment statement in the program which performs a calculation. *(1 mark)*

(ii) Write a declaration statement that appears in the program. *(1 mark)*

(iii) What is the purpose of the variable DayNo? *(1 mark)*

(iv) What type of data structure is DailyRejects? *(1 mark)*

(b) The program is to be extended to report whether this was a satisfactory week for the number of rejected sofas. An average of one reject each day is acceptable.

Write additional programming statement(s), in the language you are familiar with, to report one of the messages 'Investigate' or 'Inside weekly tolerance'. Use the same variable identifiers as used in the program given. *(2 marks)*

AQA, 2007

✅ Programming structure

3.1 Structured programming

1 Well-constructed programs use a structured approach for the design and coding stages.

One practical way in which the programmer will use a structured approach to programming is the use of subroutines (procedures/functions).

Give three other ways. *(3 marks)*

AQA, 2007

2 The following pseudocode represents a program that reads 10 integer numbers entered by a user and outputs the average.

```
Program CalculateStatistics

Table[10] : Array of Integers
Result : Real Number

Call Procedure ReadTenIntegers(Table)
Call Procedure CalculateAverage(Table, Result)
Call Procedure DisplayAverage(Result)
```

(a) (i) Name a parameter used in the above program. *(1 mark)*

(ii) Explain how this parameter is used. *(1 mark)*

(b) Draw a structure chart to represent the above program. *(2 marks)*

AQA, 2004

3.2 Standard algorithms

1 The algorithm below rearranges numbers stored in a one-dimensional array called List.
Ptr is an integer variable used as an index (subscript) which identifies elements within List.
Temp is a variable, which is used as a temporary store for numbers from List.

```
Ptr ← 1
While Ptr < 10 Do
  If List[Ptr] > List[Ptr + 1] Then
    Temp ← List[Ptr]
    List[Ptr] ← List[Ptr + 1]
    List[Ptr + 1] ← Temp
  Endif
  Ptr ← Ptr + 1
Endwhile
```

(a) Dry run the algorithm by completing the table opposite.

It is only necessary to show those numbers which change at a particular step.

Ptr	Temp	List										
		[1]	[2]	[3]	[4]	[5]	[6]	[7]	[8]	[9]	[10]	
		43	25	37	81	18	70	64	96	52	4	

(7 marks)

(b) What will happen when Ptr = 10? *(1 mark)*

(c) If the whole algorithm is now applied to this rearranged list, what will be the values of:

(i) List[1]

(ii) List[9]

(iii) List[10]? *(3 marks)*

AQA, 2003

☑ Checking for errors

4.1 Validation and error handling

1 Software which involves significant quantities of data entry will include validation checks.

A certain program uses a file with the following fields:

```
(HouseID, PostCode, Surname, DateOfBirth,
    Occupation, NumberOfAdults, NumberOfChildren)
```

One example of a validation check that could be applied to data being entered into this file is a Type check which will restrict entries to a certain data type.

This could be applied to the field NumberOfAdults which would accept only integers.

Select **three** fields from this file, and for each, name and describe a different validation check (excluding Type check) that could be applied to it. *(6 marks)*

AQA, 2006

4.2 Testing

1 The operations DIV and MOD perform integer arithmetic.

x DIV y calculates how many times y divides into x, for example 7 DIV 3 = 2.

x MOD y calculates the remainder that results after the division, for example 7 MOD 3 = 1.

(a) The following algorithm uses an array Result.

Dry run this algorithm by completing the trace table overleaf.

```
x ← 5
Index ← 0
REPEAT
    y ← x MOD 2
    x ← x DIV 2
    Index ← Index + 1
    Result[Index] ← y
UNTIL x = 0
```

y	x	Index	Result		
			[3]	[2]	[1]
–	5	0	–	–	–
1	2	1	–	–	1

(6 marks)

(b) What is the purpose of this algorithm? *(1 mark)*

AQA, 2002

2 (a) Dry run the following algorithm by completing the trace table.

```
x ← 5
y ← 3
Result ← 1
REPEAT
    Result ← Result * x
    y ← y – 1
UNTIL y = 0
```

x	y	Result
5	3	1

(7 marks)

(b) What is the purpose of this algorithm? *(1 mark)*

AQA, 2005

3 The following algorithm uses an array Values that contains the integers 4, 7, 9.

(a) Dry run this algorithm by using the trace table below:

```
Last ← 3
New ← 6
Ptr ← 1
WHILE (New > Values[Ptr]) DO
    Ptr ← Ptr + 1
ENDWHILE
WHILE (Last >= Ptr) DO
    Values [Last+1] ← Values[Last]
    Last ← Last – 1
ENDWHILE
Values[Ptr] ← New
```

New	Last	Ptr	Values				
			[1]	[2]	[3]	[4]	[5]
6	3	1	4	7	9		

(6 marks)

(b) What is the purpose of this algorithm? *(1 mark)*

AQA, 2005

☑ Data representation

5.1 Binary and hexadecimal numbers

1 Using 8 bits to represent an integer, convert the denary numbers 95 and –73 into binary using two's complement. Show in binary the result of adding these two binary numbers. *(4 marks)*

2 (a) Show how the denary numbers 53 and –75 will be represented. *(2 marks)*

   (b) Show the result obtained when 53 is added to 75 using this representation. Comment on your answer. *(2 marks)*

3 (a) Convert the denary number 1032 into binary and store the result in a 16-bit word. *(2 marks)*

   (b) Write down the hexadecimal equivalent of your binary number from part (a). *(2 marks)*

4 (a) Convert the denary number 1026.75 into fixed-point binary and store the result in a 16-bit word with 4 bits after the binary point. *(2 marks)*

   (b) Write down the hexadecimal equivalent of your binary number from part (a). *(2 marks)*

5 (a) Convert the fixed-point binary number 0100 0010 0001 0100 into denary; assume 6 bits after the binary point. *(2 marks)*

6 The binary pattern 1011 1110 0100 could be interpreted in a number of different ways.

   (a) State its hexadecimal representation. *(1 mark)*

   (b) State its value in denary if it represents an unsigned fixed-point number with 4 bits after the binary point. Show your working. *(3 marks)*

   (c) State its value in denary if it represents a two's complement integer. *(2 marks)*

AQA, 2005

7 The binary pattern 0100 0000 1110 can be interpreted in a number of different ways.

   (a) State its hexadecimal representation. *(1 mark)*

   (b) State its value as a decimal number if it represents a signed binary integer using two's complement representation. *(1 mark)*

   (c) State its value as a decimal number if it represents an unsigned fixed point number with four bits after the binary point. *(2 marks)*

AQA, 2007

5.2 Character coding schemes

1 (a) Using the ASCII code table shown in Table 1, what is the **7-bit binary ASCII** code for character 'B'? *(1 mark)*

(b) When a parity bit is included, character codes are stored as 8-bit binary numbers where the most significant bit is a parity bit. The system will use even parity.

Describe how the parity bit is used during data transmission of a single character. *(2 marks)*

AQA, 2007

Table 1 *ASCII code table*

Character	Decimal	Character	Decimal	Character	Decimal
<space>	32	I	73	R	82
A	65	J	74	S	83
B	66	K	75	T	84
C	67	L	76	U	85
D	68	M	77	V	86
E	69	N	78	W	87
F	70	O	79	X	88
G	71	P	80	Y	89
H	72	Q	81	Z	90

2   (a) Use the ASCII code table given in Table 1 to look up the ASCII code for character 'V'.

   (i) What is its representation when written in 7-bit binary? *(1 mark)*

   (ii) What is its value when expressed in 8 bits with the eighth bit an odd parity bit? *(1 mark)*

   (b) A programming language help file describes the Chr() function as follows.

   Chr() takes a single integer value as its parameter.

   The function returns the ASCII character represented by the parameter.

   Example: Chr(65) will return value 'A'

   (i) What is returned by Chr(68)? *(1 mark)*

   (ii) What value is assigned to variable MyChar when the following two statements are executed?

```
Value := 9
MyChar := Chr(65 + Value)
```

(1 mark)

AQA, 2006

3   (i) The ASCII value for the character '0' (zero) is 48. What character is represented by 0011 0100? *(1 mark)*

   (ii) Name **one** other standard coding system for coding information expressed in character or text-based form. *(1 mark)*

AQA, 2005

4   Parity bits are used to ensure the accuracy of stored data.

   (i) What is meant by even parity? *(1 mark)*

   (ii) Briefly describe how parity bits are used. *(2 marks)*

AQA, 2004

5 The ASCII coding system uses seven bits to code a character.

The character digits 0 to 9 are assigned the decimal number codes 48 to 57.

An extra bit is used as a parity bit.

A computer system uses the most significant bit (MSB) as a parity bit for each byte and works with even parity.

(i) What is the bit pattern if the digits 37 are to be stored as characters? *(3 marks)*

(ii) Explain how the parity bit is used by this computer system. *(2 marks)*

AQA, 2003

6 The ASCII coding system uses 7 bits to code a character. The eighth bit is used as a parity bit. Explain how a parity bit is used when transmitting ASCII codes using even parity. *(3 marks)*

AQA, 2002

7 The ASCII code for the character '3' is the decimal number 51.

(i) What is the ASCII code for the character '5'? *(1 mark)*

(ii) If 8 bits are used to store one character, what is the bit pattern when the string '25' is stored in a 16-bit word? *(2 marks)*

AQA, 2002

5.3 Bitmapped and vector graphics

1 (a) How can a black and white image be represented as a bitmapped graphic? *(2 marks)*

(b) What change needs to be made to (a) to represent a 256-colour image? *(1 mark)*

AQA Specimen paper

2 (a) Fig. 1 overleaf shows a number of drawing objects from the toolbox of a vector drawing program.

(i) For object 1 and object 2, state **two** properties common to both types of object, which would be recorded when used in a drawing. *(2 marks)*

(ii) State **one** other property for object 1 which would be recorded when used in a drawing. *(1 mark)*

(iii) Graphics can be created with either vector graphics software or bitmapped software. If the graphic is enlarged it may become distorted if created with bitmapped software but show no distortion if created with vector graphics software. Explain this statement. *(2 marks)*

(b) Fig. 2 overleaf shows the file type options available when saving a file with bit-mapped graphics software.

(i) How many bits are used to store each pixel if the resolution selected is as shown ('16 color bitmap')? *(1 mark)*

(ii) '256 color' images are stored with 1 byte per pixel. Explain this statement. *(1 mark)*

(iii) Read again the statement in part (ii). A picture with size 1024 by 768 pixels is saved as a '256 color' image. Calculate the picture size in Kilobytes. *(1 mark)*

(iv) Black and white (monochrome) bitmapped files store each pixel with a single bit. A black and white image of size 512 by 256 pixels has a calculated file size of 16 Kilobytes. The actual file size is larger than this calculated size as the bitmap file contains other data. What is this other data? *(1 mark)*

AQA, 2006

3   Describe **one** method used to compress images.   *(3 marks)*

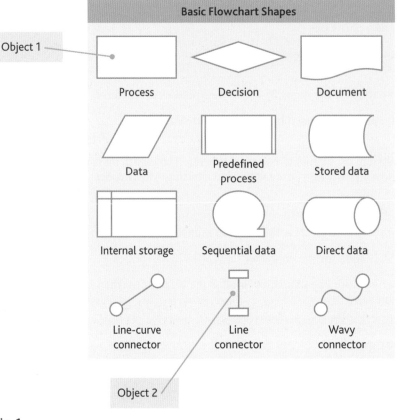

Fig. 1

Fig. 2

5.4 Representing sound in a computer

1   Traditionally, sound was recorded in analogue form, such as on vinyl records. For digital audio systems, the signals received from the microphone are sampled and the measurements of the amplitude can be stored as digital data. To reproduce the sound, the digital data is fed through a digital-to-analogue converter.

(a)   Give **two** factors which affect the quality of sound.   *(2 marks)*

(b)   What is possible when using the digital method of representing sound that could not be done with sound recorded in analogue form?   *(1 mark)*

(c)   What is sound synthesis?   *(1 mark)*

AQA, 2003

2   Computer systems store not just information representing numbers and characters, but also sounds and images.

      A microphone converts sound into an electrical signal which may be recorded.

      (i)   Explain how the electrical signal from the microphone is converted into a form which can be stored in a computer system.   *(3 marks)*

      (ii) What piece of hardware is required to convert the digitally recorded sound before it is amplified and played back through loudspeakers?   *(1 mark)*

                                                                                          AQA, 2003

3   Sound can be stored in a computer system. In order to store signals from a microphone in a form that the computer system can use, a special piece of hardware is needed.

      (a)   Give the name of this special piece of hardware.   *(1 mark)*

      (b)   Describe the way that sound is coded in a computer system.   *(2 marks)*

                                                                                          AQA, 2004

☑ The system life cycle

6.1 Stages in hardware and software development

1   The development of computer-based systems is commonly broken down into a number of stages collectively called the *systems life cycle*. Briefly describe the following stages of this cycle.
      Systems Analysis
      Systems Design
      Implementation
      Testing
      Evaluation   *(5 marks)*

                                                                                          AQA, 2000

2   A snack dispensing machine is being designed which will give change when a customer inserts more money than the cost of the snack chosen. The machine only accepts £2, £1, 50p, 20p 10p and 5p coins. All snacks cost a multiple of 5p. The machine should give the change in as few coins as possible. A programmer is asked to write a routine CalculateCoinage(Change). The routine will take as a parameter the amount of change to be returned. The routine will then calculate how many of each coin are required.

      Choose **three** suitable sets of test data for the parameter Change, which adequately test the functionality of this routine. Justify your choice in each case.   *(6 marks)*

                                                                                          AQA, 2006

▦ Unit 2

☑ Machine-level architecture

7.1 *Logic gates and Boolean algebra*

1   A certain industrial process uses an electrical control circuit to switch off the process when four measurements reach critical values. Boolean variables A, B, C and D are used to indicate for each measurement whether it is critical or not. The process must be stopped if A and B become critical at the same time or if A, C and D become critical together. The output from the control circuit is Q, another Boolean variable. Write a Boolean equation for Q in terms of A, B, C and D.

                                                                                          (4 marks)

2   A1, A2, B1, B2 and Q are Boolean variables.

(a) Construct a truth table for the logic gate circuit shown in Fig. 1. *(5 marks)*

(b) Express Q in terms of A1, A2, B1 and B2 for the logic gate circuit shown in Fig. 1. *(3 marks)*

(c) If A1 and A2 represent a two-bit binary number and B1 and B2 represent another two-bit binary number what use has this circuit? *(1 mark)*

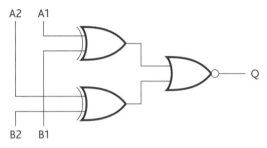

Fig. 1 *Logic gate circuit*

3 Simplify $A.(\overline{A} + B) + A.\overline{B}$. Show each stage of your working. *(4 marks)*

4 (a) The alarm in your kitchen will sound if it senses heat or smoke. State which logic gate would be used to determine whether the alarm will go off. *(1 mark)*

Draw up the relevant truth table. The outline of the truth table is done for you.

Senses heat	Senses smoke	Alarm
0		
0		
1		
1		

(2 marks)

(b) Logic gates are represented in diagrams using these symbols:

(i) Draw a logic diagram for the Boolean expression $A.(\overline{A} + B)$. *(3 marks)*

(ii) Simplify the expression using the laws and theorems of Boolean algebra. *(3 marks)*

(iii) Draw a logic diagram for the simplified expression. *(1 mark)*

AQA specimen paper

7.2 Computer architectures

1 Some of the internal components of a computer system are processor, read only memory, random access memory, address bus, data bus, clock. The diagram below shows how these are connected.

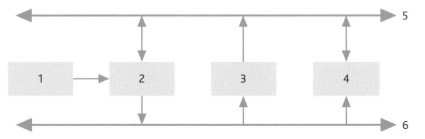

(a) Give the correct name for **each** of the six numbered items in the diagram above. *(6 marks)*

(b) Which **one** of the above components limits the number of memory locations? *(1 mark)*

(c) Which **one** of the above components limits the amount of data that can be transferred in one go? *(1 mark)*

2 Some of the components of a computer system are

Internal components
Clock 1
Data Bus 2
Address Bus 3
Main Memory 4
VDU Controller 5
Keyboard Controller 6
Disk Controller 7

Peripherals
Keyboard 8
Monitor 9
Secondary Storage 10

(a) The diagram below is partially filled in. Complete the diagram by writing a number from the list above in **each** empty circle. *(6 marks)*

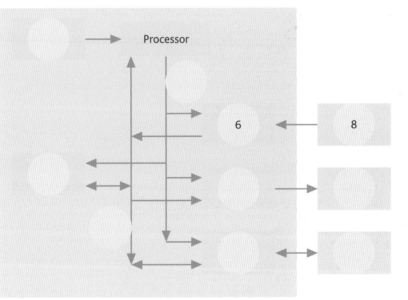

(b) The above computer system uses the *stored program concept*. Explain this term. *(1 mark)*

AQA, 2005

7.3 Basic machine code operations and the fetch–execute cycle

1 A processor with a machine code instruction format of 16 bits uses 6 of these bits for the op-code and the remaining 10 bits for the operand.

(a) What is the highest memory address that can be addressed by an instruction? *(2 marks)*

(b) How many different op-codes can this processor have? *(2 marks)*

(c) The main registers involved in the fetch–execute cycle are the program counter (PC), the current instruction register (CIR), the memory address register (MAR) and the memory buffer register (MBR). List the steps of the fetch–execute cycle using register transfer notation. *(6 marks)*

2   Here is a fragment of assembly language program written for an instruction set that uses 4 bits for an op-code and 8 bits for an operand:

```
LOAD  #100
STORE 254
ADD   #25
ADD   254
STORE 255
LOAD  254
```

(a) Devise binary codes (op-codes) for the operations LOAD, ADD and STORE shown in this assembly language program. Your codes should take account of the addressing modes employed. *(5 marks)*

(b) Now, using your op-codes, translate this fragment into its equivalent machine code. *(6 marks)*

3   Explain what the program fragment in Question 2 does when translated into machine code and executed. *(6 marks)*

4   Here is a memory dump for a machine code program expressed in hexadecimal:

500	1003
501	800D
502	1006

Op-codes of this program occupy 4 bits, operands 12 bits.

(a) What are the op-codes expressed in binary used by this program fragment? *(2 marks)*

(b) Give **one** reason for obtaining a memory dump. *(1 mark)*

(c) Give **one** reason for expressing a memory dump in hexadecimal. *(1 mark)*

5   (a) Explain what is meant by an instruction set. *(2 marks)*

(b) A high-level program was compiled into machine code and executed successfully on computer A. The machine code was then transferred onto a different computer, computer B. When an attempt was made to run this program on computer B the error message 'Attempt to execute an illegal instruction' appeared on B's visual display unit. What is the most likely cause of this error message? *(2 marks)*

✅ Computer systems

8.1 Hardware devices

1   (a) For **each** of the following situations in a small business, give **one** appropriate storage medium from this list: flash memory, CD-R, hard disk, DAT tape, floppy disk. Justify your choice.

        (i) Storage of applications and data used on a daily basis. *(2 marks)*

        (ii) Regular overnight backup of data. *(2 marks)*

        (iii) Archiving several megabytes of data. *(2 marks)*

(b) What would you expect of a printer that was to be used to print photographs as well as routine documents? Give **three** features. *(3 marks)*

AQA, 2007

2   The figure below shows a label from an item sold in a shop. The data from this label is captured by a computer system at the checkout.

(a) What input device would have been used in the shop to read this label? *(1 mark)*

5 000171 034700 >

(b) (i) Give one advantage of having the label read by the input device given in (a) rather than having the numbers keyed in by the shop assistant. *(1 mark)*

(ii) This type of code is used to identify items in many different situations. State one advantage that it has over a character code that makes it suitable for this task. *(1 mark)*

AQA, 2007

8.2 Classification of software

1 (a) Define the term software. *(1 mark)*

(b) Table 1 shows a list of software types with an example.

Complete the entries in the table. All entries **must be different.**

Table 1

Software category	Example
Programming language translator	(i)
(ii)	Disk defragmenter
(iii)	A DLL file that is used by several applications programs
General-purpose applications program	(iv)

(4 marks)

AQA, 2007

2 Table 2 lists a number of items of software.
Complete the table by adding the letter which best describes each item of software.
No letter should be used more than **once.**

Table 2

Software	Description (letter below)
Income tax calculation software	
Translator software for the C++ programming language	
Word processing software	
Operating software	

A – System software   E – Utility software
B – Assembler software   F – General-purpose application software
C – Bespoke software   G – Special-purpose application software
D – Interpreter or compiler software *(4 marks)*

AQA, 2007

3 Fig. 1 and Fig. 2 below show two versions of the same program.

a

Move	#45,	R0
Move	#4,	R1
Move	#96,	R2
Add	R2,	R1
Add	R1,	R0

100	00101000 00101101
101	00101001 00000100
102	00101010 01100000
103	10100001 00000000
104	10100000 00000000

Fig. 1   **Fig. 2**

(a) What generation of programming language is shown in Fig. 1? *(1 mark)*

(b) What generation of programming language is shown in Fig. 2? *(1 mark)*

(c) What would be a suitable heading for the column labelled **a** in Fig. 2? *(1 mark)*

(d) What software will be needed to translate the program code shown in Fig. 1 to the program code shown in Fig. 2? *(1 mark)*

(e) What is the relationship between the program instructions shown in Fig. 1 and the program instructions in Fig. 2? *(1 mark)*

AQA, 2006

4 (a) Application software can be subdivided into general-purpose, special-purpose and bespoke software.

    (i) Give a type of general-purpose application software package. *(1 mark)*

    (ii) What is meant by a special-purpose application software package? *(1 mark)*

(b) A school is planning to introduce an electronic registration system. The management have the choice of buying a readily available software package or having bespoke software written for them.

    (i) What is meant by bespoke software? *(1 mark)*

    (ii) Give **one** advantage and **two** disadvantages of bespoke software over readily available software. *(3 marks)*

AQA, 2003

5 (a) What is meant by

    (i) hardware *(1 mark)*

    (ii) software? *(1 mark)*

(b) Is an operating system hardware or software? *(1 mark)*

(c) Is a data bus hardware or software? *(1 mark)*

AQA, 2003

6 There are a large number of programming languages. System software such as compilers, assemblers, interpreters are used to translate programs into machine instructions.

(a) Explain the different ways in which a compiler and an interpreter operate.

    (i) a compiler *(1 mark)*

    (ii) an interpreter *(1 mark)*

(b) If both a compiler and an interpreter are available for a particular programming language, under what circumstances would it be preferable to use:

(i) a compiler *(1 mark)*

(ii) an interpreter? *(1 mark)*

(c) In what way does an assembler differ from a compiler? *(1 mark)*

AQA, 2003

7 Machine code is the first generation of programming languages. All other generations of programming languages need a program translator before the program can be executed. Name a type of translator suitable for:

(i) second-generation language programs *(1 mark)*

(ii) third-generation language programs. *(1 mark)*

8 (a) Machine code is the first-generation programming language. What is the second generation? *(1 mark)*

(b) A programmer writes a program in a second-generation programming language. What has to be done to this program before it can be executed? *(2 marks)*

(c) Some high-level languages are classified as imperative. What is meant by imperative? *(1 mark)*

(d) Give an example of an imperative high-level language. *(1 mark)*

(e) What is the relationship between an imperative high-level language statement and its machine code equivalent? *(1 mark)*

(f) Give **two** disadvantages of programming in first- and second-generation programming languages compared with imperative high-level languages. *(2 marks)*

AQA, 2002

✔ The Internet

9.1 Structure of the Internet

1 Explain the difference between the Web, the Internet and an intranet. *(6 marks)*

2 An organisation wants to set up a web site. They decided on a suitable domain name.

(a) Why do they need to register this domain name with an Internet registry? *(1 mark)*

(b) The Domain Name System allows the use of domain names instead of IP addresses to locate a website. Explain how the Domain Name System makes this possible. *(1 mark)*

AQA specimen paper

3 Using electronic e-mail over the Internet is an example of a client–server system.

(a) Explain the term **client–server**. *(3 marks)*

(b) The sending and receiving of e-mails uses various protocols.

(i) Explain the term **protocol**. *(1 mark)*

(ii) Bob is a student travelling in his gap year. His sister Alice, e-mails a greeting to him on his birthday not knowing where he will be on that date. Explain, by including the main protocols involved, how Bob is able to pick up Alice's message. *(5 marks)*

AQA specimen paper

4 A Telnet client is connected to a Telnet server. Networking software running on one of the hosts displays the information in Table 1 on the host's console:

Table 1 shows the IP address and port number of established connections otherwise it shows the listening port number.

(a) What is the IP address of the Telnet server? Justify your answer.   *(2 marks)*

Table 1 *Network status*

Protocol	Local address	Foreign address	State
TCP	140.234.1.25.23	202.101.10.4.1055	Established
TCP	*.23	*.*	Listening

(b) For the established Telnet connection, give **one** example of a socket address.   *(1 mark)*

(c) Explain **one** purpose for which Telnet is used.   *(2 marks)*

9.2 Web site design

1   Look at this HTML for a web page:

```
<html>
  <head>
    <title>Exam Questions</title>
  </head>
  <body>
    <h1>Exam Questions</h1>
    <p>      Exam questions
             assess understanding</p>
             The end.<br />
    <a href=www.domain.co.uk>Examination hints</a>
  </body>
</html>
```

(a) Draw a labelled diagram to show the appearance of the web page in a web browser.   *(7 marks)*

(b) Write a style rule to be included in an external style sheet to set paragraph text to red.   *(1 mark)*

(c) Name **two** other kinds of style sheets.   *(2 marks)*

2   Look at this HTML for a web page:

```
<html>                                    <a href="link1.html">Go one</a>
  <head>                                  </p>
    <title>Test</title>                   <p class=greenStyle>
    <link rel="stylesheet" type="text/css"  <a href="link2.html">Go two</a>
        href="Style.css" />               <br />Hello World!
  </head>                                  </p>
  <body>                                   </body>
    <p>                                  </html>
```

The external style sheet `Style.css` contains two rules:

```
.greenStyle {color : green; font-style : italic}
p.greenStyle a{text-decoration : underline}
```

(a) Draw a labelled diagram to show the appearance of the web page in a web browser.   *(7 marks)*

(b) State **one** difference between a class selector and an ID selector.   *(1 mark)*

(c) What **two** changes would need to be made to the style rules to change the class selector to an ID selector?   *(2 marks)*

3   Name **three** different types of style sheet.   *(3 marks)*

4   Name and describe **three** different types of colour scheme used in web page design.   *(3 marks)*

☑ Consequences of uses of computers

10.1 Legal and ethical issues

1   A company stores all its data in an online information retrieval system. Some of this data is personal data about the employees; some of it is confidential data about the business. All staff have authorised access to those parts of the system which they need to carry out their job role.

   (a) (i) Describe **two** distinct steps that should be taken to minimise unauthorised access by staff to those parts of the system they have no need to access in order to carry out their job role.   *(4 marks)*

      (ii) How could such unauthorised access be detected?   *(1 mark)*

   (b) What safeguards should be used to keep the data protected from loss or corruption due to:

      (i) hackers   *(1 mark)*

      (ii) viruses   *(1 mark)*

      (iii) a system failure caused, for example, by a power cut?   *(1 mark)*

   (c) Describe **one** further safeguard which needs to be in place to enable the company to get back into operation swiftly and effectively after a serious problem causing a complete system failure.   *(1 mark)*

AQA, 2007

3   Schools and colleges keep many electronic records of personal data on their students.

What is meant by the term 'Personal Data' as used in the Data Protection Acts of 1984 and 1998?   *(1 mark)*

AQA, 2007

4   Among the legislation which affects computer users are the following:

A. The Copyright, Design and Patents Act 1998

B. The Computer Misuse Act 1990

C. The Health and Safety (Display Screen Equipment) Regulations 1992

D. The Data Protection Act 1998

E. The Regulation of Investigatory Powers Act 2000

In the following situations, actions are taken in order to comply with one or other of the above Acts and Regulations. In each case, identify the relevant legislation which is being followed.

   (a) In the firm where Amelli works the state and condition of all workstations are checked once a year.   *(1 mark)*

   (b) Mary started a new job and gave details such as address and next of kin. She was given a printout of her record on the firm's computer and saw that her address was incorrect, so she pointed this out to her supervisor. The following day she was given an amended version and saw that the error had been corrected.   *(1 mark)*

   (c) John downloaded a new piece of software from the Internet. While installing it, he was invited to register – and pay – for it. He did so straight away.   *(1 mark)*

(d) Manesh started a new job. During his induction process it was explained very carefully to him that the network manager made spot checks on the e-mails that staff were receiving and sending from their workstations. *(1 mark)*

AQA, 2006

5   Chris, a temporary employee in the Personnel Department of ABC plc, guessed the Personnel Director's User ID and password, and logged into the computer system. Chris then changed the salary details of some of the employees on the company's payroll file.

(a) What **two** offences did Chris commit under the Computer Misuse Act of 1990? *(2 marks)*

(b) Chris had been left alone in the office. Describe **three** methods of security the company could have used to prevent or detect what had happened. These should not inhibit the normal running of an office. *(3 marks)*

AQA, 2004

6   Most methods of data encryption involve the use of a key or keys. The EU and some governments want to make it law that these keys should be made available to 'trusted' third parties. Explain why this might be seen as a good thing or bad thing by each of the following. Your conclusion should be clear from your explanation.

(a) The individual citizen *(1 mark)*

(b) A large multi-national corporation *(1 mark)*

(c) Governments *(1 mark)*

AQA, 2004

7   A well-known software company has constructed a media player to query an online database at the company's headquarters. It retrieves the titles of tracks on audio CDs for display in the media player's window. In the process it assigns a unique identifying digital fingerprint to the computer playing the audio track.

In a separate transaction, the company can then link this digital fingerprint to an e-mail sent from the same computer. This links the user's e-mail address to the music interests of the user for marketing purposes.

(a) Explain one benefit to

(i) the user *(1 mark)*

(ii) the software company *(1 mark)*

(b) Why might the use of the link be considered unethical? *(1 mark)*

AQA, 2003

8   Name the legislation that applies in the following cases.

(a) An Examination Board allows a software reseller access to its database of centre names and addresses so that the reseller can market its products directly to centres that teach AS Computing. *(1 mark)*

(b) A company using an encryption algorithm in one of its software products receives a demand for royalties from another software company that claims that it invented the encryption algorithm. *(1 mark)*

(c) A user sends an attachment to an e-mail which when opened infects the recipient's computer with a virus. *(1 mark)*

(d) A company has its computing equipment seized by the police for using unlicensed commercial software. *(1 mark)*

AQA, 2003

9 The growing level of public concern over data stored in computer systems led the government to pass The Data Protection Act 1984. The Act was introduced to protect the right of individuals to privacy.

 (a) Give **three** reasons relating to the nature of computing systems that give rise to this concern. *(3 marks)*

 (b) Name **two** other Acts that relate to computer systems. *(2 marks)*

AQA, 2003

10 Computer software is now covered by the Copyright, Design and Patents Act 1988. State **three** provisions of the Act that apply to copyrighted software. *(3 marks)*

AQA, 2002

11 In some countries government agencies routinely monitor the content of e-mail routed over the Internet.

 (a) Give two reasons why some governments may allow this to happen. *(2 marks)*

 (b) Suggest one way in which an individual may make it difficult for any such agency to read the content of a particular e-mail sent over the Internet. *(1 mark)*

AQA, 2002

12 A small film production company makes training videos for sale to schools and colleges. It uses a computer to add background music, downloaded from a particular site on the Internet, to its training videos. The editing software that it uses was found on another site on the Internet.

 (a) Name the legislation that this company might be breaking and describe one possible way in which this might be happening. *(2 marks)*

 (b) The company wishes to distribute its training videos in digital form so that they can be played directly through a computer system.

 (i) State the most suitable medium for this purpose. *(1 mark)*

 (ii) Name **two** peripherals excluding video monitor, mouse and keyboard that the computer system must use to play back a training video. *(2 marks)*

 (c) The company also offers a microfilming service to companies dealing in personal information. The personal information is transferred to microfilm. The recording, processing and use of personal information is governed by legislation. Name this legislation and state **one** principle of this legislation that relates to the integrity of the personal data and one that relates to its security. *(3 marks)*

AQA, 2002

Index